"The icon who is Andrea Nguyen has written yet another cookbook that will inevitably become stained from all the recipes I will cook from it. With *Ever-Green Vietnamese*, Nguyen shows us how to bring a range of highly delicious, vegetable-forward Vietnamese flavors into our own kitchens."

—**ANDY BARAGHANI**, author, *The Cook You Want to Be*

"I consider all of Andrea Nguyen's books on Vietnamese cuisine to be my guiding lights when it comes to cooking the cuisine of my family's home country, and *Ever-Green Vietnamese* is no different. It provides wonderful validation for vegetarians and vegans who want to maintain a soul connection to Vietnamese food and culture. That nuoc mam recipe alone is worth the price of admission."

—**SOLEIL HO**, critic-at-large, *San Francisco Chronicle*

"If you're looking for a modern, plant-centric take on Vietnamese cooking, Andrea Nguyen delivers. I've cooked more from this book than any other this year and had a blast doing it. This is a masterful resource rooted in tradition, brimming with fresh inspiration."

—**HEIDI SWANSON**, James Beard Award–winning author, *Super Natural Every Day* and *Super Natural Simple*

"Andrea Nguyen's finesse with tofu, smart veganized swaps for common seasoning staples, and tips on how to work with everyday ingredients are a highlight of this book, as are the recipes. I can't wait to make the tofu 'bologna' for a banh mi and the magical sesame salt that I will absolutely be using on every serving of steamed fresh greens. Her techniques are simple and smart, and I know eating more plants will be an even tastier endeavor now that she is my guide."

—**BEN MIMS**, cooking columnist, *Los Angeles Times*

"As a recip Nguyen's writings and recipes many times for guidance and the reassurance that comes with her vast knowledge and authority. *Ever-Green Vietnamese* feels incredibly modern in its approach but also carries the weight of her expertise. These plant-forward recipes are as timeless and essential as her advice has always been."

—**CARLA LALLI MUSIC**, author, *That Sounds So Good* and *Where Cooking Begins*

"Fresh herbs and vegetables have long been pillars of Vietnamese cuisine, but here Andrea Nguyen centers them in umami-rich recipes that are not only mouthwatering but also intelligently healthy. Her approach isn't based on adaptation or compromise but rather on the imaginative evolution of Vietnamese flavors."

—**MONIQUE TRUONG**, author, *The Sweetest Fruits*

"More than a Vietnamese vegetarian cookbook and reference guide, *Ever-Green Vietnamese* provides a thoughtful and fresh foundation to cooking for the soul, the heart, the gut, and the environment."

—**MINH PHAN**, chef and founder/creative director, Michelin-starred restaurant PHENAKITE and porridge + puffs

"If I feel like cooking Vietnamese food, Andrea Nguyen is the person I turn to. Through her cookbooks, she has been a presence in my kitchen for years."

—**DIANA HENRY**, James Beard Award–winning cookbook author and journalist

Ever-Green
Vietnamese

Andrea Quynhgiao Nguyen

Photographs by Aubrie Pick

Ever-Green
Vietnamese

**SUPER-FRESH RECIPES, STARRING
PLANTS FROM LAND AND SEA**

TEN SPEED PRESS
California | New York

For my father, who answered my questions until the end. And for my mother, who continues to stoke my culinary curiosity.

Contents

Pantry Secrets   25

Veggie-Packed Mains   235

Tempting Sweets and Sips   263

COMING FULL CIRCLE

In the late summer of 2019, I hit a wall. I felt cruddy after years of eating everything that I wanted, all in the name of professional research. A strange bulge in my lower abdomen sent me to the doctor, who suggested that I had a hernia, then ordered an ultrasound and referred me to a surgeon. That took several weeks, during which my anxiety level rose as I consulted "Dr. Google" and my family. The bulge subsided by the time I met with the surgeon, but I still didn't feel great. He reviewed the ultrasound, examined me, and said, "You don't have a hernia. Tell me what's been going on."

Verging on tears of relief and in an outpouring of what probably sounded like gibberish, I explained my career and stress level, the result of a busy work life filled with traveling and consuming too much and too many foods not meant to be eaten together. Wherever and whenever, I ate out of curiosity, obligation, and pleasure. Also, my fifty-year-old body was going through perimenopause. Hormonal shifts were wildly driving the bus. "I think I need to slow down, rest up, and change my diet," I blurted as he nodded. The emotional unloading cleansed me like a terrific shower.

Up to that point, my omnivorous meals included some whole grains and decent amounts of vegetables. Evaluating my options, I ruled out overly regimented diets because I'm not a virtuous eater every day (rice and sweetened condensed milk are wonderful). Raised Catholic, I always went without meat during Lent, but even then, when I refrained from it, I enjoyed plenty of fish and didn't gravitate toward exclusively plant-based foods. However,

decades of cooking had taught me how a little fish sauce, chicken, or pork can turn a meh dish into a wow one. My problem was that I didn't cook and eat that way enough. What if I simply prepared food with less meat and upped my vegetable intake?

I re-visited and re-imagined favorite Vietnamese dishes to spotlight members of the vegetable kingdom. Regardless of whether the dish was vegan, vegetarian, or vegetable-forward with some meat, my overarching goal was to build savory depth and fun experiences, respectively described as đậm đà and hấp dẫn, Viet terms that refer to tastiness. I had a blast veganizing fish sauce, noodle soups, and other popular dishes as well as devising recipes to celebrate Vietnamese ways with produce and grains. Sometimes I created a new dish, such as Char Siu Roasted Cauliflower (page 227), which you may stuff into steamed buns (see page 117) or banh mi (see page 128).

I also reached back to my high school days, when, after my four siblings had left for college, my parents and I shared many low-meat meals. I thought those were anomalous, but, in retrospect, the meals embodied my parents' cultural food pleasures, which were homey, comforting, and humble. Recipes such as Peppery Caramel Pork and Daikon (page 249), Creamy Turmeric Eggplant with Shiso (page 203), and Greens with Magical Sesame Salt (page 201) offer my modern takes on enduring savors.

I realized that I didn't have to give up foods that I love, but rather needed to better respect and cultivate the exciting flavors, textures, and colors in plants. Compared to what I had cooked in the past, the new dishes were lighter and more refreshing. They tasted delicious, and I felt good without feeling deprived. Choosing more plants over animals seemed natural, a cinch. I was so proud of myself. I checked in with my mother, pitching my life-changing ideas about Vietnamese low-meat and vegetarian cooking. She was happy that I felt well but also said, "Meat was expensive in Vietnam. We cooked with mostly seafood and vegetables. That's how it was. We ate more meat after we came to America because here, meat is more affordable than seafood."

I was six years old in 1975 when we fled Vietnam and resettled in the United States. My early memories of food spanned the Pacific—from the open-air markets of Saigon to the supermarkets of Southern California. I wasn't aware of the shift in my mother's cooking as I delighted in her rotation of roast chicken, beefsteak, grilled pork, and other meaty delights. Veggies were on the table but, as it turned out, not as much as they traditionally would have been. My siblings and I also reveled in having greater access to soda pop, potato chips, butter, and sugar. We had changed our eating habits. I had gotten derailed, taken a decades-long detour, and finally returned home at the table, so to speak. Switching to a plant-forward diet in midlife basically brought me back to my cultural food roots.

Of course, Vietnamese cuisine is not all about beef-laden bowls of pho and meaty stuffed sandwiches. Viet culinary culture has been and continues to be shaped by scrappy cooks who make the most of limited resources, the majority of which are harvested from the earth. The cuisine—with its inherent customization, rich Buddhist traditions, and emphasis on vegetables, herbs, fruits, and plant-based proteins—is a natural mechanism for cutting back on meat and developing a greener approach to living.

I'm not alone in adopting a pro-produce lifestyle. Plant-based foods have been trending upward for years, and more Americans are moderating meat consumption but not giving it up altogether. Buddhism has historically guided Viet vegetarianism, but in Vietnam, some people are choosing it for health and environmental reasons; organizations such as Green Monday Vietnam plug into the global Meatless Monday campaign.

Curious about how such trends aligned with my online community, I surveyed folks. Of the more than 1,500 respondents, nearly one-fourth were flexitarian, and two-thirds were omnivores. More than half saw themselves eating less animal protein in the future and, increasingly, people were diversifying their cooking to welcome diners with mixed dietary restrictions or preferences. More than three-fourths said they would be interested in a vegetable-forward cookbook. Their many thoughtful suggestions matched my lifestyle and culinary philosophy of balancing new and old concepts in meaningful, practical ways.

Enthusiasm for vegetable-centric cooking seeded and fueled this book's creation. I made this for you, me, and others for whom we've yet to cook. You don't have to be Viet to identify with *Ever-Green Vietnamese*. You just need to explore the potential of vegetables from land and sea and, if you're open to it, occasionally leverage the power of animal protein. That lies at the heart of my undogmatic plant-focused kitchen, which dovetails with the flexibility found in much of Viet cooking.

In Vietnamese, *chay* means "vegetarian." This book isn't 100 percent vegetarian, but the word appears often. When attached to a food term, chay signals a plant-based iteration. For example, nước mắm chay and phở chay indicate vegetarian or vegan fish sauce and pho, respectively. Vegetarian eateries are nhà hàng chay (a formal restaurant) or quán chay (a casual joint).

Vegetarianism isn't marginalized in Vietnam. People who ăn chay (eat vegetarian) may be full-time, part-time, or occasional vegetarians. They may abstain from eating animal protein for religious, health, or ecological reasons. They may eat mostly veggies along with some seafood. Or, they may tinker with vegetarian cooking to create trompe l'oeil dishes that make people do double takes. And, if there's an agenda in promoting Viet vegetarianism, its approach isn't moralistic but rather focused on gentle persuasion. Cue Buddhist vegetarian restaurants and temples that generously offer tantalizing fare to anyone interested. Perhaps they'll coax people into leading kinder lives? Chay foodways welcome everyone into the kitchen and to the table. That open spirit guides this book. As a non-extremist who can't stop loving food and cooking, I share this with you: A plant-forward diet has helped me better negotiate midlife physiological changes and perimenopausal symptoms. I also shed about fifteen pounds in the process.

Recipes in *Ever-Green Vietnamese* employ minimal animal protein. For instance, there's no separate pork and beef chapter, and dairy-free options are included. Eggs remain because they're a perfect food and it's tricky to find a silver-bullet swap. To underscore the flexible nature of the recipes, vegetarian seasonings such as soy sauce are used alongside homemade vegan or store-bought fish sauce. Commercially made alternative meat products are overprocessed and overpriced, plus their textures and flavors are defined by manufacturers, who aim their innovations toward popular uses such as burgers, meatballs, and dumplings. Rather than create recipes for commercial products that will likely change in the future, I focus on a timeless, affordable protein source—tofu. You'll pan-fry, whirl, and crumble it for recipes such as Peppery Vegan Bologna (page 53), a chay version of a Viet mainstay that can be featured in sandwiches and other dishes.

I employ the contemporary techniques of pressure cooking, oven-frying, and air-frying to make recipes faster to prepare and more healthful. Flavor enhancers that many Viet cooks rely on, such as monosodium glutamate (MSG) and Asian mushroom seasoning, are judiciously used in pivotal roles. Along with trusty recipes, you'll also find informative headnotes, bonus tips, and practical sidebars. With the essential input of my volunteer testers, I aimed to make these dishes as doable as possible.

Like my last cookbook, *Vietnamese Food Any Day*, this one tilts toward accessible ingredients and cooking methods. However, sometimes I may ask you to shop at an Asian market because you need a particular ingredient to make a dish sing and a substitute from the mainstream grocery won't suffice.

Cooking and eating today means that you do not have to stay in one cultural lane. I hope you'll incorporate *Ever-Green Vietnamese* into your repertoire and be part of Vietnam's delicious, wholesome food story.

KEY ADVICE, EQUIPMENT, AND INGREDIENTS

It is easy to skip this initial part of a cookbook but please don't! This is where I share how this book is organized and how the recipes were developed so you can make the most of all the content.

Key Advice

When it comes to writing and using cookbooks, I'm all about easing into the content. Given that, initially check the Key Ingredients section for items already in your pantry or that are easily obtained in your area. Cook recipes using what's within reach and then, as needed, obtain ingredients that are more difficult to find to prepare the other dishes.

Each chapter introduction sets the scene with cultural insights and a summary of recipes to take you on your cooking adventure. When picking recipes, know that I typically start a chapter with simple or basic techniques and then nudge you toward more complex "stretch" methods that may be culturally unique or worthwhile cooking projects. Regarding small collections of focused recipes, such as those using rice paper, the easier ones also come first.

These pages are packed with information. Look for technical tidbits and serving suggestions as well as storage tips and bonus variations in the Notes sections. Information in the margins highlight extra insights. Let's start with a few pointers for dealing with a recipe's nitty-gritty.

Substitute with Care When you're cooking with lots of vegetables, there's great flexibility. Recipes suggest ingredient swaps that either I or my recipe testers tried out. They don't cover every alternative but serve to guide your creativity.

Organize Prep for Efficiency You don't have to linearly use a recipe. Initially review it to identify and do advance prep work, such as soaking mushrooms or seaweed, making dipping sauces, frying tofu, or washing lettuce and herbs. While one part of the dish cooks, can something else be prepped? If raw animal proteins are involved, chop the vegetables beforehand to minimize mess and cross-contamination. Minimize dishwashing. Gather ingredients that will be simultaneously added to a pan into one bowl or onto a small baking sheet.

Measure, but Don't Fret Use dry and liquid measuring cups, plus a scale for weight measurements because it never lies. A few recipes call for detailed measurements.

MEASURING UP: WHAT ARE BRIMMING, MOUNDED, OR HEAPING AMOUNTS?

For me, a "brimming" quantity is a nearly overflowing, generous amount. Recipe tester Alyce Gershenson's husband defines it as "whatever won't fall off the top of the cup." That'll work too.

A "mounded" amount is more than brimming. When measured, the ingredient forms a low mound that resembles a hill. You won't ruin a recipe if your hill differs much from mine. However, if your hill is high, you're approaching a mountainous "heaping" quantity.

WHAT IS THE DIFFERENCE BETWEEN RIPPLING AND SHIMMERING OIL?

Many recipes tell you to begin cooking after the oil is hot enough that it shimmers, but that sort of soft sheen can be hard to spot. I find it easier to look for oil that ripples. What does all that mean? After adding oil to a pan that's heating up, look for the oil to naturally spread out, gliding, glistening, and—very soon thereafter—rippling. The rippling signals that things are hot but not overly so. To gently cook an ingredient, such as cut onion for soup, I opt for oil that's barely rippling; if it's at a full-tilt boogie ripple, I lower the heat a bit and stir a little more. If the oil smokes, I immediately take the pan off the heat and let it cool for a spell. Whether you favor shimmering or rippling oil, you're aiming for a sufficiently hot surface to cook on.

Know Your Stove and Cookware My testers and I prepared these recipes on home kitchen stoves. In general, we used burners with moderate power, between 9,000 and 12,000 BTUs. If you cook with more oomph, your cooking time may be faster than what the recipe suggests. Pots and pans heat differently too. Let the visual and tactile cues that I give help you gauge your progress and then adjust the heat as needed.

Follow the Recipe, More or Less The first time you make a dish, follow the recipe to a T. After you understand its parameters and benchmarks, make personal tweaks and note your changes. You'll have made my recipes yours!

Key Equipment

There's no need for unusual gadgets to cook most of the food in this book. Tools and appliances such as a digital scale, food processors (small and regular size), a blender, pressure cooker, range of pots and pans, and microwave oven are used. Two recipes require a Chinese steamer (see pages 113 and 117), while others can be made with a collapsible metal steamer rack. Along with saucepans and skillets, a cast-iron stovetop grill pan is helpful. For stir-frying, a 14-inch wok is great, but a big nonstick or carbon-steel skillet works fine too. A 5- or 6-quart pot is great for boiling lots of noodles or dumplings.

BASIC PAN SIZES

Small saucepan: 1- to 1½-quart capacity
Small skillet: 8 inches wide
Medium saucepan: 2- to 3-quart capacity
Medium skillet: 10 inches wide
Large saucepan: 4-quart capacity
Large skillet: 12 inches wide

To deal with the fuzzy areas of cookware, know that a saucepan typically has a long handle but may have looped handles instead. I suggest cookware size and type in recipes, but use what you have, and if needed, adjust the cooking time or heat level.

VEGETABLE CLEAVER LOVE

I'm not going to lie by saying that cooking with vegetables is a breeze. There's a lot of knife work involved to craft beautiful, delicious food. Standard chef's knives are fine, and a food processor can help, but consider adding a vegetable cleaver to your knife collection. A meat cleaver's heft is meant for chopping through bones but a vegetable cleaver's thin, lightweight blade will enable you to speed through chopping, slicing, and mincing soft ingredients.

At first, the cleaver may look scary. Have it professionally honed before using because a sharp knife is safer than a dull one. If the handle is short, use a pinch grip for better control: position your dominant hand where the blade meets the handle, with your thumb on one side of the blade and index finger on the other side (and your remaining fingers naturally gripping the handle). With a well-designed vegetable cleaver, you barely exert effort to cut a carrot into matchsticks, finely chop lemongrass, or split a sweet potato. A cleaver smashes ginger and garlic with ease and renders onion into small dice as if the allium were butter. It's great for precisely butchering tofu and boneless meats too. The wide blade also functions as a bench scraper to transfer lots of prepped ingredients.

My favorite vegetable cleavers have blades that are roughly 8 inches long and 3½ inches tall. Chan Chi Kee has produced excellent cleavers for decades. Dao Vua crafts good cleavers from recycled materials. Milk Street sells its unique Kitchin-to, a cross between a Japanese vegetable knife and a Chinese cleaver. Choose stainless steel if you don't want to care for a carbon-steel blade. Use a ceramic rod to keep the cleaver sharp between more rigorous honing sessions.

MORTAR AND PESTLE

I own six mortars and pestles, but the go-to one that sits on my counter is smallish, made of marble, and of a provenance that I can't recall, although I know I purchased it at a discount store. This mortar's bowl has an opening that measures about 4 inches wide and 2¾ inches deep. Its unpolished interior is somewhat bumpy, a perfectly abrasive surface. The bowl's construction and width-to-depth ratio serve my routine needs, such as crushing and grinding small

amounts of peanuts, sesame seeds, and chiles as well as turning half an avocado into guacamole. Nothing goes flying out of it.

Mortars and pestles are personal purchases, so at the store, pretend to use it to ensure it feels comfortable. Consider its weight. Will you mind grabbing and washing it for years to come?

Key Ingredients

It's a fantastic time to cook Vietnamese food. Grocery-store inventories are more diverse than ever, thanks in part to rising interests in global flavors and healthful lifestyles. That's why most recipes in this cookbook do not require shopping at an Asian market. However, you may occasionally need or want to pop in to a Chinese, Southeast Asian, Pan-Asian, or international market. If there's an Asian community nearby, its Asian market is likely filled with treasures.

The range of Asian markets can confuse, however. When shopping specifically for Vietnamese groceries, consider a market's location, type, and customer base. For instance, a grocer in Little Saigon will be robust, offering both popular and somewhat obscure brands beloved by its community. Because there are cultural overlaps, Chinese, Thai, and Filipino markets often carry a solid range of basics for preparing Viet dishes. Pan-Asian chains, big and small, such as 99 Ranch Market, H Mart, Shun Fat Supermarket, and Uwajimaya, stock the go-to ingredients and brands to cover most Asian cuisines, including Vietnamese. Enormous international markets, such as Buford Highway Farmers Market outside of Atlanta, carry a stunning array of popular as well as slightly under-the-radar brands. Large Korean and Japanese grocers may have some Viet basics. South Asian markets are good for sourcing spices but tend not to carry many Viet basics.

Wherever you're shopping, peruse endcaps and shelves from high to low because displays change.

If you can't find something, ask! I've listed preferred brands where appropriate but, as inventories shift, be open-minded and try unfamiliar items, such as products sold under a store's own name, which are often quite good. Shopping online is another option, but you'll miss out on the unexpected gems at a brick-and-mortar store.

This guide covers ingredients most often used in this book. Look to the recipes for information on lesser-used ingredients worth considering. Asian grocery shopping is fun. Choose your own adventure.

CONDIMENTS AND OILS

When you're cooking with a lot of vegetables, which lend varied, complex flavors, you don't need many special condiments or oils to make food sing.

Fish Sauce Vietnamese cuisine would be lacking without fish sauce. Choose between the standard variety sold at many markets or the vegetarian option available at Vietnamese grocers. Check ingredient lists, especially if you're gluten-sensitive. (Vegan fish sauce currently sold at mainstream markets lacks the salty umami oomph for my needs, so I make my own; see page 29.) **Suggested brands:** Dynasty (earthy, savory), La Bo De (vegan, has soy, only at well-stocked Viet markets), Megachef (salty-sweet, labeled "anchovy sauce"), Red Boat (excellent and artisanal), Son (pure and artisanal, mostly at Viet markets), A Taste of Thai (flat color, good flavor), Thai Kitchen (okay flavor and fine in a pinch), Viet Huong Three Crabs (a perennial favorite, a little saltier than others).

Hoisin Sauce This sweet, salty, slightly spicy sauce is often used for dipping sauces and marinades. If you're gluten-free, see the miso workaround in the recipe Notes. **Suggested brands:** Koon Chun (salty-sweet and punchy), Lee Kum Kee (sweet-salty and lovable).

Hot Sauce (chile-garlic sauce, sambal oelek, sriracha) Chile sauce adds zip any time. Chile-garlic sauce is bright and moderately hot; sambal oelek is earthy hot; sriracha is tangy hot. For Viet food, choose chile-garlic sauce (labeled "tương ớt tỏi Việt-Nam") or make my fermented version, page 37. The Viet Chile Sauce on page 39 is fiery but milder than sriracha. **Suggested brands:** Cholimex (sold at Little Saigon markets), Fix, Huy Fong, Tabasco.

Maggi Seasoning Sauce and Bragg Liquid Aminos Maggi Seasoning sauce, a Swiss-made condiment introduced by the French to Vietnam, where it became a beloved staple, adds its unique meaty flavor to many foods (banh mi, fried eggs, and a bowl of rice, for example). At supermarkets, Maggi and its worthy substitute, Bragg Liquid Aminos, are often in the Asian section. East and Southeast Asian grocers may carry different kinds of Maggi (such as Chinese-, French-, and Vietnam-made). The Chinese version is most common in America. Pricier French Maggi has MSG and is preferred by many Viet expats. Produced as a soy sauce stand-in, Maggi from Vietnam is lighter in flavor and color than the others. Maggi is formulated for different target cuisines, so try different kinds if you're curious.

> Sub coconut aminos for soy sauce or Maggi. If you do, you may need extra salt and perhaps a squeeze of lime juice or a dash of vinegar to negotiate the condiment's mild saltiness and sweet notes.

Sesame Oil Unrefined toasted sesame oil, sold at supermarkets and Asian markets, help Viet dishes sing. Ones imported from Japan tend to have extra-deep, nutty flavor. If you seldom use the oil, refrigerate it. To substitute for sesame oil, try a flavorful option such as unrefined peanut or walnut oil. **Suggested brands:** Dynasty, Kadoya, Maruhon, Spectrum.

Soy Sauce Full-sodium soy sauce is used for my recipes. Ones labeled "light" are light in color (versus the inkier "dark" soy sauce), not lite or lower in sodium. Use a gluten-free one, if you like. Should you prefer low-sodium soy sauce, you may need additional salt in the finished dish. **Suggested brands:** Kikkoman (regular or gluten-free), Kimlan (gluten-free multigrain), Lee Kum Kee, Pearl River Bridge (light, superior light, or premium), San-J (tamari).

NOODLES AND RICE

Mainstream supermarkets often stock Asian noodles and rice in the international food aisle, but you shouldn't overlook the standard rice section. Asian markets usually separate noodles and rice into two or more areas because there's so much variety; check these aisles plus the front and sides of the store.

> While Japanese and a handful of Chinese noodles have spot-on cooking directions, most Asian noodles do not. Go rogue to judge the timing and doneness yourself. You'll be a better cook.

Fine Rice Noodles (bánh hỏi) Delicate, vermicelli-size bánh hỏi rice noodles resemble thin woven rectangular pads. They are often paired with grilled seafood, roast pork or duck, and grilled meaty dishes, such as the wild betel leaf rolls on page 259. Once only available fresh, they are now obtainable as dried noodles at Chinese and Little Saigon markets. Follow the quirky detailed package instructions to rehydrate the wiry noodle pieces to tender deliciousness. **Suggested brands:** Three Ladies, Tufoco Bamboo Tree.

Flat Rice Noodles (bánh phở, Chantaboon/Jantaboon rice sticks, pad Thai noodles) The pho and hủ tiếu noodle soup recipes in this book feature flat rice noodles, which in Vietnamese are called bánh phở. At supermarkets or Asian markets, look for boxes or plastic packages of narrow noodles that are as wide as linguine (small) or fettuccine (medium); either size will work for my recipes. The labels may be in Chinese, English, Thai, or Vietnamese. **Suggested brands:** Annie Chun's, A Taste of Thai (sold at mainstream supermarkets); Bangkok Elephant, Caravelle, Sun Voi, Three Ladies, Tufoco Bamboo Tree (mostly sold at Asian markets).

Glass Noodles (saifun, bean threads) These Chinese gluten-free noodles are typically stir-fried and added to brothy soup, but Viet cooks also use them as a filling ingredient. Called miến, in Vietnamese, glass noodles absorb other flavors like a sponge and swell up during cooking to fill in gaps in dishes, such as imperial rolls (see pages 103 and 106) and Vietnamese "meatloaf" (see page 251). They're also good for mimicking pork skin (see page 75). When shopping, look for glass noodles made from mung bean and potato starches (or just mung bean starch). They cook up relatively soft and pick up flavors well. Such noodles look opaque white (not plasticky with a sheen). "Long Kow" is often on the label to signal quality (the noodles are historically shipped through Longkou, a port city in northeastern China), but always check the ingredients list for the starches used. Glass noodles mostly come as Twinkie-size bundles, as shown on page 86; a medium one weighs about 1½ oz, and a large one is roughly 2 oz. It's okay if yours is in between. These noodles go by many names in English; saifun is the Chinese name seen on many packages. **Suggested brands:** Dynasty, Golden Star, KA-ME (sold at mainstream supermarkets); Long Kow, Orchids (mostly sold at Asian markets).

When shopping for rice noodles at mainstream supermarkets, check the Asian foods section and the regular or gluten-free pasta section and look for noodles made from all rice. At an Asian market, peruse the wondrous dried noodle aisle.

Rice (jasmine and broken) Most Vietnamese people enjoy long-grain rice daily. For terrific flavor and aroma, select brown or white jasmine rice. Rice grown in Thailand is consistently excellent. See page 65 for a perfect stovetop rice recipe. Broken rice is sold at Chinese and Southeast Asian markets. **Suggested brands:** Dynasty (white and brown), Gold Star (white and brown), Lotus Foods (white and brown), Three Ladies (white, brown, and broken), a market's private label (check the regular rice and Asian sections).

Rice Flour When recipes call for white or brown rice flour, use varieties sold at mainstream supermarkets. Dry-milled (often stone-ground) and relatively coarse, supermarket white- and brown-rice flours function well in certain recipes to create crunchy coatings. Rice flour imported from Thailand is water-milled and powdery soft. It's similar to what is used in Vietnam and perfect for the crunchy Huế Rice Crepes on page 81. At an Asian market, look for regular Thai rice flour sold in plastic bags labeled with red lettering that includes "bột tẻ," which indicates that the bột (flour) was milled from gạo tẻ (long-grain rice). Bags labeled in green contain bột gạo nếp (glutinous rice flour), which will not work for the crepes; ditto for mochiko sold in boxes. **Suggested white and brown rice flour brands:** Arrowhead Mills, Bob's Red Mill. **Suggested Thai rice flour brand:** Erawan.

Rice Paper (bánh tráng) Selecting rice paper can be a crapshoot because they're not all the same, and Chinese and Vietnamese markets may carry many brands. For the recipes in this book, choose sturdy rice paper. I prefer Three Ladies and Tufoco Bamboo Tree brands, which many other Viet cooks also swear by. Each six-sheet serving of these brands weighs about 68g, signaling that they are relatively thick; use those benchmarks if you decide (or have) to shop off-brand. Sturdy rice paper is easier to manipulate for rice-paper rolls and, moreover, it is the key to tricky dishes, such as Grilled Rice-Paper "Pizzas" (page 109), both types of oven-fried imperial rolls (see pages 103 and 106), and Shiitake-Cauliflower Steamed Rice Rolls (page 77).

Resist using thin rice paper (often labeled bánh tráng mỏng), which is delicate, hard to manipulate, and may cause mishaps. Brown rice paper is usually fine for unfried gỏi cuốn rice-paper rolls. **Suggested brands:** Dynasty (at supermarkets, good but shy of sturdy), Three Ladies (sold at Cost Plus, Asian Markets, and online), Tufoco Bamboo Tree (only at Little Saigon markets).

Round Rice Noodles (maifun, bún, rice vermicelli, rice sticks) Made mostly of rice and water, these round noodles are the basis for rice noodle bowls (see page 256) and other favorite dishes. In Vietnamese, they are called bún, but packages may say maifun (the Chinese name) or vermicelli. Ideally, purchase a brand made with just rice and water. When the noodles contain starch, they are not as tender but will be fine in dishes. Like Italian pasta, bún comes in small (capellini), medium (thin spaghetti), and large (spaghetti) sizes. Except for the Vegan Spicy Huế Noodle Soup on page 163, which requires large noodles, you'll be using the small size. Packages may contain the noodles as straight sticks or folded over flats of long noodles, as pictured on page 234. **Suggested brands:** Dynasty, Gold Star, Jovial, Tinkyáda (sold at mainstream supermarkets); Pagoda/Bún Tháp Chùa, Sailing Boat, Three Ladies, Tufoco Bamboo Tree (sold at Asian markets).

PRODUCE

Regarding fresh produce, farmers are increasingly cultivating different kinds of Asian vegetables, so check local farmers' markets.

Chiles (Fresno, jalapeño, serrano, Thai) Firm, unblemished chiles with caps attached signal freshness. A refrigerated stash of chiles keeps well for at least 2 weeks. I've kept Thai chiles frozen for 1 year. Unless specified otherwise in a recipe, retain the seeds and heat-laden fleshy pith and ribs that contain most of a chile's capsaicin. Fresh chiles vary in heat level, depending on the cultivar and growing conditions. Use the recipes' chile quantities as guidelines and adjust accordingly.

CHILE CHOPPING POINTERS

Unless I'm prepping a huge amount of chiles, I don't wear gloves because they are unsustainable and can be cumbersome. To chop a chile, hold it by its stem while quartering it from near the stem to the tip, then cut crosswise into the size needed for the recipe. To slice, hold the chile by the stem and simply cut crosswise or on the diagonal. Regardless of cut, keep a hold of the last stem piece to usher the prepped chiles onto your knife blade and transfer them to wherever you want them. Should you touch the inner membranes or seeds, wash your hands with soap and coarse salt.

Garlic Store-bought peeled garlic is convenient, but freshly peeled tastes better. Peel one or two heads of garlic and refrigerate the cloves in an airtight container for up to 2 weeks. A medium garlic clove yields about 1 tsp chopped; put the clove through a garlic press and you'll have ½ tsp. Dealing with oddball-size garlic cloves? Remember this: 1 Tbsp of garlic weighs about 10g.

Ginger Choose heavy hands of ginger with as few side knobs as possible (they're extra work to peel). Break off a bit to check for bright yellow flesh, a sign of robust flavor. Refrigerate unpeeled ginger in a resealable bag in the vegetable bin for up to 1 month. Peeled ginger chunks keep for 1 week, or freeze for up to 3 months. Ginger size varies: A 1-inch-long knob of chubby ginger weighs roughly 1 oz. Use more if needed.

Herbs Amply used like a leafy green vegetable rather than a cutie garnish, fresh herbs play a major role in Vietnamese cuisine. You can more than get by with cilantro and mint, but explore other herbs as recipes suggest. Check farmers' markets and Chinese or Vietnamese grocers. Jot down the Vietnamese names because, other than cilantro, mint, and Thai basil, standard English names are rarely used at Asian markets. The herbs may be sold as bunches or in sealed trays.

When you can't find a specific herb, experiment with what is available. Try Italian, purple, or lemon basil, for example. Substitute Japanese shiso for Viet tía tô; Korean perilla has a much milder flavor. Consider sorrel, French tarragon, and flat-leaf parsley too. Or grow your own. Source seeds from vendors such as Kitazawa Seed Co. and Truelove Seeds; also check Etsy. Little Saigon markets may sell plants in spring and summer.

Keep herbs perky and ready to use. With the exception of any kind of basil, trim ½ inch from the stem ends of whole herb sprigs, wash the sprigs, and then roll them in a clean, dry dish towel to gently remove most of the moisture. Stand the sprigs in 1½ inches of water (I use recycled 1-qt yogurt tubs), loosely cover them with a recycled produce bag, and refrigerate for about 1 week, changing the water every 3 or 4 days. (Alternatively, wash, spin, and store

Vietnamese HERBS

Vietnamese balm / kinh giới looks dainty but adds beautifully bright lemongrass-y, minty accents.

Vietnamese shiso / tía tô leaves are flat and bicolor, deep green on top and reddish purple underneath. Sometimes called Vietnamese perilla, it offers hints of mint, tarragon, and basil.

Thai basil / húng quế offers anise and cinnamon notes that linger beautifully in Saigon-style pho; it may be labeled rau quế.

Cilantro / ngò is the most-used herb in Viet cooking, so always have some on hand.

Rice paddy herb / ngò om lends a citrusy, cumin-y finish to brothy soups (some like it for pho), but I've included it in guacamole too. This delicate herb is sold mostly at Little Saigon markets.

WASH FRESH MUSHROOMS?

Cultivated mushrooms play a starring role in this cookbook. Should you wash them? It's always up to you. If you wash mushrooms, consider your approach and the type of mushroom, and adjust the cooking time to compensate for the extra moisture that they will have absorbed.

Some people advise wiping off any organic matter used to cultivate the mushrooms. Others call for gently rinsing under cold running water followed by drying (a salad spinner is the perfect tool). A quick washing of whole button mushrooms resulted in a weight gain of roughly 2 percent, according to chef and author J. Kenji López-Alt. The moisture gain is negligible, *Cook's Illustrated* confirmed in its tests, adding that precut mushrooms will absorb more water, so wash them close to cooking time.

(I've let them soak for up to 24 hours). Start in the morning or do it overnight; cover and chill the bowl if you want. Rehydrated mushrooms keep well in the fridge for 1 week, so feel free to prep way in advance. Squeeze them to remove excess moisture before chopping. If the stems aren't too hard, use them too. Decant and save the soaking liquid to use in recipes. Dried shiitakes vary in size, so I measure them by weight for accuracy. **Suggested brand:** Wei-Chuan.

The neutral flavor, ebony color, and crunchy slithery texture of dried black fungus and wood ear mushrooms make them especially appealing. Usually grayish on one side, black fungus is thinner and more delicate than wood ear mushroom, which often sports one tan side. They are interchangeable. Labels may confusingly read "black fungus," "fungus," or even "black wood ear mushroom fungus." Buy the fungi as whole or odd-shaped pieces, not as sliced strips, which hamstring your prep options. Measuring the frilly dried fungi can seem cumbersome, but your recipe won't be dramatically altered if you're slightly off. Soak the fungi in hot tap water for about 15 minutes, or until they're soft and expanded; use soon or refrigerate for up to 1 week (discard or decant and repurpose the mild-tasting soaking liquid). **Suggested brands:** Richin Trading, T&H Trading.

Onions (green, yellow, and red) Onion sizing can make me cry at the keyboard and confound me at the grocery store. Here are my shopping and prep guidelines.

- **Green onions:** Green onions are the same as scallions. Gauging from the white root base, a small green onion is ¼ inch wide, a medium one is about ⅜ inch thick, and a large one is ½ inch wide or bigger.

- **Yellow and red onions:** A small onion (4 to 5 oz) is racquetball-size, a medium one (6 to 8 oz) is the size of a tennis ball or baseball, and a large onion (10 to 11 oz) approaches softball-size.

Seaweed (kombu, nori, and wakame) Glutamate-rich sea vegetables are fabulous for adding umami to food. The recipes in this book call for popular kinds of seaweed commonly used in Japanese and Korean cooking. Dark, stiff kombu may be labeled "dried kelp" or "dried seaweed"; packages of affordable "dashi kombu" work fine for my recipes. Any white, powdery coating you see on seaweed's surface is mannitol, a mild sugar that's part of kombu's umami; it is not dirt or mold that requires rinsing, although you may wipe it off with a damp towel, if you like. Do a little math to measure kombu; for instance, a 6 by 6-inch piece is the same as a 9 by 4-inch piece because they both yield 36 square inches of kelp.

The same nori sheets used for sushi may be ground into a seasoning (see page 27) or added to rice-paper rolls (see page 103) as a briny accent. Frilly bits of cut wakame inject piscine personality into vegan fish sauce and soup broths. When shopping at Chinese markets, check the Japanese or Korean section for these seaweed types; they are usually not shelved with Chinese seaweed. Dried seaweed keeps well for a very long time. If you're using locally harvested seaweed, adjust soaking or cooking times as needed.

Suggested kombu and wakame brands: Shirakiku, Wel-Pac.

> Attention, Asian market shoppers! When in doubt about which brand to choose, select one in the mid-to-high price range. Competition is stiff and, in general, the differences in prices reflect quality.

Shallots A member of the onion (allium) family, shallots lend great complexity to food, but when they are unavailable or unaffordable, substitute onion (as suggested in the recipes). Get the most from shallots by selecting firm, solid clusters. Individual bulbs vary in size, so use the measurements in the recipes to check quantities.

SPICES

Spices figure prominently in Vietnamese cooking. For instance, sea salt is required for making fish sauce, peppercorns lend pungent heat alongside chiles, and spice blends help create signature flavors. Many cooks consider flavor enhancers as essential too.

Chinese Five-Spice Powder When warm, earthy notes are needed, Viet cooks use this spice blend. It should smell savory-sweet, not evocative of pumpkin pie. Buy it or use the recipe on my website (Vietworldkitchen.com/evergreentips) to craft your own. **Suggested brand:** Spicely.

Curry Powder (Madras-style) Experiment with different curry blends to find your ideal. I prefer ones listing sweet-citrusy coriander as the first ingredient. They have a touch of heat too. Some curry powders contain salt, so my recipes assume that yours does; if your blend is salt-free, add a little additional salt. Recipes also have an option for blending your own with coriander, garam masala, and turmeric. **Suggested brands:** Spicewalla (mostly online), Sun Brand (contains salt).

Flavor Enhancers (monosodium glutamate and mushroom seasoning) More than a century old, monosodium glutamate (MSG) has an overblown bad rap. Some recipes in this book need a flavor enhancer to zhuzh things up. (I explain why I'm for enhancers and MSG on page 28.) If you don't want to use MSG, look for mushroom seasoning at Asian markets; the beigy granules are more potent than the umami mushroom seasoning blends sold at supermarkets. Kinoko Yugo Fusion has a shiitake flavor; Imperial Taste and Po Lo Ku are more neutral. **Suggested MSG brands:** Ac'cent (sold at mainstream supermarkets), Ajinomoto (sold at Asian markets). **Mushroom seasoning brands:** Imperial Taste, Kinoko Yugo Fusion, Po Lo Ku (all sold at Asian markets).

Pepper (black and white) For best flavor, buy whole peppercorns and grind them in small batches, then store in a small jar. My recipes refer to pepper as "recently ground" because unless I'm garnishing, I don't grind pepper on the spot. To grind pepper and other spices, use a dedicated, basic (inexpensive!) electric coffee grinder; after each use, clean it by grinding 2 tsp of raw rice. Look for large, plump Tellicherry peppercorns for more complex flavor. Vietnam grows excellent pepper. **Suggested brands:** Burlap & Barrel, Diaspora Co., Penzeys, Spicely, house brands of reputable spice shops.

Salt Fine sea salt has a clean flavor, and its size mirrors what most Viet cooks use. I use brands with roughly 550mg of sodium per ¼ tsp. Peruse your salt's label and scooch quantities up or down. Kosher salt varies; when substituting the popular Diamond Crystal brand for fine sea salt, double the quantity in the recipes. **Suggested brands:** Diamond Crystal (kosher), La Baleine, Hain Pure Foods.

VINEGARS (APPLE CIDER, RICE, WHITE)

Recipes in this book employ three kinds of vinegar. Unfiltered apple cider vinegar (ACV) has a savory, complex fruity flavor that's nice in Nước Chấm Dipping Sauce (page 32). Within its class, unseasoned rice vinegar from Japan offers the brightest and cleanest flavor. Distilled white vinegar is terrific for Viet pickles. **Suggested brands:** Bragg, Kirkland (both reliable for ACV); Heinz (bright white vinegar flavor); Marukan (excellent, clean rice vinegar flavor).

OTHER ESSENTIALS

Along with the ingredients mentioned previously, these are also very handy for making the recipes in this book with ease. You may have them already.

Coconut Milk and Coconut Cream When it comes to coconut milk, select cans or boxes of a full-fat, unsweetened variety, usually found in the supermarket Asian food section or an Asian market's canned vegetables and fruit aisle. Check the label to gauge richness: Super-rich coconut milk has about 14g of fat per ⅓-cup serving. When using packaged coconut cream, stir it to combine before measuring; or scoop the firm-ish cream from an unshaken can of coconut milk that's been left undisturbed overnight (or longer). If the coconut milk or cream contains guar gum, it's there to help emulsification. (At supermarkets, coconut water and oil are shelved

with juices and other oils, respectively.) **Suggested brands:** 365 Everyday Value (Whole Foods brand), Kara, O Organics (Albertsons brand), Simple Truth (Kroger brand), Thai Kitchen, Trader Joe's (less fat but bright, fresh flavor).

Molasses Regular dark molasses is used in this book's recipes, most often as a colorant. Its mild flavor is not aggressive, and its color is not too dark. **Suggested brands:** Grandma's, Brer Rabbit.

Sweetened Condensed Milk For the best expressions of alluring sweetened condensed milk, buy full-fat products containing only milk and sugar. If you prefer a dairy-free option, choose sweetened condensed coconut milk, which may include a bit of salt. Look for them in the baking aisle at supermarkets; they may be stocked near the coffee and tea section at Chinese and Southeast Asian grocers. **Suggested brands:** Borden Eagle Brand, La Lechera (intense, sweet, lush flavor), Longevity Brand (the Viet favorite), Magnolia (made by Borden, too, it is a bit more luscious than Eagle), Nature's Charm (excellent vegan coconut version).

Tofu (refrigerated or fermented) It's no surprise that tofu is the main protein in this book. In Vietnamese, there are three regional terms for blocks of tofu: northern đậu phụ, central đậu khuôn, and southern đậu hũ. I favor đậu hũ because it is the most commonly used outside of Vietnam.

Shop for silken, medium, medium-firm, firm, extra-firm, and super-firm tofu in the grocery store's produce department or near the dairy case. Super-firm tofu is often labeled "high protein" and sold in vacuum-sealed packages with minimal water. The other kinds of chilled tofu come in tubs. With extra-firm tofu, brands sold as two-block packages tend to be firmer than single-block ones. East and Southeast Asian markets have the biggest tofu selection, including medium and medium-firm tofu, which are wonderfully tender and not typically available at mainstream grocers. Many of my recipes call for a 14- or 16-oz package of tofu because, interestingly, the smaller package often contains one full pound. If there is a difference, it will not majorly impact your cooking outcome. However, when a recipe specifies a weight measurement for the tofu, use a scale to ensure you have enough. Don't waste time with pressing tofu for these recipes. Just open the package and pour out any water. Many markets sell their own brands of tofu, which are likely very good. **Suggested brands:** 365 Everyday Value (Whole Foods brand), House Foods, Nasoya, Simple Truth (Kroger brand), Trader Joe's, Wildwood.

Fermented tofu, called fǔ rǔ, in Mandarin Chinese, and chao, in Vietnamese, is a cheeselike powerhouse of umami-laden seasoning with a touch of funk that is sold at Chinese and Vietnamese markets. In the condiment aisle, look for jars labeled "fermented bean curd." If the cubed contents seem sketchy, know that a mainstream vegan cheese product line contains chao. Compared with Japanese tofu known as misozuke, Chinese versions are svelte and more complex. Always check best-by dates for freshness before purchasing. White fermented tofu (pictured on page 253) is used in this book. If you like extra heat, opt for white fermented tofu with chile. Use a fork or a teaspoon to retrieve the tofu (it may not come out whole); mash to measure it. I sometimes use the brine in recipes too. Once the jar has been opened, store in the fridge, where it will continue to age and be edible for up to a year. **Suggested brands:** Cache'de Chef, Hwang Ryh Shiang, Wei-Chuan.

> When shopping in Little Saigon enclaves, check the Vietnamese tofu shop (lò đậu hũ) to pick up snacks, fried tofu, and freshly made brick-shaped loaves of firm tofu (use within two days or store in water for up to a week).

ON SUGAR AND SUGAR SUBSTITUTES

Many people want to consume less granulated sugar, and this book's recipes include sugar swaps (agave syrup and mild honey are my go-to's) that work well to yield the results that I want. Except for the caramel sauce on page 34, you can't ruin the savories by subbing a different kind of sweetener than what is specified. Try coconut sugar or palm sugar, for example. However, when tinkering with sugar substitutes, know your sweetener's sweetness relative to granulated sugar; for instance, use less strong-tasting honey but perhaps double the amount of pure maple syrup.

Even within the realm of granulated sugar, there is a flavor difference—while white granulated sugar yields a brighter color, it has a flatter taste than organic granulated sugar. For caramel sauce, which is partly used as a colorant, I use white sugar. But when I'm finessing the savory-sweet flavor of noodle-soup broth, I favor organic granulated sugar (and agave syrup). Weight-wise, 1 cup of organic granulated sugar weighs more than 1 cup of granulated white sugar! And functionally, granulated sugar's chemistry works well for a broad range of sweets, which is why I stick with granulated sugar for baked goods and candy, and weigh it, as suggested in recipes.

Pantry Secrets

MUCH OF THE SOUL OF A COOKBOOK LIES IN its collection of low-key recipes that are often text-heavy, under-photographed, and seemingly too boring for cooks to notice. However, you're reading these words, so you haven't overlooked a key part of *this* book.

Herein are some secret weapons—the recipes that I reach for repeatedly to craft dishes full of vibrant flavor, color, and texture. They play essential roles in my kitchen and will hopefully do the same in yours. Some are needed for defining Viet flavors, others are great for adding sparkly notes, while a handful facilitate faster meal prep. They collectively set the stage for the foodways expressed in this book and beyond.

Foundational recipes start things off. For instance, I keep ground-up nori on hand to construct the vegan umami backbone of my sate sauce and to lend briny notes to dishes such as fried rice. Many people asked me how I would deal with fish sauce in a mostly vegetarian Vietnamese cookbook. That was my initial consideration too!

The solution is having an incredible vegan nước mắm recipe that may be used as an equal swap with standard fish sauce. Vegan and nonvegan recipe testers—as well as my picky family—were mighty impressed by what can be made from seaweed, pineapple juice, salt, and a flavor enhancer. Even if you do not follow a vegan diet, the recipe is fun for contemplating how to build umami for Vietnam's iconic condiment.

For this book, I retooled my nước chấm dipping sauce recipe to help cooks yield more consistent, knockout flavors. This version of the ubiquitous Viet condiment keeps for weeks and serves as a mother sauce for two variations, enabling you to assemble recipes and experiment with ease.

Make bittersweet caramel sauce for iconic, deeply savory-sweet entrées that belong to a category of braised and stewed dishes called kho. It's simply a matter of cooking up sugar, water, and a tiny bit of something acidic. The result seeds Viet comfort foods.

From there, segue onto a spicy path and prepare chile-centric sauces to inject last-minute zip into your creations. A squirt of Viet-style hot sauce, a spoonful of lightly fermented chile-garlic sauce, or a plop of toasty chile-lemongrass sate sauce adds Viet-ish notes in remarkable ways. Treats such as rice-paper rolls and crunchy Huế rice crepes are quicker to put together if you keep a batch of mildly spicy peanut-hoisin sauce in the freezer.

Not all flavor accents need to be heat-laden to be big. A jar of Kewpie-ish mayonnaise, whether it's eggy or vegan, enriches banh mi and other snacks. A small batch of freshly fried shallots is welcome any time, but it will send bánh cuốn steamed rice rolls (see page 77) and grilled romaine salad (see page 183) over the top.

When it comes to making meals easier, have some homemade building blocks on hand. A stash of fried tofu is always in my fridge. You can accomplish much with tofu after it has been fried into sturdy, tasty pieces. I used to deep-fry tofu because that's what is commonly used in Vietnamese cooking, but pan-frying works well and is more healthful. The flavor and intended uses of store-bought plant-based meat products do not often align with Viet cooking, so I came up with my own. The umami tofu crumbles and vegan bologna are wholesome, versatile, and cost-effective.

And when I want to quickly put a Viet imprint on dishes, I often reach into my fridge for a jar of pickles. Daikon and carrot pickles are the standard, although you can use beets and jicama to change up the color and flavor, if you like. Pickled shallots are a northern Viet tradition, and I created the spicy pickled fennel to highlight a newcomer on the Viet vegetable scene.

The pickled mustard greens recipe comes from my mother, who recalled a story about Auntie Ngôn, her friend who married a man who ate only Western food. While Auntie Ngôn perfected American dishes for him, such as meatloaf, she prepared old-school Viet fare for herself. Dưa cải chua pickled mustard greens were among her mainstays. She enjoyed their bite, light fermented funk, and crunch as a comforting salad-y side dish. Without a yard to wilt the greens under the sun in the traditional way, which compacted them before brining and fermentation, she air-dried the greens on her coffee table.

Mom knew Auntie Ngôn didn't want to give up her favorites in America. I'm with Auntie Ngôn on linking food with identity; I think of her whenever I put up a batch of pickled greens, a soulful part of the Vietnamese table. Explore this chapter's recipes and you'll see that they're wonderful for Viet food and much more.

¼ tsp fine sea salt

½ oz sushi nori sheets

Rong Biển Xay

Nori Dust

Keep this in your umami toolbox for whenever you want a vegetable-based, piscine savory depth or a speckly dark garnish. Try it on fried rice or rice porridge, for example. It's a stand-in for dried shrimp in the sensational lemongrass-y sate sauce on page 40.

Nori dust's fishiness can initially be off-putting. Recipe tester Hugh McElroy, who has followed a vegan diet for years, remarked that despite his initial skepticism, the dark flecks turned out to be "an amazing component in other dishes." Aside from dishes in this book, I've added the dust to grilled cheese sandwiches along with a dab of sate sauce, a smear of umami mayonnaise (see page 48), and a sprinkling of chopped green onions.

Put the salt in the jar of a blender. Tear the nori sheets into 1- to 2-inch pieces, dropping them into the blender jar. Blend from low to high speed until the nori looks like graphite-colored glitter. If needed, pause the machine to stir or shake the jar. When done, let the foggy dust settle for a minute before removing the lid. Using a funnel, transfer the nori to an airtight container. Use immediately, or cap and store.

Notes

Equipment Instead of using a blender to grind the nori, you may use a small food processor. Tear the nori sheets into pieces no bigger than 1 inch.

Lifespan Keeps well at room temperature in a cool, dark place for up to 6 months.

FLAVOR ENHANCERS AND WHY I'M PRO-MSG

My mother, who is eighty-eight, keeps a huge canister of Ac'cent in a cupboard alongside the salt and pepper. The container holds monosodium glutamate (MSG), a flavor enhancer that Viet cooks have been using since before she was born. It's a staple that was rationed during food shortages; in the late 1970s, some Viet expats mailed MSG (bột ngọt, "sweet powder") to struggling family members in Vietnam so they would have a precious item to sell or trade.

For most of my culinary life, I've been neutral about flavor enhancers, generically called hạt nêm (seasoning granules) in Vietnamese. My savory dishes, made with fish sauce and animal proteins, both deliciously rich in glutamates, were terrific without enhancements. However, while working on this book, I sometimes got into a veggie-centric bind and needed an ingredient to finesse the flavors that I expect in Vietnamese cooking. If adding additional salt only made the dish harshly salty, I reached for a flavor enhancer. BAM! A subtle, extra-wonderful đậm đà (boldly savory) taste appeared. Recipes in this book don't often call for flavor enhancers, but when they do, add a little to take a dish from good to great.

When considering flavor enhancers, Viet cooks mostly choose between MSG and MSG-less seasoning granules derived from mushrooms and other vegetables. Both amplify the flavors of food, but the beige granules cloud liquids and, depending on their taste, may overwhelm. Crystalline MSG doesn't cloud broths and plays well with other ingredients without taking over. I keep several flavor enhancers on hand but use MSG the most.

What is MSG's magic? Based on the flavor properties of seaweed and created in 1908 by Japanese chemist Kikunae Ikeda, MSG is concentrated, commercially made glutamic acid, which, when dissolved in food, adds savory deliciousness—umami, a term coined by Ikeda. Glutamic acid is a nonessential amino acid produced by the human body; it is also naturally present in many ingredients and foods. Our bodies do not identify MSG's glutamic acid as being different from its natural kin.

Is MSG harmful? On a daily basis, we eat about 13 grams of naturally occurring glutamate versus roughly 0.5 gram of added MSG, as reported by *EatingWell* magazine. Research spanning from the 1970s to today shows no definite link between MSG and reported symptoms, such as heart palpitations, headaches, and sweating. That said, a small number of people have short-term reactions, many of which are mild. Consuming a large amount of MSG on an empty stomach may result in side effects, but that's not a common situation. I adore processed foods with MSG, such as Doritos and Top Ramen, but I don't eat them often. Cooking from scratch allows me to keep my MSG consumption at a low to moderate level.

How to use MSG? A flavor enhancer is not a flavor *replacer*. To build umami, I use MSG along with salt, sugar, and other ingredients. Flavor-enhanced food ideally tastes fabulous but still like itself. Because of weight differences, apply a 1-to-2 volume ratio of MSG to Asian mushroom seasoning granules. A teaspoon of flavor enhancer has a much saltier hit than a teaspoon of salt. When experimenting, decrease the normal salt amount by about one-third and make up the difference by gradually adding MSG and tasting along the way.

Where to buy MSG? See page 20 for sourcing and storage tips.

¼ cup dried wakame

2 by 3-inch piece dried kombu, snipped into 10 to 12 pieces

1½ cups room-temperature filtered water (use what you drink)

¾ cup pineapple juice (see Note)

¼ cup fine sea salt, plus 1½ tsp

2 Tbsp MSG, or ¼ cup Asian mushroom seasoning

1 Tbsp Marmite

Nước Mắm Chay

Vegan Fish Sauce

Fishless fish sauce sounds like an oxymoron but it's common in Vietnamese vegetarian cooking, in which the staple may simply be referred to as nước mắm, without the formality of chay attached. Vegan fish sauce currently sold at mainstream markets tastes too mild for my recipes. The most convincing renditions, sold at Little Saigon markets, come from Vietnam and feature doctored-up pineapple juice. After analyzing the ingredient lists, I created this preservative-free, accessible recipe. It takes roughly 1½ hours (most of which is nonactive cooking) to construct an umami scaffolding that has a WOW effect on your palate.

Tangy, sweet pineapple juice mimics fish sauce's fermented soft lilt. Two kinds of seaweed add piscine, glutamic notes from the ocean. Sea salt and flavor enhancers build a strong savory foundation; salt alone produces a spiky finish, but if you add monosodium glutamate (MSG) or mushroom seasoning you get umami magic with less sodium. Marmite contributes meaty depth and attractive color. Employ this vegan fish sauce as a 1-to-1 substitute for standard nước mắm. See page 19 for seaweed sourcing tips.

Create briny, fruity foundations
In a mixing bowl or large liquid measuring cup, soak the wakame and kombu in the filtered water for 1 hour (expect them to expand a lot in size). Meanwhile, strain the pineapple juice through a paper coffee filter (I use a pour-over setup with a size #2 filter) into a smaller bowl or measuring cup; this also takes roughly 1 hour.

Strain and cook the fish sauce
Pour the seaweed water through a fine-mesh strainer set over a 1- to 1½-qt saucepan, pressing the wakame and kombu to expel all the liquid (see Note on how to use the leftover seaweed). Add the strained pineapple juice, ¼ cup salt, MSG, and Marmite. Set the mixture over medium heat and warm, stirring or whisking, until the solids dissolve (check by feel because the surface will be cloudy; it rarely reaches a gentle boil in my kitchen).

(CONTINUED)

Precision in measuring is critical for a few of the seasonings in this sauce. If you have a kitchen scale, check metric weight measures to verify amounts for the following: 12g wakame, 64g salt, and 26g MSG or mushroom seasoning.

Cool and tweak the flavor

Set the liquid aside to cool for 5 to 10 minutes (any white foam will eventually dissipate). Taste and, if you prefer saltier fish sauce, add the remaining salt by ½ tsp, up to 1½ tsp.

The sauce will be cloudy. If you don't mind that, you're done and it is ready to use. Otherwise, line the mesh strainer with a paper towel, set over a small bowl, and pour the sauce through. (For clearer results, you may filter in two or three batches through a pour-over setup and coffee filter, but it takes much more time.) Let cool completely before using.

Notes

Ingredients For the pineapple juice, choose one that is not made from concentrate, such as Dole. A 6-oz can contains ¾ cup.

Lifespan Refrigerate the fish sauce in a capped jar for up to 3 months. Bring to room temperature before using.

Leftovers Keep the seaweed refrigerated for up to 3 days to repurpose for the cucumber and carrot salad variation on page 182, or add it to a brothy soup or porridge, such as the ones on pages 144 and 148.

SAUCE BASE

½ cup lukewarm water, plus more as needed

2 Tbsp agave syrup, mild honey, or granulated sugar, plus more as needed

2½ Tbsp unfiltered apple cider vinegar, plus more as needed

2 tsp fresh lime or lemon juice, plus more as needed

3 Tbsp fish sauce (store-bought or vegan version, page 29), plus more as needed

―――

2 to 3 tsp chile-garlic sauce (see page 37), or 1 or 2 Thai or serrano chiles, thinly sliced (optional)

1 large garlic clove, minced (optional)

¼ cup coarsely grated carrot (optional)

Nước Chấm

Nước Chấm Dipping Sauce

Take the time to perfect this tangy-salty-spicy dipping sauce and you can turn practically any dish toward Vietnam! Although *nước chấm* literally means "dipping liquid" in Vietnamese, it's not just for dunking. This amber condiment may be drizzled onto rice plates (see page 75) and spooned into rice noodle bowls (see page 256).

Cooks have myriad ways to make this sauce, and the best approach to personalizing it is to first make a versatile tangy base. For decades I constructed a limeade foundation, but I recently switched to an easier vinegar base accented by fresh citrus. Unfiltered apple cider vinegar has a savory note and is functionally more consistent than citrus juices, which vary in tartness and make finessing the sauce harder. Agave syrup and honey dissolve fast and yield a pleasant roundish mouthfeel, but if you don't have either of those handy, sugar is a staple in nearly all kitchens. This recipe helps you craft your own version of nước chấm; the sauce base ingredient quantities serve as starting points for your tweaks. After you get the hang of things, you'll be making this Viet condiment on the fly. See Variations for how to use the base for gingery nước mắm gừng and mắm tôm chấm (made with fermented shrimp paste).

Finesse the tangy base

To make the sauce base: In a small bowl, stir together the water, agave syrup, vinegar, and lime juice. Taste to make sure there's a tart-sweet foundation. Add additional sweetener and vinegar or juice in ½- or 1-tsp increments, depending on your palate. Taste and dilute with a splash of water if you go too far.

When you're satisfied, add the fish sauce. Is it salty enough? If not, add more fish sauce 1 tsp at a time. The amount used depends on the type and brand and your flavor preferences. Aim for a big flavor finish because the sauce will coat unsalted or mildly salted ingredients, such as lettuce and herbs. Once you get it the way you like it, jot down your formula for future reference.

Add extras

Add enough of the chile-garlic sauce for heat, garlic for pungency, and carrot for color, slight crunch, and a touch of sweetness. Set the sauce on the table so diners may help themselves, or portion it into individual dipping sauce bowls.

———

Notes

Ingredients Concerned about consuming too much sugar? Replace the water with a relatively sweet coconut water, such as Harmless Harvest brand, and decrease the sugar by about 25 percent. Or, replace half (or all) of the sweetener with a sugar substitute.

In a pinch, swap in unseasoned rice vinegar for the apple cider vinegar.

Lifespan The base may be refrigerated in a capped jar for up to 1 month. Re-taste and, if needed, squeeze in citrus juice or add fish sauce to freshen. Finish with any extras up to 8 hours before serving.

Variations To make ⅔ cup of Ginger Dipping Sauce, combine ½ cup of the sauce base with 2 Tbsp packed minced peeled ginger, 1 to 2 Tbsp lime juice, and 2 to 3 tsp finely chopped seeded Fresno or jalapeño chile. Let sit for 15 minutes before serving with seafood, roasted or poached chicken, or chicken pho (see page 161).

For 1 cup of Fermented Shrimp Sauce, whisk together 1 Tbsp fermented shrimp paste (mắm tôm, see Note, page 242; or substitute anchovy paste) and ¾ cup of the sauce base. Season with 2 to 3 Tbsp fresh lime juice. Add one or two sliced Thai or small serrano chiles, if you wish. Serve with Crispy Pan-Fried Turmeric Fish Noodle Salad (page 241), or dip fried tofu in it.

2 Tbsp water, plus ¼ cup

⅛ tsp unseasoned rice vinegar, apple cider vinegar, or distilled white vinegar

½ cup granulated cane sugar

Nước Màu

Caramel Sauce

If you perfect three basics—nước chấm dipping sauce, cooked rice, and this caramel sauce (pictured, at left, on page 36)—you'll be on your way to being a boffo Vietnamese cook. Respectively called nước màu (color water) and nước hàng (merchandising water) in southern and northern Vietnamese, this is not rich, sweet caramel sauce for adorning ice cream, but rather pleasantly bittersweet, nearly burnt sugar. Its inky color and deep flavor suggest the well-browned edges and corners of a good steak, a rack of ribs, and the bits that you scrape up from a pan during deglazing. When used for an array of cozy Vietnamese main dishes called kho, this slightly thick caramel sauce imparts a savory depth that defines soulful Viet food. In marinades, the sauce adds a lovely mahogany color. Although I have quick fixes for nước màu in recipes, I encourage you to make it from scratch to create true Viet savors. Along with this detailed method, there's a how-to video at my website: Vietworldkitchen .com/evergreentips. Go for it!

Prep a cooling station

Choose a 1- to 1½-qt heavy-bottomed saucepan, preferably with a light-colored interior to make it easier to monitor progress. Fill a large bowl or pot with cool water to come halfway up the outside of the pan.

Melt the sugar

In the saucepan, combine the 2 Tbsp water, vinegar, and sugar. Set over medium heat and cook, stirring with a heatproof spatula or metal spoon; when the sugar has nearly or fully dissolved, stop stirring. Let the sugar syrup bubble vigorously for 5 to 6 minutes, or until it takes on the shade of light tea. Now, turn the heat to medium-low to slow the cooking. Turn on the exhaust fan to vent the inevitable smoke. (Don't worry if sugar crystallizes on the inside of the pan. But if the residue from the bubbling sugar syrup gets crusty, add a drop of vinegar to correct it.) For even cooking, you may occasionally lift and swirl the saucepan.

Choosing cane sugar
over beet sugar is
better for consistent
caramelization.

Watch the caramelization

Cook the syrup for about 2 minutes longer, until it is the color of dark tea. Beyond that, watch carefully during the next 1 to 2 minutes as the sugar darkens by the second. Monitor the cooking and, to control the caramelization, frequently pick up the saucepan and slowly swirl the syrup.

When a dark reddish cast sets in, let the sugar cook a few seconds longer to a color between inky red wine and black coffee. Remove from the heat and set the pan in the bowl of cold water to stop the cooking. Expect the pan bottom to sizzle upon contact.

Cool, dilute, and use

Leaving the pan in the water, add the remaining ¼ cup water to the sauce. The sugar will seize up, which is okay. When the dramatic bubbling stops, briefly set the pan on a dish towel to blot off water, then set the pan over medium-high heat. Cook briefly, stirring to loosen and dissolve the sugar. Remove the pan from the heat and return it to the bowl of water. Leave in the water for about 1 minute, stirring to stop the cooking process. Let the caramel sauce cool to room temperature. Use the sauce immediately, or transfer it to a small heatproof jar, cap the jar, and store.

Note

Lifespan Store in a cool, dark place indefinitely.

VIET CHILE S[...]

4 to 6 medium or 3 to 4 large garlic cloves, coarsely chopped (use the maximum amount for pungency)

8 oz Fresno, red jalapeño, cayenne, or other medium-hot red chiles, cut into ½-inch pieces (see box, page 13)

1½ Tbsp light or dark brown sugar

Fine sea salt

¼ cup unseasoned rice vinegar, plus more as needed

1½ tsp agave syrup or mild honey, plus more as needed

Tương Ớt Tỏi

Chile-Garlic Sauce

If you're familiar with Huy Fong's brand of chile sauces with its iconic rooster logo, this one (pictured opposite, at right) is a more nuanced version of its Viet-style tương ớt tỏi. For years, my staple homemade chile-garlic sauce was a quickie that I blended up and cooked, but one time when I left the raw chile mixture out to ferment for a spell, it developed a complex, tastier depth that made me want to eat it by the spoonful. (I knew better than that.) Moreover, the aging process offered a fun way to coax and control flavor from a handful of humble fruits. I typically sniff and taste it daily to gauge doneness. The final cooking softens its edges a tiny bit. Jars of this chile sauce make a nice gift.

Pulse the garlic and chiles

In the bowl of a food processor, combine the garlic and chiles. Add the brown sugar and 1½ tsp salt and then pulse until a coarse mixture forms. Transfer to a clean 1-pt container (I prefer a glass canning jar because it is easy to monitor progress and is odorless, affordable, and a cinch to clean). Cap or cover with a lid.

Let mature

Set the sauce aside at room temperature for 3 to 10 days, stirring daily or every other day with a clean metal spoon and then re-covering. The chile sauce is ready when it develops a complex, sweet heat that you can smell and taste; bubbles may appear in the mixture. The initial raw sharpness should mellow a bit and settle into a deep savor. When the room temperature is consistently coolish (lower than 72°F), move the sauce to a sunny spot to capture some warm rays, and be patient. (Once, many years ago, a bit of fuzzy mold appeared, and I removed it with a fork. If that happened today, I'd also transfer the mixture to a different clean container and continue.)

For a slight vegetal edge, trim all the chile stems, but add the star-shaped green parts to the processor too.

(CONTINUED)

Cook to finish

Scrape the chile mixture into a 1- to 1½-qt saucepan and set over low heat. Stir in the vinegar and agave syrup, bring to a vigorous simmer, and then adjust the heat to maintain that bubbly cooking for 3 to 5 minutes to meld the flavors. Remove from the heat and set aside to cool and concentrate for about 10 minutes. Taste and adjust the flavor with agave syrup ½ tsp at a time, salt by the big pinch, and vinegar 1 tsp at a time. Aim for a fruity-hot, salty, slightly tart flavor. Let cool completely before using, or transfer to a clean jar, cap, and refrigerate.

Notes

Equipment Choose your fermentation container wisely. For example, metal containers (other than stainless steel) can react to the acidity of the sauce. Plastic vessels can permanently absorb flavors.

Ingredients For extra-edgy fire, add twenty red Thai chiles. Trim and chop them just like their larger kin, pulsing them in the processor with the other ingredients.

Lifespan Keep refrigerated for up to 6 months and enjoy at room temperature. The flavor deepens a bit after it sits for a month or so.

2 garlic cloves,
coarsely chopped

4 oz Fresno, jalapeño, or
other medium-hot chiles,
cut into ½-inch pieces (see
box, page 13)

¾ cup water, plus more
as needed

3 Tbsp tomato paste

2 Tbsp agave syrup or mild
honey, plus more as needed

2 Tbsp distilled white vinegar,
plus more as needed

Fine sea salt

¼ tsp xanthan gum (optional)

Tương Ớt

Viet Chile Sauce

Despite the popularity of sriracha at Viet American restaurants, the go-to chile sauce in Vietnam isn't as bold and fiery. With a little tomato involved, it's sweet, fruity, and friendly hot. Thai-style sriracha is great for the mayonnaise variation on page 48, but why not go all in with a Viet-style hot sauce? This recipe (pictured on page 36, center) is my take on the ones made in Vietnam. It's easy to prepare and, like the Chile-Garlic Sauce, it lends foods exciting heat without overpowering them.

Simmer the sauce

In a 1- to 1½-qt saucepan, combine the garlic and chiles. Add the water, tomato paste, agave syrup, vinegar, and ¾ tsp salt to the pan. Turn on the exhaust fan to deal with the volatile chile fumes that will soon float in the kitchen air. Set the pan over medium heat and bring the sauce to a simmer, then turn the heat to medium-low and let simmer steadily for about 4 minutes to combine the flavors and soften the chiles. Taste, and if it's too spicy-hot, add additional agave syrup 1½ tsp at a time. The amount depends on the spiciness of the chiles and your palate; the finished sauce will taste sweeter than it does during cooking, so don't overdo it now. Continue cooking for 4 minutes longer.

Cool and puree

Remove the pan from the heat and let sit for 3 to 5 minutes to settle the sauce and concentrate its flavor. Transfer the sauce to a blender and puree to a very smooth texture. To thicken it slightly, sprinkle with the xanthan gum, and briefly re-blend. If the sauce isn't smooth enough, pass it through a fine-mesh strainer.

Revisit and tweak

Let the sauce sit for 10 minutes, uncovered, to develop flavor. Taste and add additional agave syrup ½ tsp at a time to tame heat, vinegar ½ tsp at a time to brighten, salt by the pinch to add a savory edge, and water 1 Tbsp at a time to dilute flavor or texture. Transfer to a jar and let cool, uncovered, to room temperature before using or capping and refrigerating for up to 6 months.

Choose red chiles
for a cheery look;
green jalapeños yield
a sienna color.

When chiles are
extra-hot, omit
about one-fourth of
the fleshy, whitish
pith and any attached
seeds when chopping.

1½ oz chopped lemongrass
(see page 44)

⅓ cup coarsely chopped
shallots

1 Tbsp coarsely chopped
garlic

2 Tbsp dried red pepper
flakes

¾ cup neutral oil (such as
canola or peanut)

¼ cup Nori Dust (page 27)

1 Tbsp granulated sugar
(preferably organic for more
complex flavor)

1 tsp fine sea salt

1½ tsp Vegan Fish Sauce
(page 29), or 2 tsp soy sauce

Sốt Sa Tế Chay

Vegan Sate Sauce

Want to elevate your vegetarian cooking game? Make this rich-tasting, umami-laden condiment. You've likely encountered something similar when eating hủ tiếu, bún bò Huế, or pho. It's based on oily Chinese sha-cha sauce, a supposed riff on Southeast Asian sate sauce. After arriving in Viet kitchens, it evolved into a dark, savory, spicy concoction but kept the sate name. Confusing semantics aside, just make this!

For the conventional Viet version, called sốt sa tế, I use lemongrass, shallot, dried shrimp, fish sauce, and soy sauce. For this knockout vegan version, I turned to ground nori to replace the dried shrimp and used homemade vegan fish sauce (or soy sauce) instead of standard fish sauce. The nori gently fries in the oil to inject its brininess and add body into the resulting heady mixture, which is like XO sauce crossed with chile crisp. This recipe encourages experimentation so that you may develop your own version. Finish food with this condiment, plopping it into porridge (see page 148) and noodle soups (see pages 154 to 167), mixing it into plain or fried rice, and garnishing crunchy garlic bread (see page 132), oven-blasted sweet potatoes (see page 209), or even dal and hummus—use it whenever you desire an exciting flavor burst.

Mince the aromatics and fry

In a small food processor, pulse the lemongrass into finely minced bits. Add the shallots and garlic and blitz into a fine minced texture. Scrape the mixture into a 1- to 1½-qt saucepan, then stir in the red pepper flakes and neutral oil. Set over medium-low heat, stirring occasionally. After bubbles ring the edge, cook the mixture for 8 minutes, stirring or swirling the pan, until it turns orange-red, sweetly fragrant, and no longer raw-smelling.

For precision, weigh the lemongrass. Prep three medium or two hefty stalks to obtain what's needed.

Add the umami finish

Stir the nori dust, sugar, salt, and fish sauce into the oil. Lower the heat slightly for the sauce to percolate like the sound of steady, gentle rain for 6 to 12 minutes, stirring frequently; the cooking time depends on your preference. For a svelte, briny finish, turn off the heat at around 6 minutes. For a slightly toastier quality, push cooking up to 9 minutes. For a crisper, fun result that won't be as briny, proceed with caution, frying a few minutes more, until a slightly dark-reddish cast appears and the mixture feels somewhat crisp when stirred. (To hedge or experiment, stop cooking early, let cool briefly and test, then re-cook if you want to crisp up things. Or pause the cooking to scoop out half of the sauce, then continue frying the rest and compare results!) When you're satisfied with your savory-spicy creation, remove the pan from the heat and let the sauce gently settle and cool completely before using or transferring to a lidded jar for storage.

Notes

Ingredients If only frozen minced lemongrass is available, measure out ¼ cup (packed) to obtain the 1½ oz required. Lemongrass from a tube does *not* make this condiment sing.

Of course, you may use regular fish sauce, if you like.

Lifespan Refrigerate for 6 months. Enjoy at room temperature to let the flavors bloom.

¼ cup hoisin sauce

3 Tbsp peanut butter (preferably creamy and salted; see Note)

1 tsp ketchup or tomato paste (for a brighter hue)

1 Tbsp neutral oil (such as canola or peanut)

2 garlic cloves, minced and mashed or put through a garlic press

½ tsp dried red pepper flakes, or ¼ tsp cayenne pepper

1 cup lightly salted chicken broth or vegetable broth

1 tsp fish sauce (store-bought or vegan version, page 29) or soy sauce (optional)

2 Tbsp finely chopped unsalted roasted peanuts, 1 tsp toasted sesame seeds (any kind), or a combination (optional)

Tương

Peanut-Hoisin Sauce

When it comes to unfried rice-paper rolls like the ones on page 98, you can use nước chấm dipping sauce for a quickie accompaniment, or spend a little extra time to cook up this sauce. It's charmingly rich, sweet, salty, and slightly spicy. In Vietnamese, *tương* means "fermented bean sauce," but in my home, the term is shorthand for *this* sauce. I base mine on a central-Viet one that's traditionally crafted with liver and served with the crunchy rice crepes on page 81. Peanut butter yields a similar earthy, rich flavor. If broth is handy from other prep, use it. Diluted bouillon base or plain water will work too. This sauce keeps very well and, aside from recipes in this book, it's great for dipping raw or cooked vegetables, serving with grilled or pan-fried tofu, or even dressing a salad.

Sizzle, then simmer

In a small bowl, stir together the hoisin sauce, peanut butter, and ketchup. In a 1- to 1½-qt saucepan, combine the neutral oil, garlic, and red pepper flakes, then set over medium-low heat. After the mixture gently sizzles for 1 minute and turns orange, slide the pan to a cool burner to slow the cooking. Stir in the hoisin–peanut butter mixture and combine well. Set the pan over medium heat, then stir in the chicken broth. Bring to a swift simmer, then lower the heat slightly and cook for 2 minutes, stirring now and then, until the sauce has thickened enough to nicely coat the back of a spoon.

Cool and concentrate

Remove the pan from the heat and let rest for 15 minutes, uncovered, before tasting. If you want an anchoring savory note, season with the fish sauce, ½ tsp at a time. Partially cover and let cool to room temperature; the sauce will thicken and deepen in flavor. Present it in a bowl garnished with the peanuts and sesame seeds, if desired.

Notes

Ingredients If peanuts are problematic, use sunflower seed butter or soy nut butter, which come close to matching peanut butter's roastiness.

If the finished sauce is thin after resting for 10 minutes, bring to a simmer and thicken with 1 tsp cornstarch mixed with 1½ tsp water.

Lifespan The sauce may be refrigerated for up to 5 days, or frozen for 1 month. Reheat to a pourable state over medium-low heat, adding a splash of water if needed.

Variation For Gluten-Free Peanut-Hoisin Sauce, swap out the hoisin sauce for a mixture of 3 Tbsp dark miso (such as red miso), 2 Tbsp agave syrup or mild honey, ½ tsp toasted sesame oil, and 1 pinch Chinese five-spice powder.

Lemongrass POINTERS

Batonlike lemongrass (sà) confounds many cooks. How do you render the stalks usable for recipes? Here are a few tips.

Buying Look for lemongrass at mainstream super-markets, Asian grocers (especially Chinese, Southeast Asian, and pan-Asian markets), and some farmers' markets. Lemongrass may be sold by the single stalk, as bunches, in tubes, and in frozen tubs (at Viet markets).

If possible, buy fresh lemongrass. Choose firm stalks, not bendy ones. Check the cut bottoms for freshness. A medium stalk measures no wider than ½ inch, and a hefty large one is about ¾ inch at its thickest point. After trimming, one medium lemongrass stalk yields roughly 2 Tbsp chopped or 1½ Tbsp grated lemongrass. A large stalk yields about 3 Tbsp chopped, or 2 Tbsp grated.

Storing Keep lemongrass refrigerated in a plastic bag for up to 1 week, or trim and freeze for up to 3 months (go ahead and buy a bunch at the Asian market!). Fresh is best, but you can sometimes get by with lemongrass paste, sold in tubes.

Growing Lemongrass (*Cymbopogon citratus*) loves sun and well-drained soil. Plant some in a pot and bring it indoors if you have harsh winters. You may root fresh stalks or buy starter plants; note that lemongrass's cousin is citronella grass (*Cymbopogon nardus*), which looks the same but is not edible.

Homegrown lemongrass stalks may be skinnier than store-bought ones, but they'll taste brighter. The leafy tops have great flavor, so fold and tie them into a bundle to add to soups, stews, curries, and the like. Wear long sleeves and gloves to harvest lemongrass because the bladelike leaves are wickedly sharp.

Prepping Lemongrass may hide bits of dirt between its top layers, so give it a rinse before using. When prepping this citrusy aromatic, use a sharp knife and keep this in mind: You can't chew what you can't chop. A vegetable cleaver (see page 6) or a heavy chef's knife are my tools of choice.

To trim a stalk, chop off the green, woody top section and the tough base. Remove loose or dry, tough outer layers and save them for making broth or tea. The usable section will be 4 to 8 inches long, depending on the stalk size.

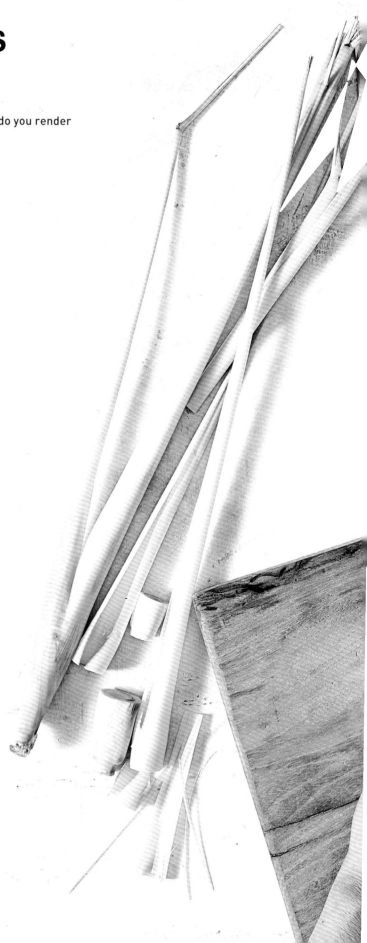

Want to chop the trimmed stalk to use soon? Slice it into 4-inch sections, halve each lengthwise, cut crosswise into half-circles (do your best to cut thin pieces), and then chop in a rocking motion to yield the desired texture. (If you like, whack the stalk with a meat mallet or a heavy saucepan to break up the fibers before cutting; if a pyramid-shaped piece pops out of the bottom, discard it.)

Minimize knife work by grating the stalk with a rasp grater, such as a Microplane, and then chopping the pieces that eventually splay open. Use 1½ Tbsp grated lemongrass for every 2 Tbsp chopped lemongrass.

For advance prep, freeze a bunch of trimmed lemongrass in a ziplock bag for up to 3 months. Or, chop the trimmed stalks into ¼-inch pieces and then blitz to a fine mince-like texture in a small or full-size food processor, processing ½ to 1 cup at a time (depending on the size of your machine). Add 1 Tbsp neutral oil and pulse to combine. Freeze in a storage container for up to 3 months.

Using Fresh versus Frozen versus Tubed versus Ground Apply a 3-to-4 ratio when subbing frozen minced lemongrass or lemongrass paste (from a tube) for freshly chopped lemongrass (for example, 3 Tbsp frozen or tubed lemongrass for ¼ cup freshly chopped). Fresh is best for certain recipes in this book, and I will indicate as such in those instructions. Ground dried lemongrass is subtle and I don't use it much.

Brimming ⅓ cup thinly sliced
shallots

3 Tbsp neutral oil (such as
canola or peanut)

Hành Phi

Fast-Fried Shallots

Caramelized slices of fried shallot adorn many Vietnamese dishes, lending sweet pungent notes. Ardent cooks, like my mother, fry a lot of shallots in advance, but they're never as good as when freshly made. Shallots cultivated abroad tend to be moister than ones in Vietnam, which means frying takes longer.

I've tried shortcuts, such as frying sliced dried shallots imported from Vietnam, but unfortunately they lack flavor. The Maesri brand of fried shallots from Thailand is good and so are European-made fried onions from Trader Joe's and Lars. That said, when I want to send a dish over the top, I fry a small batch of hành phi. Microwaving the shallots first quickly removes some moisture, so you spend less time frying (see Note if you don't use a microwave). When frying a double batch, use a 10-inch skillet.

Partially dry the shallots

Line a microwavable plate with a paper towel. Separate the shallots into pieces (you may have rings or half circles), dropping them on the paper towel; it's okay to leave itty-bitty, tight pieces intact. Spread out the shallots, overlapping them as needed. Microwave on high power for 60 to 90 seconds, until the slices are roughly half their original size. Expect steam and light brown streaks on some pieces.

Remove the paper towel and shallots from the plate and let cool to room temperature, 2 to 3 minutes. You can gently fluff them with your fingers to further separate the pieces as they cool.

Fry, cool, and crisp

Set a fine-mesh strainer in a medium bowl and place near the stove.

In a 1- to 1½-qt saucepan, combine the neutral oil and shallots, stirring gently a few times to combine. Set over medium-low heat and, after gentle sizzling begins, let the shallots cook for about 4 minutes, stirring or swirling frequently for even cooking. As the frying action ramps up and if you fear it getting out of hand, turn down the heat slightly to better monitor progress; it's better to fry longer and gentler.

When roughly half the shallot pieces are golden brown, remove the pan from the heat and continue stirring and swirling as the shallots keep darkening. After about 30 seconds, when most of the shallots are golden, pour them into the prepared strainer. Let cool for about 3 minutes, until crisp (shake the strainer and the shallot pieces should rattle), before using. If the shallot pieces aren't crisp, briefly and carefully re-fry them in the oil. Save the strained fragrant oil for other dishes such as fried rice (see page 67).

Notes

Equipment If you don't have a microwave, pat the cut shallots with a paper towel to remove moisture and fry a little longer. You'll have less oil remaining.

Lifespan These fried shallots are best the day they are made. When they're covered with parchment paper and kept overnight at room temperature, their flavor dulls slightly. If they soften, briefly re-fry with a touch of neutral oil over medium-low heat.

1 large egg, near or at room temperature (see Note, page 287)

1 big pinch garlic powder, or 1 small garlic clove, minced and mashed or put through a garlic press

Fine sea salt

¼ tsp MSG, or ½ tsp Asian mushroom seasoning (see Note), pounded to a powder

1 tsp Dijon mustard

1½ tsp agave syrup or mild honey

1 Tbsp fresh lemon juice or vinegar (distilled white or unfiltered apple cider), plus more as needed

1 cup neutral oil (such as canola or peanut)

Sốt Bơ Trứng

Umami Q.P. Mayonnaise

To enrich banh mi and other dishes, nowadays many cooks in Vietnam favor Kewpie mayonnaise. When I set out to mimic the cult condiment, my husband saw how easy it was to make with an immersion blender and dubbed it "quick prep" mayo, hence the homonym acronym. My fabulous rendition is slightly sweet with savory depth, thanks to MSG (what's used in Kewpie). See facing page for a vegan version.

Prepare the mayo

In a 2-cup container (such as a liquid measuring cup or a glass jar) that's wide enough to fit an immersion blender, combine the egg, garlic powder, ¼ tsp salt, MSG, mustard, agave syrup, lemon juice, and neutral oil. Insert the immersion blender to touch the bottom, then operate on high speed, gradually pulling up the blender as the ingredients become well incorporated, thick, and creamy.

Taste and tweak

If needed, blend in pinches of salt (for savoriness), squirts of lemon juice (for tang), or water by the teaspoon (for softer texture). Transfer to a jar, if needed, and let sit for 30 minutes to develop flavor before using.

Notes

Equipment To make in a stand blender, put all the ingredients, except the oil, in the blender jar. Replace the cap in the lid with a funnel. Blend for 5 to 10 seconds, then slowly add the oil in a thin stream. When all the oil has been incorporated, about 2 minutes, the mayo should be creamy and spreadable.

Ingredients Instead of MSG or mushroom seasoning, use 1 tsp fish sauce or Marmite. The flavor will not be equal, but you'll have an umami boost.

Lifespan Keeps well in the refrigerator for up to 1 week.

Variations Add 2 pinches ground turmeric with the salt to mimic the cheery version at banh mi shops. For Umami Sriracha Mayonnaise, omit the mustard and sweetener, use the vinegar instead of lemon juice, and add 2 Tbsp sriracha. Blend as directed.

8 oz silken tofu

6 Tbsp neutral oil (such as canola or peanut)

¼ tsp plus ⅛ tsp xanthan gum, plus more as needed

Fine sea salt

1 big pinch garlic powder, or 1 small garlic clove, minced and mashed or put through a garlic press

Mounded ¼ tsp MSG, or mounded ½ tsp Asian mushroom seasoning (see Note, facing page), pounded to a powder

2 tsp Dijon mustard, plus more as needed

2 tsp fresh lemon juice or distilled white vinegar, plus more as needed

1½ tsp agave syrup or mild honey

Sốt Bơ Trứng Chay

Vegan Umami Mayonnaise

This eggless version of the umami mayo on the facing page isn't a quick-prep recipe because you must drain the silken tofu for a spell and whisk the xanthan gum binder with oil before whirling all the ingredients into a tasty, spreadable vegan condiment. For xanthan gum, shop at natural foods and specialty markets; check the bulk foods section to buy a small amount. With one tofu package, make this sốt bơ trứng chay, plus the sriracha variation opposite.

Prep the tofu and oil-xanthan mixture

Cut the tofu into 1-inch chunks and place them on a super-thick layer of paper towel (I fold an extra-large sheet to make six layers) or a double-folded non-terry dish towel. Let drain for 5 minutes if using water-packed silken tofu, or 10 minutes if using custardy tofu. Meanwhile, in a small bowl, whisk together the neutral oil and xanthan gum. Blot the excess moisture from the tofu.

In a 2-cup container (such as a liquid measuring cup or a glass jar) that's wide enough to fit an immersion blender, combine the tofu and oil-xanthan mixture. Add a mounded ¼ tsp salt, the garlic powder, MSG, mustard, lemon juice, and agave syrup. Insert the immersion blender to touch the bottom, then operate on high speed, gradually pulling up the blender as the ingredients become well incorporated, thick, and creamy. It should be ploppable. If it's runny, blend in another 1 or 2 pinches xanthan gum.

Taste and tweak

If needed, adjust with pinches of salt (for savoriness), a bit of mustard (to curb the tofu flavor), or a splash of lemon juice or vinegar (for tang). Transfer to a jar, if needed, and let sit for 1 hour to firm up and develop flavor before using.

Notes

Equipment To make in a stand blender, put the ingredients in the blender jar as directed. Blend for 30 seconds, scraping as needed, until thick and creamy.

Lifespan Keeps well in the refrigerator for up to 1 week.

Custardy silken tofu can be messy, so I often drain it on layers of paper towel instead of my usual dish-towel approach.

8 oz super-firm tofu

1 Tbsp white or brown
rice flour

¼ tsp MSG, ½ tsp Asian
mushroom seasoning,
or 1½ tsp nutritional yeast

⅛ to ¼ tsp fine sea salt (less
if using MSG or mushroom
seasoning)

1 Tbsp fish sauce (store-
bought or vegan version,
page 29), Maggi Seasoning
sauce, Bragg Liquid Aminos,
or soy sauce

1½ Tbsp neutral oil (such as
canola or peanut)

Thịt Bằm Chay

Umami Tofu Crumbles

Alternatives to ground-meat products are formulated for certain uses, such as hamburgers. Given that lighter-flavored ground pork is the go-to for many Viet foods, I developed this natural, inexpensive, and versatile substitute (pictured opposite, at bottom) for thịt bằm (minced meat). It's handy for snacks, fried rice, bao, and more.

Coating nubs of super-firm tofu with coarsely ground supermarket rice flour creates the bumpy texture of cooked ground meat. This is a family-friendly recipe. Recipe tester Jenny Sager's one-year-old enjoyed helping crumble the tofu.

Crumble and season the tofu

Blot the tofu dry with a dish towel, then cut or break it into approximately 1-inch chunks. Over the sink, in batches of one or two chunks, give them a squeeze with one hand to slightly mush them, flicking excess water into the sink. (Instead of using bare hands, you may re-use the dish towel to squeeze and crush the tofu.) Using your fingers, crumble the tofu into smaller pieces that resemble very coarsely ground meat (think chili grind with some tiny bits), dropping it into a medium bowl.

Sprinkle the rice flour, MSG, and salt onto the tofu, then stir and toss to coat. Stir in the fish sauce and 1 Tbsp of the neutral oil. Let sit for 5 minutes.

Fry the crumbles

In a 10-inch nonstick, carbon-steel, or cast-iron skillet over medium heat, warm the remaining 1½ tsp neutral oil. Add the seasoned tofu and give things a stir. When you hear gentle sizzling in the skillet, lower the heat slightly and cook the tofu for 5 to 7 minutes, stirring frequently. As the tofu cooks, the jagged pieces cohere to resemble bumpy clusters of ground meat; scrape the spatula against the pan's rim to return any sticking bits to the mixture. The tofu will darken or brown a bit, depending on the liquid seasoning chosen (Maggi, Bragg, and soy sauce darken more than fish sauce). You can keep cooking it further, but it may dry up too much. Aim for moist crumbles. Remove from the heat and let cool for about 5 minutes to further meld the flavors before using, or let cool completely and refrigerate for up to 1 week.

This recipe yields 8 oz from one-half package of tofu, so use leftover tofu for the wontons on page 89. Or cook up a double batch in a 12-inch skillet.

1 (14- or 16-oz) package extra-firm tofu, water poured off

Mounded ¼ tsp fine sea salt

1 Tbsp neutral oil (such as canola or peanut), plus more as needed

Đậu Hũ Chiên

Pan-Fried Tofu Slabs

When tofu gets fried, it gains personality—a golden appearance, nutty rich flavor, and sturdy exterior. The result is delicious right out of the pan, but the point of this recipe is to help you create a supply of tofu prepped ahead of time that you may slice, simmer, or stir-fry. Pan-fried tofu (pictured on page 51, at top) lends protein and meaty texture to dishes, all the while taking on surrounding flavors. I often make a double batch so there's plenty for easy weeknight meals.

Cut and salt the tofu

If the tofu came as one block, quarter it. If it came as two longish blocks, halve each crosswise. Now, slice each of the four blocks into three slabs (they'll be roughly ½ inch thick). You'll have twelve rectangles or squares, depending on the initial tofu block's size and shape.

Arrange the slabs close to one another in a gridlike fashion, then sprinkle half the salt on the top sides. Turn the slabs over and repeat. Arrange them on a dish towel and let drain for about 15 minutes. (In moderate or cool conditions, I've left the tofu uncovered for hours.)

Pan-fry the tofu

In a 12-inch nonstick or carbon-steel skillet over medium-high heat, warm the neutral oil. Meanwhile, blot excess moisture from the tofu with a dry area of the dish towel.

When the oil ripples, add the tofu pieces, shaking the skillet to ensure they get coated in oil. Fry for about 3 minutes, occasionally shaking the skillet for even cooking. Flip the tofu when it turns golden brown underneath (check by looking at the edges). Fry the other side for 3 minutes, until crispy golden brown. If the skillet looks dry, add a whisper of oil.

Transfer the pan-fried tofu slabs to a cooling rack (or lean them against the rim of a plate or a baking sheet) so that air can circulate to cool and dry them. Use while warm or at room temperature or refrigerate for up to 5 days.

Salting tofu facilitates water release and seasons it too. It's akin to dry-brining meats, and the result is tastier fried tofu.

To use firm tofu, pan-fry over medium-low heat to coax a crispy, nutty finish from the higher-moisture tofu.

To re-crisp the tofu, pan-fry on medium heat for about 1 minute per side.

16 oz extra-firm tofu

¾ cup lightly packed vital wheat gluten, plus more as needed

3½ Tbsp cornstarch, plus more as needed

3 Tbsp nutritional yeast

1½ Tbsp fish sauce (store-bought or vegan version, page 29)

1 Tbsp neutral oil (such as canola or peanut)

1 large garlic clove, coarsely chopped

1½ tsp granulated sugar

Fine sea salt

½ to ¾ tsp black peppercorns (use the maximum amount for a hot edge)

Giò Lụa Chay

Peppery Vegan Bologna

Silky and somewhat springy, this sausage is Vietnam's go-to convenience meat, known in the north as giò lụa, and in the south as chả lụa. However you would use bologna, hot dogs, and Spam—in sandwiches, fried rice, noodle soups, and salads, for example—you could use giò lụa. All that potential can be found in a chubby log cooked in a sheath of banana leaf (parchment paper is a fine substitute).

To make conventional bologna using pork, beef, or chicken, I simply whirl the ingredients in a food processor. Tackling a vegetarian version for this book wasn't easy. Many Viet cooks bind tofu skin into a log for giò lụa chay, but the results aren't convincing. I wanted an easier approach. This recipe required multiple trials over the course of three months; you're benefiting from my *many* mistakes. (My husband was the harshest critic!) This recipe uses key ingredients available at most mainstream markets: Vital wheat gluten, sold at health food stores, is what seitan is made of. Extra-firm tofu, particularly Wildwood brand (it is denser than its peers), consistently works well.

Make the bologna paste

Fill a 4-qt saucepan two-thirds full with water, set over high heat, bring to a boil, then turn the heat to medium and cover to keep hot.

Meanwhile, use a dish towel to blot excess moisture from the tofu block, then break the tofu into chunks and drop into the bowl of a regular-size food processor. Add the vital wheat gluten, cornstarch, nutritional yeast, fish sauce, and neutral oil.

Using a mortar and pestle, swirl and mash the garlic, sugar, and ½ tsp salt into a paste. Add the peppercorns and pound into a coarse texture. Scrape into the processor and process. After a beige, doughlike paste ball forms around the blade, continue for another 10 seconds; about 30 seconds total. If a ball doesn't form, add a generous 2½ Tbsp vital wheat gluten, 1½ tsp cornstarch, and ⅛ tsp salt; process for about 5 seconds to stiffen. Let the mixture rest in the machine for 3 to 5 minutes to develop elasticity.

(CONTINUED)

For good results, use a scale to measure with metric precision for the following: 106g vital wheat gluten, 28g cornstarch, and 12g nutritional yeast.

Shop for frozen or fresh banana leaf at Asian and Hispanic markets.

Prep the banana leaf

Using scissors, cut banana leaves (fresh or thawed) into two 8 by 10-inch pieces, omitting the stiff or dark areas. For easy manipulation, measure and cut the 10-inch edge across the leaf grain. Quickly dunk the leaf pieces in the pot of hot water to soften and make pliable, then blot or wipe off excess moisture.

Cut two 12-inch squares of aluminum foil and set on your work surface, positioned with one of the corners pointing toward you like a diamond. Atop each foil square, set a leaf, smoother-side up and with one of the 8-inch edges closer to you. (Alternatively, replace the leaf with parchment paper and place atop the foil as directed; it's convenient but lacking in aroma.)

Shape and wrap the bologna

Lightly dust your work surface with 1 tsp vital wheat gluten. Using a dough scraper, transfer the tofu mixture onto your board, cut it in half with the scraper, and then lightly knead and shape each half into a 5-inch-long chubby log resembling a russet potato; as needed, dampen your hands to neaten the log. Set each log near the 8-inch edge of banana leaf (or parchment paper) closest to you.

Roll up the sausage in the leaf and then fold down the ends. Position one log on the bottom corner of a foil square and then roll it up a full turn. Now, fold in the foil sides and finish by rolling the entire thing in foil. Securely tie with one or two lengths of kitchen twine. Repeat with the other log and foil square.

Boil, cool, and slice the bologna

Drop the logs into the hot water, turn the heat to high for a vigorous boil, and let cook for 45 minutes, replenishing the water as needed and rotating the sausages. Expect them to bob and expand; the foil often darkens too. Transfer the sausages to a plate, then put straight in the fridge to cool for about 4 hours, before using. Unwrap and discard the banana leaf (or parchment) to serve or use in other dishes. (Chilled bologna is easier to thinly slice.)

Notes

Equipment If you don't have a mortar and pestle, mince and mash the garlic with a knife; gather the peppercorns into one small flat pile and carefully crack them with the bottom of a heavy saucepan.

Lifespan Refrigerate the sausages for up to 1 week. To freeze them for 3 months, I keep the foil and twine intact and put them in a ziplock bag for good measure.

1 lb daikon or jicama

6 oz carrot or beet,
or a combination

1 tsp fine sea salt

2 tsp granulated sugar,
plus ½ cup

1¼ cups distilled
white vinegar

1 cup lukewarm water

Đồ Chua

Đồ Chua Pickle

Literally meaning "sour stuff," this is the quotidian Vietnamese pickle—the one you've spotted and eaten countless times in banh mi, on rice plates, and in other dishes. This flash pickle is typically made with daikon and carrot, but some people use jicama instead of daikon for a crunchy-sweet result. Whether you're a fan of the root or tuber, experiment with đồ chua. For example, tint the pickle a fuchsia hue by using purple carrots. Use red or gold beets instead of carrot for a glorious magenta- or golden-colored pickle. Seek inspiration at farmers' markets and from seed catalogs.

Cut and soften the vegetables
Peel and cut the daikon into matchsticks about 3 inches long and ¼ inch thick (the width of an average chopstick). Peel and cut the carrot into sticks a little skinnier than the daikon.

Put the daikon and carrot in a bowl and toss with the salt and 2 tsp sugar. If using daikon, go ahead and massage and knead it for 3 minutes (or set aside for 20 minutes), until it has softened enough that you can bend a piece to make the ends touch without breaking. (If using jicama, which breaks when massaged, just set it aside for 20 minutes.) Rinse the vegetables with water, drain in a mesh strainer or colander, and then press or shake them to expel excess moisture. Transfer to a 1-qt jar.

Brine and pickle
In a liquid measuring cup or a medium bowl, stir together the remaining ½ cup sugar, the vinegar, and lukewarm water until dissolved. Pour enough of the liquid into the jar to cover the vegetables, saving any excess for salad dressing. (If using daikon, let sit for 1 hour; if jicama is featured, refrigerate for 1 or 2 days to fully develop the flavors.) Drain before serving.

Choose dense daikon with firm, smooth skin, which are signs that it enjoyed good growing conditions and will likely taste more sweet than bitter. Precut jicama may be sliced into matchsticks for this pickle.

For a similar daikon bite, use kohlrabi, purple-top turnips, or watermelon radishes. Peel and cut them into sticks as usual.

Note

Lifespan Refrigerate the pickle in an airtight jar for up to 1 month. Daikon may develop a strong flavor, so open the jar and let it air before serving.

1 lb small firm shallots

2 Tbsp fine sea salt

1¼ cups water

½ cup granulated sugar

1 cup distilled white vinegar

Dưa Hành

Pickled Shallots

These rosy, relatively tame shallots (pictured on page 59, center left) are a northern Viet Tet must-have; but why enjoy them only once a year? They are great for salads, cheese boards, and gin on the rocks. Of course, they are stupendous with charcuterie, such as the bologna and pâté on pages 53 and 92, respectively.

Peel and cut the shallots

Bring a kettle of water to a boil. Put the shallots in a small bowl and add boiled water to cover. Let sit for 30 to 60 seconds to loosen the skins, then drain.

Trim the root and stem ends of the shallots, then peel away the dry brown skin with a knife (a regular or bird's beak paring knife is super-handy). Remove any dry-looking or soft layers under the skin; save them for broth. Separate any bulbs that are stuck together (look at the root ends). Leave bulbs that are no bigger than ½ inch wide as is, but halve the others lengthwise. Quarter the large ones as long as they don't end up bigger than 1 inch wide.

Soak overnight

In a medium bowl, combine the salt and 1¼ cups water. Add the shallots and cover the bowl with plastic wrap, pressing the plastic down to ensure contact with the salt solution. Let stand at room temperature for 6 hours to 24 hours to decrease harshness. Drain and rinse the shallots well under cold water.

Briefly cook, then allow to mature

In a 1½-qt saucepan over medium heat, combine the sugar and vinegar and bring to a rolling boil, stirring occasionally, about 1 minute or until the sugar dissolves. Add the shallots. When bubbles appear at the edge of the pan, immediately turn off the heat. Using a slotted spoon, transfer the shallots to a 1-qt heatproof jar. Pour in the hot brine to fill to the rim. Let cool completely, uncovered, then cap and refrigerate. Let the shallots mature for 4 or 5 days before tasting. If they're too strong, let sit for 1 or 2 days longer before serving.

Note

Lifespan These keep well in the fridge for several weeks.

For a crisp outcome, select the firmest, smallest shallot clusters possible—no wider than 2 inches. (I mostly find them in the fall and early winter.)

1 lb fennel bulb(s)

½ tsp fine sea salt

1 Tbsp granulated sugar

2 tsp fennel seeds

2 garlic cloves, halved

3 to 5 Thai chiles, or 2 or 3 small serrano chiles, (use the maximum if you enjoy heat), stemmed and coarsely chopped

¾ cup distilled white vinegar, plus more as needed

½ cup water, plus more as needed

2½ Tbsp fish sauce (store-bought or vegan version, page 29), plus more as needed

Save the fennel stalks to add a mild sweetness to soup or noodle-soup broth, such as Deluxe Vegan Pho (page 158). Or, chop them for salads.

Dưa Củ Hồi

Racy Pickled Fennel

Fennel seeds are part of some northern-style beef pho broths and in Chinese five-spice blends, but fresh fennel bulbs remain relatively new in Vietnam. I developed this recipe (pictured opposite, at bottom), after reading on a Viet vegetable website that some old-fashioned cooks pickle fennel. Fennel seeds amplify the bulb's sweet licorice flavor. Garlic, chile, and fish sauce build a bright vibe that's racy. This pickle is great in banh mi with mint or basil instead of cilantro, and ribbons of crisp iceberg or romaine in lieu of cucumber.

Slice and massage the fennel
Halve the fennel bulb(s) along the grain; if the pyramid-shaped core seems tough, trim it. With the cut side down, thinly slice the fennel lengthwise into pieces no thicker than ¼ inch. Put the fennel into a big bowl and sprinkle with the salt and sugar. Massage the fennel for about 3 minutes until it turns wet and a pale jade-green, and many pieces are easily bendable. Its volume will have decreased by about one-third.

Add the seasonings and brine
Using a mortar and pestle, grind and pound the fennel seeds to a fine texture. Add the garlic and chiles, then continue pounding to create a heady, coarse paste. Scrape into the bowl of fennel pieces, then add the vinegar, water, and fish sauce. Using tongs, mix together; there will be barely enough liquid to cover. If you're short on liquid, mix up a bit more vinegar, water, and fish sauce to add to the mixture.

Let sit before eating
If serving the pickle soon, let sit for 20 minutes, turning the fennel several times to expose it to the brine. The fennel will become tangy, crunchy, and pungent with a nice, sweet anise note. Serve without the brine. Or, transfer everything to a jar, push the solids down to submerge, cap, and refrigerate.

Note

Lifespan Keeps for up to 1 month; the color mellows, but the flavor remains.

2 lb big gai choi (mature Chinese mustard greens)

5 green onions

7½ cups warm water

1 Tbsp plus 1 tsp distilled white vinegar

2 Tbsp fine sea salt

2 tsp granulated sugar

1 tsp MSG, or 2 tsp Asian mushroom seasoning (optional, for a savoriness that some renditions have)

Dưa Cải Chua

Pickled Mustard Greens

With a mild horseradish-like bite, slight fermented funk, and delicate crunch, pickled mustard greens (pictured on page 59, top right) are enjoyed in many parts of Asia. Vietnamese people often eat it as a side dish, like a permanent, ready-made salad. The greens are classically paired with boldly flavored dishes, such as kho simmered in caramel sauce (see page 217) and other salty preparations. Served that way, it cuts richness. However, you can let the pickle star in soup (see page 142). Like kimchi, it's very versatile; I've chopped the pickled greens to add to tofu "egg" salad.

For the best flavor and crisp texture, head to a Chinese or Vietnamese market for gai choy, mustard greens that are typically sold in bags or bound in rubber bands to keep the heads intact. Select "big gai choi" because the greens are more mature and spicier than "little gai choi," though you may use the younger ones if they are biggish; slender gai choi with roots is too tender. Big gai choi leaves are veiny with thick ribs and wavy wide tops, which, when scraggly, are often trimmed (don't be deterred by their odd look). You may substitute a broadleaf mustard, like Florida broadleaf or Japanese big red, but the texture isn't as hearty; resist pickling curly leaf mustard, which turns unpleasantly chewy.

Strategically cut the vegetables

Trim a thin slice from the bottom of the mustard greens, then separate the large leaves. Cut each leaf into big bite-size pieces: Aim for 3- to 4-inch pieces for leafy, soft parts and cut the midribs a bit smaller since they are thicker. Halve the super-thick stem sections lengthwise and then crosswise, as you see fit. The center cores may be halved or quartered lengthwise, depending on their size. Put everything into a 6-qt pot or something similar that's suitable for pickling. Cut the green onions into sections about as long as your index finger, then add to the mustard greens. Mix them around a bit, gently pushing down to compact.

For this pickle, I typically use a lidded 6-qt Cambro food storage container, which is ample for one batch. A Dutch oven would work too. Get your container together before starting because these pickles come together fast.

Add the brine and seasonings

In a large bowl, stir together the water, vinegar, salt, sugar, and MSG (if using) to dissolve the solids. Then pour this brine over the vegetables.

Weight and wait

Set a plate (or anything that will fit) on top of the vegetables to weight them down and keep completely submerged. Depending on the container, you may use two items, such as a silicone mat plus a plate. Cover the container, then set in a dry, dark place (a pantry or cabinet) for 2 to 5 days to mature. Use less time for a strong mustardy bite.

It's fine to uncover the container to check the progress. Expect the greens to soften and remain underwater without a weight, but you can keep them weighted if they still float a little. Using a clean metal spoon, stir the contents—a few bubbles may appear. When done, the mustard greens will be yellow-green, emit a sharp tangy aroma, and have a mild horseradish-like bite. You'll no longer need the weight to keep them submerged in the opaque greenish yellow brine. The length of the fermentation depends on the air temperature and your preference. It's fine to age it a day or two longer.

Once you're satisfied, cover tightly (or transfer to smaller containers) and refrigerate. When serving the greens as a side dish, drain them and retain the green onions, if you like.

Notes

Lifespan Refrigerate for up to 2 months. The mustard greens mellow over time.

Variation To add complexity to the brine, add 5 large garlic cloves (halved) for pungency, and 6 to 8 partially split Thai or serrano chiles for heat.

Rice Transformations

OF ALL THE STAPLES IN MY KITCHEN, RICE IS arguably the most important. I've often positioned the rice chapter toward the back of my books because it is commonly served with other food. In truth, rice is a major player in Viet culture, and in a book celebrating vegetables, the rice chapter deserves prominent placement.

There are two Vietnamese words for rice: Raw grains are called gạo. Cooking them to release their fragrance and chewy-sweet starchiness elevates them to cơm. A meal is called bữa cơm, and ăn cơm denotes eating. Rice may also figure into a tender greeting. In a *Time* essay on the complexities of love, novelist Viet Thanh Nguyen wrote about overhearing a man on a cell phone say, "Con ơi, Ba đây. Con ăn cơm chưa?" ("Hello, child. This is your father. Have you eaten rice yet?") Chef Minh Phan shared with me that her parents still welcome her home by inquiring if she has eaten rice. Rice symbolizes sustenance, love, caring, and humanity.

Rice is also incredibly practical. It may be simply boiled into a fluffy mainstay, fancied up for feasts, or transformed into multidimensional dishes. It can be toasted and pounded to inject nuttiness into foods. It can be fermented. It is soaked and then ground for rice paper and noodles. Vietnam is one of the world's leading rice exporters, and many kinds of rice are used in Vietnamese cooking. But in the spirit of making the most of what you've got in your pantry, this chapter focuses on long-grain rice. It's the everyday grain for Vietnamese people and you can hardly tire of it because there are wondrous things to do with it.

Rice is mostly eaten with other dishes, but a bowl of fragrant, tender-firm rice with sprinklings of fish sauce, drizzles of nước chấm, or a pat of butter and Maggi Seasoning sauce embodies Viet comfort food to me. For that reason, this chapter kicks off with a method for making a perfect pot of rice. People are often surprised that I don't regularly use a rice cooker, but I'm better at cooking rice because I've done it many times on the stovetop.

Batches of over- or undercooked rice (they happen at least once a year!) keep me on my game. As Ligaya Mishan put it in a *New York Times* article about the merits of crispy scorched rice, "Cooking has always been, on some level, a matter of trial and error, a game of chance." I would add that there's always another pot of rice to make. Don't sweat it while you practice your craft via the 10-10-10 Perfect Rice recipe on page 65.

Keeping cooked rice in your fridge is like having money in the bank. Rice can easily be turned into fried rice for a quick lunch or dinner. The vegetable-friendly fried rice offers a template for creatively using the produce in your fridge and garden. It's versatile, like fried rice ought to be.

The clay-pot rice is a wonderful cheat of sorts because the "broth" is made overnight with no tending on your part, and there is no actual clay pot involved. The result is splendid and achievable on a weeknight, although the dish is special enough for a party or holiday gathering.

I adore standard Hainan chicken and rice, but I also have a veganized version that features crispy fried tofu, gingery-garlicky rice, and a simple soup, plus several sauces. It's a long recipe but doesn't require too many ingredients, and you may prep the components in advance, or multitask if you want. I developed the recipe with minimal equipment during a full kitchen remodel in the midst of the 2020 pandemic. It was rewarding to employ readily available ingredients to craft a comforting, fun meal.

To explore an unusual type of rice, cook up couscous-like cơm tấm (aka rice grits, middlins, or broken rice; see page 10), a welcome departure for Vietnamese people who eat rice daily from smallish bowls, wielding chopsticks at share dishes. These nubby grains are typically served to each diner as a bountiful Saigon-style rice plate featuring a mound of the white rice topped with rich green onion oil, plus a main or two along with pickles, cucumber, tomato, and nước chấm. Cơm tấm is eaten with a fork and knife to easily mix the rice with the sauce and to cut or stab at other items. With no sharing required, the glorious plate signals self-indulgent consumption.

Cơm tấm restaurants exist, but if you have a bag of gạo tấm on hand, create your own broken-rice rice plate. The recipe in this chapter spotlights a trompe l'oeil of a beloved classic featuring bì, a delightfully tasty mixture of pork-skin slivers, poached pork, and ground toasted rice.

The last two recipes further reveal the possibilities of rice. One is a modern hack for bánh cuốn rice rolls that involves overhydrating rice paper instead of steaming batter into individual rice sheets. After I showed my octogenarian mother the easy method, she labeled it a game changer that liberated her from a tedious skillet method that she'd used since coming to America in 1975.

The chapter concludes with one of my favorite rice treats—crunchy fried rice crepes. Delightful bánh khoái are from the city of Huế in central Vietnam. Cook them from batter made with rice flour from Thailand, soaked raw rice, or supermarket rice flour. Wrapped in lettuce with herbs and dunked into an earthy bean sauce, the crepes are utterly delicious. They'll fill your home with the aroma of delectably fried rice.

Options and variations are built into these recipes so that while you perfect them, you may also make them your own.

2 cups white jasmine rice or similar-type long-grain rice

2½ cups water

Cơm

10-10-10 Perfect Rice

My mom taught me to cook rice in an electric rice cooker, but I didn't really learn how to cook rice until I prepared Vietnam's daily grain in a pot on the stove. You can observe and tweak the cooking—it'll lead to a better understanding of how to coax the grains to best express their tender-chewy selves. Some people boil and drain rice like they do pasta, but that rids too much of the sweet starches that define the grains' cozy texture and flavor. I prefer an approach that involves a heavy pan and a gradual lowering of the heat. To easily remember the method's cooking and resting times, one of my longtime recipe testers, Alex Ciepley, dubbed them the "10-10-10." Use the mnemonic to cook rice in the same pot and eventually you'll just eyeball the water level.

The main recipe is for long-grain, white jasmine rice (what many Vietnamese cooks prepare nowadays), but the Notes include details on cooking broken rice and brown jasmine rice (see page 10 for buying tips). To yield grains that aren't too firm or too soft, I opt for a 4-to-5 ratio of rice to water. Salt isn't typically added to plain rice because other dishes will season the grains at the table.

Wash the rice

Put the rice in a 2- to 3-qt saucepan and add water to cover by about 1 inch. Stir the grains with your fingers to loosen the surface starch, then pour off the water (I save it to water my garden). Repeat two or three times, or until the water is nearly clear (it will never be crystal clear). Dump the rice into a mesh strainer, shake to drain the excess water, and return the rice to the pan.

Simmer, then cook

Add the 2½ cups water to the pan and bring to a boil over high heat, stirring occasionally to prevent clumping. Lower the heat slightly to maintain a brisk simmer for 1 to 3 minutes, stirring often to scrape the bottom and circulate the grains, until they turn glossy on top. A few craters forming is normal. Turn the heat to low, cover the pan, and cook for 10 minutes.

(CONTINUED)

To ensure good heat conductivity, cook rice in a heavy-bottomed saucepan with a tight-fitting lid. When halving this recipe, use a 1½- to 2-qt saucepan.

Washing rice yields fresh-tasting grains. If your rice is fortified with vitamins and minerals, consider not washing it.

Rest, fluff, and rest again before serving

Turn off the heat and let the rice sit for 10 minutes. Uncover and fluff with chopsticks, a fork, or a spatula to circulate the grains. Re-cover and let rest again for 10 minutes to firm up the grains and finish cooking. Keep covered and warm for up to 30 minutes. Re-fluff before transferring to a serving bowl.

Notes

Ingredients To cook broken rice (gạo tấm), use the same rice-to-water ratio as for white jasmine.

Technique If the finished rice is too firm and dryish, sprinkle with water, cover, and set over low heat for 10 minutes to hydrate; then fluff. If the rice is mushy, when you make your next batch, decrease the water by 1 Tbsp per 1 cup rice. Tinker to find the best ratio for your tastes and the rice itself (for example, new-crop rice requires slightly less water than usual).

When making white or brown rice specifically for fried rice, turn the cooked rice onto a rimmed baking sheet, spreading it out to allow the grains to dry quickly so they will fry up nicely. Let cool completely, uncovered, for 1 to 2 hours, before frying. Or, cover the baking sheet and refrigerate overnight.

Lifespan Leftover rice keeps splendidly in an airtight container in the fridge for up to 5 days, or in the freezer for 1 month. To reheat, sprinkle with a little water, loosely cover with a silicone lid (or parchment or wax paper), and then microwave on high power in 30- to 60-second blasts. If the grains compress, let them briefly cool, fluff, and then serve.

Variation To prepare Thai-grown brown jasmine rice, use a 2-to-3 ratio of rice to water. Wash and rinse 2 cups brown jasmine rice and return the rice to the pan. (The bran is intact, so one rinse will do to remove impurities; don't expect any starch to be released.) Add 3 cups water, bring to a boil, and then turn the heat to medium. Let simmer briskly, partially covered, for about 5 minutes, stirring occasionally, until the liquid is an opaque light beige and slightly thick. Turn the heat to low, cover completely, and cook for 20 minutes. The rest remains the same, with resting and fluffing as directed.

SPICY VINEGAR

1 Tbsp unfiltered
apple cider vinegar or
unseasoned rice vinegar

1 Tbsp water

1 tsp chile-garlic sauce
(see page 37)

———

3 Tbsp fat (neutral oil,
coconut oil, butter, fried
shallot oil, and so on)

2 garlic cloves,
finely chopped

2 Tbsp chopped yellow onion,
shallots, or green onions,
white parts only (optional)

2 cups chopped mixed
vegetables (such as carrots,
green beans, celery, or
mushrooms)

3 cups chopped leafy greens
(such as bok choy, kale,
cabbage, or Swiss chard)

Fine sea salt

3 cups cooked rice, cold or
at room temperature

1 Tbsp fish sauce (store-
bought or vegan version,
page 29), soy sauce, Bragg
Liquid Aminos, or Maggi
Seasoning sauce, plus more
for serving

2 Tbsp chopped green onions,
green parts only (optional)

Mounded 1 Tbsp Nori Dust
(page 27; optional)

¼ cup hand-torn or coarsely
chopped fresh herb leaves
(such as cilantro, basil, mint,
or shiso; optional)

2 batches Fast Fried Shallots
(page 46), or ⅓ cup store-
bought fried shallots or
onions (optional)

Cơm Chiên Rau Thập Cẩm

Loaded Vegetable Fried Rice

Vegetable fried rice seldom has a lot of vegetables, so I packed this versatile recipe with veggies to make it extra healthful. To efficiently prep and dump the ingredients into the pan, cook like I do. First, fill a 2-cup measuring cup to the rim with cooked rice. Then rummage through the fridge for firm-ish veggies and cut up enough to halfway fill a 4-cup measuring cup; leafy greens mound the remainder of the vessel to make up to 5 cups total. As for optional add-ins, use what's on hand. In this recipe, green onions contribute color and pungency, nori lends brininess, herbs offer sprightliness, fried shallots enrich, and spiked vinegar injects spicy tang. Use all those extras, as I do, or some, or none.

Prepare the vinegar

To make the Spicy Vinegar: In a small bowl, stir together the vinegar, water, and chile-garlic sauce. Set aside.

Organize and fry the vegetables

Line up the fat, garlic, onion (if using), vegetables, greens, salt, rice, and fish sauce near the stove so you can cook quickly.

Set a 14-inch wok or 12-inch nonstick skillet on one of your largest burners over medium heat and add 2 Tbsp of the fat. When the fat ripples or melts, add the garlic and yellow onion. Briefly cook for 10 to 15 seconds, until aromatic. Dump in the chopped vegetables and leafy greens, stirring to combine well. Season with ¼ tsp salt. Turn the heat to medium-high and cook for about 3 minutes, or until the vegetables are just tender and there's little moisture visible (moisture weighs down fried rice, so raise the heat when watery veggies, such as celery, are involved). Transfer the vegetables to a platter or bowl.

(CONTINUED)

Fry the rice and finish with extras

Return the pan to medium-high heat and add the remaining 1 Tbsp fat. Add the rice and stir-fry for 2 to 3 minutes, until the rice is hot and revived. Using a spatula, spread out the rice in the pan and let it sizzle for 1 to 2 minutes, undisturbed. Stir and repeat once or twice. This develops some crispy grains and deep savor. When you're satisfied, return the cooked vegetables to the pan, drizzle with the fish sauce, and stir to combine well, about 20 seconds.

Turn off the heat. If desired, stir in the green onions and cook 10 to 15 seconds. When they're just softened, stir in the nori dust (if using). Taste and season with salt, if needed. Transfer the rice to a platter and garnish with the herbs and fried shallots, if desired.

Serve the fried rice immediately, offering the spicy vinegar for diners to sprinkle on for a bright lift.

———

Note

Variation To make fried rice with protein, add a handful of chopped Pan-Fried Tofu Slabs (page 52), Peppery Vegan Bologna (page 53), or Umami Tofu Crumbles (page 50) as the veggies finish cooking. Or, top each serving with a fried egg.

2⅔ cups water, plus more
as needed

3 by 3-inch piece kombu

1¼ oz dried shiitake
mushrooms

¾ cup chopped carrot
(pea-size pieces)

¾ cup chopped celery
(cut slightly larger than
the carrot)

1½ tsp finely chopped
peeled ginger

½ cup chopped shallots or
yellow onion

1 cup frozen shelled green
soybeans (edamame),
thawed and at room
temperature

½ tsp granulated sugar

Fine sea salt

¼ tsp recently ground
white or black pepper

1 Tbsp soy sauce

1½ tsp toasted sesame oil

1 Tbsp fish sauce (store-
bought or vegan version,
page 29)

1½ cups white Thai jasmine
rice or other long-grain
white rice

2½ Tbsp neutral oil (such as
canola or peanut)

Cơm Tay Cầm Chay

Shortcut Vegetable Clay-Pot Rice

Despite the name of this rice, I follow the lead of many modern Viet cooks and don't use an actual clay pot (some of them break easily); a heavy metal pot lacks charm but it does the job perfectly fine. I also don't labor much to make broth to imbue the rice grains with good flavor. Dried shiitake mushrooms often figure into Vietnamese clay-pot rice, so I soak a bunch overnight with kombu to yield an umami-rich "broth." The next day, I chop up the mushrooms and cook them with other vegetables to add to the rice after it cooks in the broth. That's all it takes. Serve this rice for a fancy meal or keep it casual with a side salad (sliced cucumber and jicama seasoned with salt and rice vinegar is nice). Tester Maki Tsuzuki reported that it was a hit with her omnivorous son and vegetarian friend.

Make an overnight broth

In a medium bowl, combine the water, kombu, and shiitakes. Cover and let sit overnight. The next day, remove and discard the kombu (or save it for another use such as soup or broth). Remove the shiitakes, squeezing each one to release its fragrant liquid back into the bowl. Decant (or strain) this mushroom broth into a liquid measuring cup.

Prep the vegetables and seasoning sauce

Chop the shiitake caps and any chewable stems into blueberry-size pieces. Transfer to a bowl; add the carrot, celery, and ginger; and set aside. Keep the prepped shallots and edamame nearby.

In a small bowl, stir together the sugar, ⅛ tsp salt, pepper, soy sauce, sesame oil, and 1½ tsp of the fish sauce. Set this seasoning sauce by the stove.

Cook the rice

Put the rice in a heavy-bottomed 3- to 4-qt pot and add water to cover by about 1 inch. Stir the grains with your fingers to loosen the surface starch, then pour

(CONTINUED)

Because of the broth's slight viscosity, I veer from my usual rice-to-liquid ratio and cooking method.

If you forgot to soak the kombu and 'shrooms overnight, start the soaking first thing in the morning to make the rice in the afternoon.

off the water (I save it to water my garden). Repeat two or three times, or until the water is nearly clear (it will never be crystal clear). Dump the rice into a mesh strainer, shake to drain the excess water, and return the rice to the pot. Pour in 2 cups of the mushroom broth, reserving any left over, and stir in the remaining 1½ tsp fish sauce and ½ to ¾ tsp salt (use the maximum amount if serving the rice as a main dish).

Set the rice over high heat, stirring occasionally to scrape up the bottom grains as things come to a fluttery boil. Turn the heat to medium to maintain a steady gurgly simmer for 1 to 2 minutes, or until the mixture is thick with plumped grains (expect little visible liquid when you stir). Cover the pot, turn off the heat, and let rest for 20 minutes.

Cook the vegetables

Meanwhile, set a 10-inch skillet over medium heat and add the neutral oil. When the oil barely ripples, add the shallots. Cook, stirring frequently, for 4 to 5 minutes, until the shallots turn fragrant with many golden-brown pieces. Dump in the shiitakes and chopped vegetables and cook for about 1 minute, until hot and glistening. Stir in the seasoning sauce and cook for 1 to 2 minutes, or until the carrot is crisp-tender. Remove from the heat and stir in the edamame.

Mix the veggies into the rice and finish

When the rice cooking time is over, uncover and gently fluff with a spatula. The grains should be tender-firm; if they're chalky or hard, sprinkle with 1 to 2 Tbsp mushroom broth or water. Using the spatula, mix in the vegetables to distribute well. Re-cover and turn the heat to high. After about 15 seconds, when you hear faint sizzling, turn the heat to between medium-low and low. Gently cook for 5 minutes to meld the flavors and heat through.

Turn off the heat and let the rice rest for 5 to 10 minutes. Using the spatula, fluff (doing your best to scrape and mix in any crisp grains from the bottom and sides). Serve hot or warm, scooped into a large bowl or individual bowls.

Notes

Timing Once the rice is totally done cooking, it can sit for about 30 minutes before serving.

Variation For meaty flair, replace the edamame with leftover roast chicken or pork, or cubes of pan-fried tofu (see page 52). One or two chopped Chinese sweet sausages (lạp xưởng) could be added to the shallot while it fries, as tester Laura McCarthy suggested.

UMAMI GINGER BROTH

6 by 6-inch piece kombu, snipped or torn into quarters

½ oz dried shiitake mushrooms

Chubby 1½-inch section fresh ginger, peeled, cut into thick coins, and smashed with the flat side of a knife

2 green onions, cut into 2-inch lengths and gently smashed

7 cups water

1 Tbsp fish sauce (store-bought or vegan version, page 29)

½ tsp fine sea salt

PAN-FRIED TOFU

2 (14- or 16-oz) packages extra-firm tofu, water poured out

1 tsp fine sea salt

3 Tbsp semi-refined peanut oil, neutral oil, or a blend (see Note)

2 pinches ground turmeric (optional, for sunny color)

———

2 cups raw long-grain rice (such as Thai jasmine)

¼ cup semi-refined peanut oil, neutral oil, or a blend (see Note)

2 Tbsp finely chopped shallots or yellow onion

1½ Tbsp finely chopped peeled fresh ginger

1 Tbsp finely chopped garlic

Mounded ½ tsp fine sea salt

8 oz zucchini or similar type of squash, cut into ¾-inch cubes

Cơm Gà Hải Nam Chay

Hainan-Style Crispy Tofu and Rice

When it comes to the popular Asian chicken-and-rice dish from Hainan, a Chinese island near the northeastern coast of Vietnam, many people obsess about properly poaching the chicken to spotlight its plush flesh. But, for me, this one-dish wonder is more about the sumptuous garlicky rice and various ginger-inflected sauces. The protein could be animal- or plant-based, as long as it's rich yet mild-tasting enough to let the piquant sauces pop. Many veganized versions of cơm gà Hải Nam feature mock chicken, but I prefer to pan-fry tofu so there's crispiness along with silkiness. The tofu plays super-well with the fragrant rice, delectable sauces, and gingery mushroom-laden soup. It's a knockout, comforting one-dish meal.

This recipe appears scary-long, but you can make the components days in advance to quickly assemble when you're ready. Recipe tester Hugh McElroy suggests prepping all the ginger and green onions in one go and separating them for the various uses.

Build the broth

To make the Umami Ginger Broth: In a 3-qt saucepan, combine the kombu, shiitakes, ginger, green onions, and water. Let soak and hydrate for at least 30 minutes, or, better yet, up to overnight. Partially cover the pan, set over medium heat, and bring to a boil. Then adjust the heat to a simmer, uncover, and let simmer for 15 minutes. Turn off the heat and let rest for 5 minutes.

Strain the broth through a mesh strainer into a 2-qt saucepan. Discard the kombu (or save it for another use), green onions, and ginger. Trim and discard the stems from the shiitakes, then quarter the caps and return to the broth. Season the broth with the fish sauce and salt. Cover and set aside.

Prepare the tofu

To pan-fry the tofu: If the tofu came as 1-lb blocks, quarter them and then cut each quarter into two squarish slabs. If the tofu was packaged as two blocks per pound, cut each crosswise into four squarish slabs. Regardless, you'll have

GINGERY SOY SAUCE

Chubby 2-inch section
fresh ginger, peeled
and thinly sliced

2½ Tbsp soy sauce

2 Tbsp unseasoned rice
vinegar or unfiltered apple
cider vinegar

1½ Tbsp agave syrup or
mild honey

1 Tbsp white or red miso
(optional, for depth and
thickening)

1 or 2 Thai or small serrano
chiles, thinly sliced (optional,
for heat)

**GREEN ONION–GINGER
SAUCE**

1 cup chopped green onions,
white and green parts

1½ Tbsp finely chopped
peeled ginger

⅛ tsp fine sea salt

1 pinch baking soda
(optional, to preserve color)

2½ Tbsp semi-refined
peanut oil, neutral oil,
or a blend (see Note)

———

Chile-garlic sauce (see
page 37) for serving

1 English cucumber, sliced
on the diagonal into ¼-inch-
thick pieces

2 firm-ripe tomatoes, cut
into ½-inch-wide wedges

sixteen slabs total. Arrange them in a gridlike fashion on a dish towel, season all over with the salt, and drain for 15 to 20 minutes.

Blot excess moisture from the tofu with a dry area of the dish towel. Using a knife, score the top of each slab twice, making ¼-inch-deep cuts.

Set a 12-inch nonstick or carbon-steel skillet over medium heat and add 1½ Tbsp of the peanut oil. When the oil gently ripples, add 1 pinch of the turmeric (if using), followed by eight slabs of tofu, laying each one scored-side down. Turn the heat to medium-high.

Fry the tofu for 3 to 4 minutes per side, until crispy golden brown. Occasionally swirl the skillet to distribute the oil for even cooking and then flip the tofu when you see about ⅛ inch of crisp browning form on the edges. (If the tofu sticks on the scored side, slide the skillet to a cool burner and let rest a minute to unstick, then flip.) Transfer the pan-fried tofu slabs to a cooling rack (or lean them against the rim of a plate or a baking sheet) so that air can circulate to cool and dry them. Repeat with the remaining 1½ Tbsp peanut oil, 1 pinch turmeric, and tofu.

Make the rice

Put the rice in a heavy-bottomed 3-qt saucepan and add water to cover by about 1 inch. Stir the grains with your fingers to loosen the surface starch, then pour off the water (I save it to water my garden). Repeat two or three times, or until the water is nearly clear (it will never be crystal clear). Dump the rice into a mesh strainer and drain for 10 minutes.

Meanwhile, bring the ginger broth to a near-simmer over low heat.

Set the saucepan over medium heat and, after it is dry, add the ¼ cup peanut oil. When the oil barely ripples, add the shallots, ginger, and garlic and cook, stirring constantly, for about 2 minutes, until some pieces turn golden.

Firmly shake the strainer of rice to expel any remaining water and then dump the rice into the saucepan. Stir to combine, then add the salt. Turn the heat to medium-high and stir constantly with a large spoon for about 3 minutes, until the grains feel light when stirred and many have turned chalky white.

Slide the rice saucepan to a cool burner and pour in 2½ cups of the hot broth (without the shiitake); expect sputtering. Give the saucepan a big stir, then slide it back to the hot burner, turn the heat to medium, and let simmer vigorously for 1 to 3 minutes, stirring frequently, until most of the water has been absorbed and the surface looks glossy and thick; small craters may form too. Turn the heat to low, cover, and cook for 10 minutes. Turn off the heat and let the rice sit for 10 minutes to finish cooking. Uncover, fluff with chopsticks, a fork, or a spatula to circulate the grains, and then cover (the rice will stay warm for 30 minutes).

(CONTINUED)

When gathering ingredients, you need 1 bunch green onions and a 4-oz section of ginger total.

Cook the zucchini

While the rice cooks, add the zucchini cubes to the remaining broth and let them gently cook, partially covered. Turn off the heat when the zucchini is tender, about 10 minutes, and cover to keep hot.

Make the sauces

To make the Gingery Soy Sauce: In a small food processor, combine the ginger, soy sauce, vinegar, agave syrup, and miso (if using) and pulse into a zippy brown mixture. Transfer to a dipping-sauce dish and add the chile, if desired.

To make the Green Onion–Ginger Sauce: In a small microwave-safe bowl, combine the green onions, ginger, salt, baking soda (if using), and peanut oil. Microwave on high power for about 45 seconds, or until steamy and bubbly. (Alternatively, heat the peanut oil in a 1- to 1½-qt saucepan over medium heat, until a green onion piece sizzles gently upon contact. Add the green onions, ginger, salt, and baking soda, stirring until things soften, 30 seconds.) Let cool to room temperature.

Set both sauces at the table along with the chile-garlic sauce.

Assemble and eat

Arrange the cucumber and tomatoes on a plate and set at the table. If the tofu has lost some of its crispness, re-fry over medium heat for 1 minute on each side to re-crisp. Cut the tofu into slices along the score marks. Arrange the tofu on a plate or atop the rice on individual plates. Ladle the broth into individual bowls. Bring the tofu, rice, and broth to the table.

Forks and spoons are the primary utensils for this dish, but you could add knives to make cutting the tofu easier. Invite diners to assemble some tofu, a drizzle or a plop of the sauces, and rice. It's fun to vary each bite by changing up the sauce or even combining them! Sip the broth as a chaser to wash things down, and nibble on the cucumber and tomatoes for refreshing textures and flavors.

Notes

Ingredients Delicately nutty, semi-refined peanut oil, sold at many Chinese markets, lends fragrance and flavor to this vegan version as chicken fat does in the standard version. Or try a 2-to-1 blend of unrefined peanut oil and neutral oil for a lovely dimension. Using neutral oil alone is okay, but it lacks depth.

Lifespan Prepare the broth, tofu, rice, and sauces up to 3 days in advance. Keep separate and refrigerate. Bring the sauces to room temperature before serving. Warm the broth (add the zucchini if you haven't). Briefly re-fry the tofu to re-crisp. Microwave the rice to refresh.

1½ cups broken or white jasmine rice (see page 10), plus 2 Tbsp

1¾ cups plus 2 Tbsp water

1 Tbsp neutral oil (such as canola or peanut)

8 oz peeled jicama, cut into matchsticks

½ medium carrot, cut into matchsticks

1 large garlic clove, finely chopped

Fine sea salt

1 (2-oz) bundle dried glass noodles (saifun or bean threads, see page 9)

1 Tbsp soy sauce

GREEN ONION OIL

⅔ cup chopped green onions, white and green parts

2 pinches fine sea salt

2 Tbsp neutral oil (such as canola or peanut)

———

16 pieces Pan-Fried Tofu Slabs (page 52)

½ tsp plus ⅛ tsp granulated sugar

½ tsp fine sea salt

Scant ¼ tsp white pepper

½ Vietnamese "Meatloaf" (page 251), cut as 4 wedges, or 4 fried eggs

1 cup drained Đồ Chua Pickle (page 56)

1 medium or 2 small tomatoes, sliced

1 large Persian cucumber, sliced

1 cup Nước Chấm Dipping Sauce (page 32, made with garlic and chile)

Cơm Tấm Bì Chay

Broken Rice with Vegetarian Bì

I adore broken-rice plates featuring bì (a fragrant mixture of slightly crunchy slivered pork skin, tender poached pork, and nutty ground toasted rice) but I make this vegan version more often. It's tasty, doable with grocery-store ingredients, and a cool vegan fake—glass noodles get tricked out to resemble pork-skin slivers, tofu stands in for pork meat, translucent sautéed jicama resembles pork fat, and carrot adds colorful spark. Round out the rice plate with a piece of Viet meatloaf for a true Viet experience.

Cook the rice two ways

Put the 1½ cups rice in a heavy-bottomed 2-qt saucepan and add water to cover by about 1 inch. Stir the grains with your fingers to loosen the surface starch, then pour off the water (I save it to water my garden). Repeat two or three times, or until the water is nearly clear (it will never be crystal clear). Dump the rice into a mesh strainer, shake to drain the excess water, and return the rice to the pan.

Add the 1¾ cups plus 2 Tbsp water to the pan, set over high heat, and bring to a boil, stirring occasionally to prevent clumping. Lower the heat slightly to maintain a brisk simmer for 1 to 3 minutes, stirring often to scrape the bottom and circulate the grains, until they turn glossy on top. A few craters forming is normal. Turn the heat to low, cover the pan, and cook for 10 minutes. Turn off the heat, let the rice sit for 10 minutes, fluff the rice, and then keep covered.

Meanwhile, put the remaining 2 Tbsp rice in a 12-inch nonstick skillet. Set over medium heat and cook for about 10 minutes, stirring and shaking the skillet often, until the grains are golden (a few browned ones are fine). Expect them to turn opaque and some smoke to appear. Remove from the heat and let cool for 5 to 10 minutes (they'll further darken). Using a clean spice grinder (or a coffee grinder dedicated to spices), pulse the rice to a coarse, sandy texture. Transfer to a small bowl and set aside.

(CONTINUED)

Broken rice is often served at room temperature or slightly warm, so you may make it days in advance and microwave to refresh.

Prep the vegetables and rice powder up to 2 days ahead. The noodles may be soaked up to 4 hours in advance.

The assembled bì mixture is also great in vegetarian rice-paper rolls and banh mi.

Instead of bì, feature herby roast chicken (see page 243), lemongrass tofu (see page 231), eggplant mini steaks (see page 212), or other grilled favorites.

Cook the vegetables

Set the same skillet over high heat and add 2 tsp of the neutral oil. When the oil is hot, add the jicama and cook for about 5 minutes, stirring occasionally and then more often as cooking progresses, spreading out the jicama to evenly cook after each stirring. When the jicama softens and appears about half of its original volume, add the remaining 1 tsp neutral oil, the carrot, and garlic. Season lightly with salt and continue cooking for 2 to 3 minutes longer, until the vegetables are crisp-tender; it's okay if the jicama browns a little. Remove from the heat and let rest for a few minutes before transferring to a bowl and letting cool completely.

Make the "pork skin" and green onion oil

Bring a kettle of water to a boil.

Put the glass noodles in a deep medium bowl. Pour about 2 cups of the boiled water over the noodles to barely cover. Add ½ tsp salt and the soy sauce, then stir to dissolve and untangle the noodles. Let soak and soften for 6 to 8 minutes, or until the noodles are clear and firm-chewy (al dente). Drain well and set aside to cool completely.

To make the Green Onion Oil: While the noodles cool, in a small bowl, combine the green onions, salt, and neutral oil. Microwave on high power for 45 to 60 seconds, until the green onions soften in the bubbly oil. (Alternatively, heat the neutral oil in a 1- to 1½-qt saucepan over medium heat until a green onion piece gently sizzles upon contact. Add the remaining green onions and the salt and then stir until things soften, 30 seconds.) Stir and then set aside to cool completely.

Assemble the bi

Using a serrated knife, cut the fried tofu into thin strips and put them in a bowl. Chop the noodles into 1- to 2-inch lengths and add to the tofu. Add the jicama and carrot to the bowl and sprinkle with the sugar, salt, white pepper, and toasted ground rice. Toss to combine well.

Plate and serve

Re-fluff the rice, mound it on four large dinner plates, and then top each mound with green onion oil. Surround the rice with a pile of bì, a wedge of meatloaf, a bit of pickle, and some tomato and cucumber. (If there's not enough room on the plates, present the veggies separately on a serving plate.) At the table, invite diners to season the bì and rice with nước chấm. I like to mix them all together to allow the bì to combine well with the rice. Enjoy the meatloaf as an extra-fun protein (break it up to combine with the rice, if you like) and consider the raw vegetables as palate refreshers between bites.

SHIITAKE-CAULIFLOWER FILLING

1½ oz dried shiitake mushrooms, soaked in water to cover for 6 hours

¾ cup small-dice carrot

2½ cups fresh cauliflower rice or crumbles

½ tsp fine sea salt

½ tsp recently ground black pepper

¼ tsp plus ⅛ tsp granulated sugar

2 Tbsp fish sauce (store-bought or vegan version, page 29)

2 Tbsp neutral oil (such as canola or peanut), plus more as needed

½ cup chopped shallots or yellow onion

½ cup chopped green onions, green and white parts

MSG or Asian mushroom seasoning for flavoring (optional, for umami sparkle)

———

24 (22-cm-diameter) sturdy rice papers (see Note; preferably Three Ladies or Tufoco Bamboo Tree brand)

About 3 Tbsp Fast-Fried Shallot oil (see page 46) or neutral oil

8 oz Persian or English cucumber

1 pinch kosher salt

1 pinch granulated sugar

1 cup hand-torn or coarsely chopped mixed herbs (such as cilantro and mint)

2 batches Fast-Fried Shallots (page 46), or ⅓ cup store-bought fried shallots or onions

¾ cup Nước Chấm Dipping Sauce (page 32, made with chile)

Bánh Cuốn Chay

Shiitake-Cauliflower Steamed Rice Rolls

Literally meaning "rolled cake," bánh cuốn are much more exciting than that English translation. The breakfast and lunch favorite comprises thin, translucent rice sheets prepared from fermented batter that has been skillfully steamed atop a piece of fabric. Compared with Cantonese cheung fan rice-noodle rolls, bánh cuốn are more delicate, served warm or at room temperature, and eaten with nước chấm, fried shallot, herbs, cucumber, and blanched bean sprouts.

Traditionally, steaming bánh cuốn is left to professional or hard-core home cooks. In the 1970s, Viet expats circulated a workaround for preparing the rice sheets in a nonstick skillet, which I've done for years. Recently, crafty cooks in Vietnam and elsewhere have taken to soaking sturdy rice papers to plump suppleness and then briefly steaming or microwaving them. The brilliant reason: Rice papers are simply steamed rice sheets that have been dried. The result is tender and beautiful, albeit lacking a strong rice flavor because lots of tapioca starch is used in commercial rice paper. That's not a deal-breaker for me because this shortcut is achievable and fun. Bánh cuốn may be eaten unfilled with sliced Viet bologna (see page 53) plus garnishes, but I love them as filled rolls. Riced cauliflower mimics meaty nubs in the main recipe's vegan take; remember to soak the mushrooms in advance. See the Notes for pork and shrimp filling options.

Prepare the filling

To make the Shiitake-Cauliflower Filling: Squeeze the shiitakes to remove excess liquid (save the soaking water for broth or another use). Finely chop the caps and stems and then place in a bowl. Add the carrot and cauliflower; season with the salt, pepper, sugar, and fish sauce; and stir to combine. Set near the stove.

Set a 12-inch nonstick skillet over medium heat and add the neutral oil. When the oil barely ripples, add the shallots and cook, stirring, for 2 to 4 minutes, until fragrant with many browned pieces. Dump in the mushroom mixture and cook,

(CONTINUED)

Steam or microwave the rolls? Steaming is best to gently cook and carefully monitor progress. For your steamer setup, use a wide lidded pot, such as a 6-qt Dutch oven, outfitted with a metal steamer basket (or use a Chinese steamer, see page 112). Select six plates that fit into the steamer and can be easily retrieved with tongs or a hot-plate gripper. Microwaving is easier but you must carefully watch the rolls, or they'll quickly overcook; plate size is not as crucial.

Soaking and filling the rice papers can initially seem unwieldy. Watch my quick how-to video at Vietworldkitchen.com/evergreentips.

stirring often, for about 5 minutes, until the cauliflower and carrot are tender. Add the green onions, and when they soften, remove the pan from the heat. Let rest for 5 minutes, taste, and if additional savoriness is needed, season with MSG or salt. Transfer this filling to a bowl, partially cover, and let cool to room temperature.

Soak the rice papers and make the rolls

Make the rolls in three batches to avoid a sticky pile of soaked rice papers. In a deep skillet, roasting pan, or similar vessel that is wider than the rice paper, add room-temperature (about 70°F) water to a depth of 1½ to 2 inches.

Working with eight rice papers per batch, slide each one into the water, making sure it's wet on both sides and fully submerged before adding the next. (I often slide, wiggle, then press it down.) Let the papers soften for about 10 minutes, until they turn supple, slippery, and gelatinous-feeling.

Meanwhile, select six plates that fit your steamer or microwave oven. Lightly brush the plates with some of the shallot oil.

When the papers are finished soaking, using your hands, gently separate them, keeping them in the soaking vessel (water loosens them, so keep them submerged). They'll look like floating tissues.

Using both hands, retrieve a rice paper and place it on a rimmed baking sheet, the longer side parallel to you (the rice-paper round will have morphed into an oval, so it will resemble an egg on its side). Place 2 Tbsp filling below the midline, spreading it out to span 6 inches wide. Fold in the side flaps to keep things in place. Bring up the bottom flap to cover the filling, then fold and roll upward to close. It's okay if it's not perfect; cooking rids imperfections, including small holes or tears. Place on a prepared plate. Repeat to fill and fold seven more rolls. When done, repeat the whole process to make another sixteen rolls. (If cooking with pals, soak the papers in two vessels to fill and fold simultaneously. When you're confident, advance to soaking twelve rice papers at a time.)

Cook the rolls

Brush the top and ends of the rolls with the remaining shallot oil.

To steam the rolls—If using a pot and collapsible steamer setup, fill the pot with a generous ½ inch of water (if using a Chinese steamer, fill the bottom pot with about 2 inches of water). Bring the water to a boil then lower the heat to steady the steam. Add a plate of rolls, cover, and steam for 1½ to 2 minutes, until the rolls turn translucent, soft, and slightly sticky.

(CONTINUED)

To microwave the rolls—Loosely cover a plate of rolls with parchment paper or wax paper and microwave on high power for 45 to 75 seconds.

Peek to gauge doneness; if the rolls look clear and vacuumed-sealed around the filling, they have overcooked. Decrease the cooking time (and maybe lower the heat or power) for the next plate and repeat to cook all the rolls. Let the rolls cool for 5 minutes. (Loosely cover to keep soft for up to 1 hour.)

Assemble and serve

Halve the cucumber lengthwise, scrape out the seeds, and thinly slice on the diagonal. Transfer the slices to a bowl and season with the salt and sugar. Add the herbs and stir gently to combine. Place a small pile on each bánh cuốn plate (offer any extra herby cucumber on the side). Shower fried shallots on the rolls, then present with a bowl of the nước chấm.

Serve with spoons and chopsticks (or forks). Drizzle some sauce over the bánh cuốn, cut a section of the roll with a spoon, then use a two-handed approach to gather up the section plus stray shallot bits. The herb salad refreshes with green flavors and crunch, so add a bit to each bite.

———

Notes

Ingredients If the preferred brands of rice paper are unavailable, recipe tester Alex Ciepley suggests soaking four papers at a time for 2 to 4 minutes, then cooking the rolls for 10 to 30 seconds longer. The results are fine, albeit chewier and slightly bland because there's more tapioca in thinner rice papers.

Lifespan Cover and refrigerate cooked rolls for up to 3 days. Return to room temperature and refresh by re-steaming or microwaving for about 1 minute.

Variations For Pork-Shiitake Steamed Rice Rolls, called bánh cuốn nhân thịt, soak ½ oz dried shiitakes in water to cover for 6 hours, then squeeze and finely chop the caps and stems. Just like in the main recipe, cook the ½ cup chopped shallots in oil until brown, then add 1 lb ground pork (or chicken or turkey dark meat), mashing and stirring to break it up. Season with a mounded ¼ tsp sugar, ½ tsp fine sea salt, ¾ tsp recently ground black pepper, and 1 Tbsp fish sauce. When the pork is half-cooked, about 1 minute, add the chopped shiitakes. Cook for 1 minute more, until the pork is nearly cooked, then add the ½ cup chopped green onions. When the green onions soften, remove from the heat. Let rest briefly, then taste, tweak the flavors, and let cool completely before using.

Alternatively, cook a 50/50 or 25/75 blend of ground pork and raw shrimp (chopped into pea-size pieces). Add the shrimp with the mushroom. Apply the same seasonings and cooking times. You'll make Steamed Rice Rolls with Pork and Shrimp, or bánh cuốn nhân tôm thịt, in Vietnamese.

CREPE BATTER

2¾ cups regular Thai rice flour (see page 10)

1½ Tbsp cornstarch

¾ tsp fine sea salt

¾ tsp ground turmeric

3¼ cups water

———

8 oz boneless pork shoulder, beef steak, or chicken thighs, thinly sliced into pinkie-length strips

2 tsp fish sauce (store-bought or vegan version, page 29)

½ tsp fine sea salt

½ tsp recently ground black pepper

½ tsp granulated sugar

10 oz extra-large (21/25 count) shrimp, peeled, deveined, and cut into ¾-inch chunks

1 Tbsp neutral oil (such as canola or peanut), plus 1¼ cups

3 large eggs, well beaten (optional, for extra protein richness)

½ cup chopped green onions, green and white parts

8 oz mung bean sprouts

Leaves from 2 heads soft-leaf lettuce (such as butter, Boston, or red- or green-leaf)

1 small handful mint sprigs

1 small handful cilantro sprigs

1 small handful Vietnamese shiso or balm, or other soft-leaf fresh herbs (optional)

1¼ cups Peanut-Hoisin Sauce (page 42)

Bánh Khoái

Huế Rice Crepes

Outside of Vietnam, fried crispy rice crepes called bánh khoái are nearly unknown or forgotten. But you should befriend this central Viet specialty because, compared with their popular southern offshoot, bánh xèo (sizzling rice crepes), they're easier to make and really tasty—imagine a nutty, toasty, crunchy rice shell filled with savory treasures. The crepes are hearty and primal.

Bánh khoái batter is prepared from a handful of ingredients, and most of the filling is precooked (see the Notes for alternative batter and nonmeat filling options). The most difficult part is waiting for these crepes to finish frying so you can gobble them up in lettuce-and-herb wraps with peanut-y hoisin sauce. Years ago, I traveled to Huế to taste the real deal, which were shallow-fried in long-handled five- to six-inch skillets that safely distanced cooks from the bubbling oil. Eight-inch skillets and less oil work fine in my kitchen with terrific results. When entertaining, prep all the components, do a demo, and invite guests to fry. This is a fantastic, special one-dish meal for your rice repertoire.

Prepare the batter

To make the Crepe Batter: In a medium bowl, whisk together the rice flour, cornstarch, salt, and turmeric. Make a well in the center, then whisk in the water. Set aside for 1 hour, uncovered, to thicken (see Note).

Cook the filling

Meanwhile, in a second bowl, season the pork with the fish sauce and ¼ tsp of the salt, ¼ tsp of the pepper, and ¼ tsp of the sugar. In another bowl, combine the shrimp with the remaining ¼ tsp each salt, pepper, and sugar. Set a 10-inch nonstick skillet over medium-high heat and add 2 tsp of the neutral oil. When the oil ripples, add the pork and cook for 1 to 2 minutes, until the rawness just disappears. Transfer to a small plate or bowl; discard any lingering juices.

Add 1 tsp neutral oil to the skillet and turn the heat to medium. Add the shrimp and cook, stirring, for about 2 minutes, or until they turn firm and opaque. Transfer to another small plate or bowl.

(CONTINUED)

For consistency, weigh the rice flour. You'll need 325g of Asian or stone-ground white rice flour.

Along with shrimp count, eyeball the size. Extra-large shrimp are about ⅞ inch wide at the thickest segment.

Extra-wide skillets, often called "French skillets," have more surface area to produce crepes loaded with crunch.

To be more organized, divide the cooked pork and shrimp into twelve portions for each crepe.

Set the pork, shrimp, eggs (if using), green onions, and bean sprouts along with the crepe batter and remaining 1¼ cups neutral oil by the stove. Put a wire cooling rack on a rimmed baking sheet and place on the other side of the stove to hold the finished crepes.

Fry the crepes

Set an 8-inch nonstick or carbon-steel skillet over medium heat and add 1½ to 2 Tbsp of the neutral oil. As the oil becomes rippling hot, stir the batter well before pouring ¼ to ⅓ cup of it into the skillet. Immediately swirl the pan to cover the bottom thickly. The batter will dramatically sizzle, seize, and bubble.

Avoiding the center line where you'll later fold the crepe, arrange about 2 Tbsp pork and 4 or 5 shrimp chunks onto the crepe. Drizzle with a scant 1 Tbsp egg, then scatter a three-finger pinch of green onions on top (it's fine for these softer elements to be in the middle). Cover and fry for 2 minutes, until the green onions soften.

Remove the lid and pile 1 small handful bean sprouts on one half (you'll cover some of the filling). Continue frying for 2 to 4 minutes, uncovered, to crisp the underside. Using a spatula, check that the crepe is crispy with few or no soft spots. (If it needs to fry longer, lower the heat, gently lift its edges, and drizzle more oil underneath.) You want the crepe to be crunchy; crunchy crepes are stiff when lifted with a spatula. When you're done, use the spatula to fold the crepe in half and transfer to the prepared rack to cool and drain. (If the crepe is hard to fold, transfer it to the rack and fold after it has briefly cooled; it is okay if the spine breaks.)

If you lowered the heat, raise it to medium to ensure a hot, but not smoking, skillet. Replenish the skillet with neutral oil and then repeat to fry twelve crepes total.

If you feel comfortable about the cooking, you can simultaneously fry the crepes in two or more skillets. The crepes taste best straight from the skillet, but they will stay crunchy and tasty for about 2 hours; if they soften, briefly re-fry to re-crisp. Keep them on the rack until you're ready to serve.

Assemble and serve

Arrange the crepes on platters along with the lettuce, herbs, and peanut-hoisin sauce. Pass around one or two pairs of kitchen scissors for diners to cut their crepes into manageable pieces. Tear a piece of lettuce roughly the size of your palm, place a piece of the crepe on it, add herb leaves, and then drizzle on some sauce. Gather everything into a bundle and munch away.

(CONTINUED)

Notes

Ingredients If Thai rice flour is unavailable or you're interested in trying a modification, make a batter from raw rice instead. Wash 1⅔ cups long-grain white rice once and drain well. Transfer to a blender jar, add 2¾ cups water, and let sit 1 to 4 hours to hydrate and soften. Add the cornstarch, salt, and turmeric to the blender jar, then whirl on high speed for 2 to 3 minutes, until the rice turns bright yellow and super-smooth with only a slight grittiness when rubbed between your fingers (it's okay if the batter feels warm). This batter yields a nutty, toasty flavor and good crunch.

Alternatively, replace the fine Thai rice flour with coarse, stone-ground white rice flour sold at mainstream supermarkets. Blend 1¾ cups plus 2 Tbsp coarse rice flour with the cornstarch, salt, turmeric, and 3¼ cups water on high speed for about 2 minutes, until it turns bright yellow and super-smooth. This batter fries up crisp-tender, but not as crunchy as when Thai rice flour or raw rice is used.

Regardless of your batter choice, let it rest to thicken for 1 hour before using.

Timing The batter can sit at room temperature, covered, for up to 8 hours. Otherwise, cover and refrigerate overnight, returning it to room temperature and stirring well to combine before using. The filling may be cooked up to 3 days ahead and refrigerated separately. The sauce keeps well too (see Note, page 43 for tips).

Lifespan Extra crepes can be refrigerated and re-fried but will taste a tad tired.

Variations You can put many things in these crepes as long as it's in smallish pieces and well-seasoned to stand up to the hearty rice shell. To make Vegetarian Huế Rice Crepes, use tofu and mushrooms instead of pork and shrimp. For the tofu, use 1½ cups of Umami Tofu Crumbles (page 50) and season generously with salt and pepper. Or, slice eight Pan-Fried Tofu Slabs (page 52) into ¼-inch-thick pieces; season with 1 to 2 tsp fish sauce or soy sauce, salt, and pepper; and then sear in a medium-hot skillet with 2 tsp neutral oil for 2 to 3 minutes, until lightly browned (expect a few pieces to break). For the mushrooms, thickly slice 10 oz fresh cremini, white, or shiitake mushrooms; season generously with salt and pepper; and then cook in a hot skillet for 2 to 3 minutes, until they turn soft and glistening. Pour off their cooking juices before using.

Omit the egg when making vegan crepes.

Huế Rice Crepes IN SIX STEPS

Wait for rippling hot oil, then pour in the batter.

Quickly swirl the pan to thickly coat the bottom.

Avoid the midline when arranging bulky filling.

Drizzle with egg (a pourer with a spout helps).

Briefly fry, uncover, then place the sprouts on one half.

Crispy-crunchy crepe perfection. It is stiff when lifted!

Snack Sensations

SNACKING IS AN AROUND-THE-CLOCK activity in Vietnam. Food vendors strategically time their operations to satisfy customers' peak craving hours for certain savories and sweets. People know when and where to find their favorites. Living abroad, I can't partake in all the daily street-food action, but that's okay. I'm just as happy to prepare Viet snacks at home to treat myself, family, and friends. They are joyful, thrilling foods.

In Vietnamese, there are several terms for snacks. Restaurant menus often describe them as món khai vị (food to whet the appetite) to convey formality and flair. On the other end of the spectrum is the more casual món ăn vặt (food miscellany), which frames snacks as trivial and practically inconsequential compared with the bigger meals of breakfast, lunch, and dinner.

I take a lyrical stance, preferring món ăn quà (food gifts), an intimate expression of generosity that underscores the thoughtfulness involved in feeding others. It's a term I learned from my mother, who, in spite of her busy schedule as a dressmaker, always made sure we snacked well.

This chapter includes some of my favorites, both old and new. You'll note Southeast Asian, Chinese, French, and American influences in the recipes, which, in totality, illustrate how colonialism, trade, immigration, and, now, technology have impacted Viet foodways.

The wontons and sweet potato fritters are traditionally deep-fried, but I've developed recipes to oven-fry or shallow-fry to help you make them with greater ease. Wonderful as-is, the mushroom-walnut pâté can also be worked into a wonton filling or banh mi. The multipurpose lemongrass and fermented-tofu sauce is terrific as a creamy dip and salad dressing.

Because rice paper is a defining ingredient in Vietnamese cuisine and many cooks can stumble while working with it, there are two recipes for unfried rice-paper rolls. A photographic tutorial coaches you to nimbly roll your own. To push the rice-paper limits, grill it for rice-paper "pizza," a modern street-food snack. The oven-fried chả giò (imperial rolls) are a breakthrough for those who've requested healthful, crispy fried rice-paper rolls without the hassle of deep-frying. Plus, you can prep the rolls and freeze them for months. Yes, air-frying instructions are included.

If you love steamed bao, there are versatile recipes to make small sandwiches or filled veggie buns from an easygoing dough. Your Chinese steamer will get delicious use from those recipes. When you'd rather bake your buns, make the fluffy, sweet bao, which employ sweetened condensed milk for their marvelous texture and flavor. The char siu pulled-jackfruit filling can go into the baked or steamed bao.

Prepare the savory noshes in this chapter as cocktail nibbles, a prelude to a lavish meal, or, heck, even a light lunch (add a green salad, perhaps). There are more snackable recipes in this book, including the banh mi, plus sweets and beverage chapters. No matter how you present món ăn quà, they'll be received with extra gratitude.

LEMONGRASS FERMENTED-TOFU SAUCE

¼ cup packed fermented white tofu, preferably without chile, plus brine as needed

1½ Tbsp agave syrup, mild honey, or granulated sugar

1½ Tbsp fresh lime juice, plus more as needed

1½ Tbsp minced lemongrass (see page 44)

2 to 3 Thai or small serrano chiles, finely chopped (use more for edgy heat)

2 Tbsp toasted sesame seeds (optional, to thicken and enrich)

1 to 3 tsp neutral oil (such as canola or peanut)

———

1 or 2 small watermelon radishes, or a half or whole bunch red radishes, cut as thin slices or wedges

1 or 2 medium carrots, scrubbed or peeled and sliced on the diagonal

½ to 1 lb jicama, peeled and cut into 3-inch chubby sticks

1 or 2 Persian cucumbers, or ¼ to ½ small English cucumber, thickly sliced or cut as 3-inch chubby sticks

1 or 2 small handfuls raw asparagus or green beans, trimmed and cut into 3-inch lengths

Leaves from 1 or 2 small endive

Before serving, if the veggies are limp and need perking up, fill a large bowl with water and ice, then submerge the culprits in the icy bath for a few minutes to crisp. Drain and pat dry.

Rau Củ Sống Chấm Chao

Crudités with Lemongrass-Chao Dip

For a Vietnamese take on crudités, I serve seasonal raw veggies with a dynamite sauce featuring chao (fermented tofu, see page 23), a wondrous ingredient that's akin to creamy, winy cheese. The tangy spicy, umami-rich sauce is typically served with cooked foods, but I adore it as a dip and salad dressing (see page 183). Choose at least three vegetables from the crudités options; the smaller quantities are for when all are used.

Prepare the sauce

To make the Lemongrass Fermented-Tofu Sauce: In a small bowl, using a fork or the back of a spoon, mash the tofu (expect lingering solids). Stir in the agave syrup and lime juice, then add tofu brine by the teaspoon to achieve a pleasant salty-sour-sweet-winy balance. Stir in the lemongrass and chiles.

If using the sesame seeds, use a mortar and pestle to stir, grind, and pound them into a fragrant, finely textured mixture. (Alternatively, use a small food processor or an electric spice grinder.) Scrape and stir into the sauce. Let the sauce develop flavor for about 15 minutes before re-tasting; then add enough of the neutral oil to soften, lime juice to brighten, and additional brine to intensify.

Assemble and serve

Arrange all the vegetables on a platter. Transfer the sauce to a small bowl and set in the center or on the side of the platter. Invite diners to dip and eat.

Notes

Lifespan Make the sauce up to 5 days ahead and refrigerate in an airtight container; return to room temperature to serve.

Variation Instead of chao, use 2½ Tbsp white (shiro) miso mixed with 1½ Tbsp water. Serve with the same vegetables for a Crudités with Lemongrass-Miso Dip.

FILLING

4 oz extra-firm tofu

2 Tbsp cream cheese
(dairy-free, if preferred)

2 Tbsp finely chopped
green onions, green and
white parts

1½ tsp Nori Dust (page 27)

½ tsp soy sauce

Scant ¼ tsp fine sea salt

¼ tsp smoked paprika

————

All-purpose flour for dusting

20 to 24 wonton wrappers

About 3 Tbsp neutral oil
(such as canola or peanut)

¼ cup Thai sweet chile sauce

Hoành Thánh Chiên

Smoky Tofu-Nori Wontons

I grew up stuffing wontons with pork and dipping the deep-fried wonders in fish sauce–tinged sweet-and-sour sauce, but for many Viet Americans today, their hoành thánh chiên take cues from tiki bars with a cream cheese–based crab Rangoon-ish filling. For a low-guilt, oven-fried vegetarian version, make a tofu filling with a bit of cream cheese to bind. The smoked paprika and nori impart an intriguing hamlike flavor. This crunchy snack employs a simple hack to air-fry in a regular oven. The resulting wontons are lean, so if you prefer richer fried ones, see the Notes, which also contains a mushroom pâté variation.

Prepare the filling

To make the filling: Break the tofu into two or three chunks and put in a piece of muslin or a dish towel. Stand over the sink and squeeze and massage the tofu to expel its liquid; mash it well. Transfer to a medium bowl and add the cream cheese, green onions, nori dust, soy sauce, salt, and smoked paprika. Mix well, then pat down the filling and divide it into quarters, like cutting a pie.

Fill the wontons

Position a rack in the upper third of the oven and preheat to 375°F. (If your oven has convection capability, select it for even crisper results; use 350°F if your oven does not automatically convert the temperature for convection cooking.) Line a baking sheet with parchment paper and dust it with flour.

Working with one quadrant of filling and six wrappers at a time, lay the wrappers on your work surface. Use two small spoons to scoop about ¾ tsp of filling and place it slightly off-center on each wrapper. Using a pastry brush or your index finger, paint the wrapper edges with water. Bring a corner of the wrapper to meet the opposite corner to create a triangle. Press to seal well and get rid of any air bubbles. Set the wonton flat on the prepared baking sheet, then make the remaining wontons; it's okay to stack them in layers separated by flour-dusted parchment paper.

(CONTINUED)

Have leftover pot sticker wrappers from the soup on page 151? Use them here instead of wonton skins!

For a dairy-free filling, I opt for tofu-based cream cheese.

Merge banh mi and dumplings into a tasty two-biter? Why not? In Minneapolis at Hai Hai restaurant, chef Christina Nguyen creatively stuffs wontons with cream cheese and chicken liver pâté and presents them with a passion fruit–chile sauce. Her sinfully rich snack is a wonderful occasional splurge. It inspired my lighter veggie pâté variation.

Oven-fry the wontons and serve

Set a wire cooling rack inside a large rimmed baking sheet; for the best heat circulation, choose a rack that sits nearly level with the sheet's rim. Arrange the wontons flat on the rack, knocking off excess flour and spacing each a thumb's width apart for efficient heat circulation.

Brush each wonton with some of the neutral oil on both sides (it will look glossy). Oven-fry for 3 to 6 minutes, until the wontons are gently sizzling and a few of their tips have turned blond. Flip them, rotate the pan, and continue to oven-fry for 3 to 6 minutes, until browned. Let them rest for about 30 seconds to finish crisping, then transfer to a plate. Repeat for the remaining wontons.

Like all wontons, expect the center where the filling is to soften as they sit, but the rest of the wonton will be crunchy-good, even at room temperature. (Pop them in a 350°F oven for 1 minute if you want them warmed through.) Dive in with the chile sauce for dipping.

Notes

Equipment In an air fryer, cook the wontons at 350°F for about 2 minutes per side. Since air fryers vary by model, test-fry a wonton to determine the best temperature and timing.

To shallow-fry the wontons, fill a wide saucepan, deep skillet, or wok with ¾ inch neutral oil (such as canola or peanut). Heat the oil to about 325°F, then fry the wontons in batches for 3 to 4 minutes, turning them often and spooning oil over the top until they're golden brown and crisp.

Ingredients Don't have smoked paprika? Substitute ⅛ tsp recently ground black pepper for a different kind of zip. Thin wonton skins, like the Dynasty brand, cook up deliciously crispy-crunchy; at Asian markets, "Hong Kong–style" wonton wrappers signal thinness.

Lifespan The filling keeps well in the fridge for about 3 days, so you can cook up small batches if you prefer. Unbaked wontons can be tightly covered and refrigerated up to 3 hours; it's fine to oven-fry them straight from the fridge.

Variation For Mushroom Pâté Wontons, swap out the tofu-nori filling for this combination: In a medium bowl, mix together ⅓ cup packed Five-Spice Mushroom Walnut Pâté (page 92), 2 Tbsp cream cheese, ⅛ tsp fine sea salt, and ⅛ tsp recently ground black pepper. Assemble, fry, and serve your wontons as directed.

8 oz fresh cremini or white mushrooms

¾ cup raw walnut halves or pieces

2 tsp Maggi Seasoning sauce or Bragg Liquid Aminos, plus more as needed

Brimming ¼ tsp Chinese five-spice powder

Fine sea salt

Recently ground black pepper

2½ Tbsp unsalted butter or neutral oil (such as canola or peanut)

¼ cup chopped shallots or yellow onion

1 large garlic clove, minced

⅓ cup coarsely chopped cilantro sprigs, stems included

Pate Nấm Chay

Five-Spice Mushroom-Walnut Pâté

I adore homemade liver pâté, but dealing with offal isn't always my jam. Cue this mushroom pâté, a liverless, light, and delicious spread. Walnuts produce a fatty finish, their tannins adding delicate complexity. Serve this pate nấm with a sleeve of crackers and, if handy, pickled shallots (see page 57) or daikon and carrot (see page 56). Also employ the spread for wontons (see page 89) and building banh mi (see page 128).

Chop the mushrooms and walnuts

Cut the mushroom caps and stems into large dice, about ¾ inch, and put them into a bowl. Coarsely chop the walnuts and add them to the mushrooms. Season with the Maggi, five-spice powder, ¼ tsp salt, and ⅛ tsp pepper.

Cook and process the pâté

In a 2- to 3-qt saucepan over medium heat, melt the butter (or warm the oil). Add the shallots and cook, stirring, for 3 to 5 minutes, until mostly golden.

Add the garlic and cilantro to the pan and stir to aromatize. Dump in the mushroom-walnut mixture and stir to combine. Cover, turn the heat to medium-low to facilitate gentle bubbling action, and cook for 8 to 12 minutes, stirring midway, until the mushroom pieces shrink by about half.

Uncover and cook for 1 to 2 minutes, stirring often, to concentrate the flavor. When no liquid is visible, remove from the heat and let cool for 5 minutes. Transfer the mixture to a food processor and whirl into a smooth spread.

Season, tweak, then serve

Taste and season with additional Maggi, salt, and pepper for a robust, savory, spicy finish. Let the flavors develop for about 15 minutes. Serve at room temperature.

Note

Lifespan Keeps well in an airtight container in the refrigerator for 2 weeks. If you're in a hurry, zap it in the microwave in 15-second blasts to remove the chill.

Mature, cruddy-looking cremini that have opened like parasols yield tasty results. Purposely pick imperfect mushrooms for perfect pâté.

Makes 1¼ cups, 6 servings

7-oz sweet potato (orange- or white-fleshed variety)

Fine sea salt

6 oz large (26/30) shrimp, peeled, deveined, and cut into ¾-inch chunks

¾ tsp granulated sugar

Recently ground black pepper

Brimming ¼ cup all-purpose flour (bleached or unbleached)

2 Tbsp white or brown rice flour

2 Tbsp cornstarch

⅛ tsp baking powder

1 pinch ground turmeric (include when using white sweet potato)

⅓ cup water

¾ cup neutral oil (such as canola or peanut), plus more as needed

Leaves from 1 head soft-leaf lettuce (such as butter or red- or green-leaf)

1 small handful cilantro sprigs

1 small handful mint, basil, shiso, or a combination of soft-leaf herbs

½ cup Nước Chấm Dipping Sauce (page 32)

Bánh Tôm

Crispy Sweet Potato and Shrimp Fritters

A classic Hanoi snack, these fritters are typically deep-fried with whole shell-on shrimp, but it's challenging to make them crunchy and to keep the shrimp affixed atop the fritter. For an easier method, I shave the sweet potatoes instead of cutting them as sticks and put chopped shrimp in the batter. My bánh tôm shallow-fry into wispy-crispy nests, keeping their original savory-sweet charm intact. Enjoy these as lettuce-and-herb wraps, dunked in nước chấm for a burst of contrasting flavors and textures. See Notes for a vegan option.

Prep the sweet potato

Using a vegetable peeler, remove the sweet potato skin, then shave the flesh directly into a medium bowl. Aim for ribbons no longer than 4 inches and no wider than ¾ inch; as you work, turn the potato to create bevels and to manage the size (you can cut down any too-big pieces afterward). When the remaining sweet potato gets hard to shave, switch to a knife to cut it into matchsticks about the size of a fat bean sprout.

Add ¾ tsp salt and 2 cups water to the bowl and then swish with your hand to dissolve the salt. Let the potato soak at room temperature, uncovered, while you prep the other ingredients. (The potato can hang out for up to 2 hours.)

Ready the shrimp and batter

In a small bowl, combine the shrimp with ¼ tsp of the sugar, ⅛ tsp salt, and ⅛ tsp pepper. Mix thoroughly and set aside.

In a large bowl, combine the all-purpose flour, rice flour, cornstarch, baking powder, turmeric, remaining ½ tsp sugar, and ⅛ tsp salt and, using a whisk, stir to incorporate. Make a well in the center, then stir in the ⅓ cup water to just combine. Let this batter sit, uncovered, for 15 minutes to hydrate.

(CONTINUED)

Sweet potato varieties vary a lot. For example, moist, orange-fleshed Garnets offer sweet flavor; dryish, white-fleshed Hannahs fry up a touch crisper. Regardless of type, my sweet spot is a 7-oz potato.

Precision is critical for the batter. If you have a kitchen scale, use metric measurements to verify the following: 40g all-purpose flour, 20g rice flour (either kind), and 16g cornstarch.

To gauge shrimp size, know that large shell-on shrimp are about ¾ inch thick at their widest.

When a Viet recipe involves lettuce-and-herb plus dipping sauce, ready those accompaniments in advance to save time and enjoy your food at its peak.

Finish the batter

Meanwhile, drain the sweet potato in a mesh strainer, shaking well to expel excess moisture. Spread out the potato on a dish towel and pat to remove excess moisture. After the batter sufficiently hydrates, add the potato and shrimp to it. Stir to coat and distribute well.

Shallow-fry

Pour a generous ¼ inch of the neutral oil into a 10-inch nonstick skillet and set over medium heat. Meanwhile, set a cooling rack on a baking sheet.

Test the oil by inserting a dry bamboo or wooden chopstick. If bubbles appear quickly, the oil temperature is near 350°F, the optimal cooking temperature. Using a large metal spoon, scoop up about ⅓ cup batter, then use a fork (or another spoon) to neaten and shape it into an artful flat nest about 3 inches wide. Very gently press down with the fork to make sure the batter hangs together, then use the fork to usher it into the oil. Once in the oil, move some potato pieces around to further tidy up the fritter, if you like. You should be able to fry about three fritters at a time. Fry each side for about 3 minutes, until very crisp and golden brown. Using tongs, transfer the fritters to the prepared rack to drain while you repeat with the remaining batter. Once all the fritters are fried, assess them to identify any that you may have pulled out of the oil before they were perfectly fried. Re-fry any that need crisping.

Assemble and serve

Serve the fritters with the lettuce, cilantro, mint, and dipping sauce. Let diners build their own lettuce wraps, which should contain a piece of fritter (pass around scissors or use forks or fingers to break up the fritters) and two or three herb leaves and sprigs. Dunk the whole thing in the sauce and eat.

Notes

Lifespan Fried fritters can sit on the rack for up to 4 hours. Reheat in a 400°F oven for 5 minutes until hot. Briefly rest to cool and crisp before serving.

Variation For Vegan Sweet Potato, Kale, and Nori Fritters, prep the sweet potato and make the batter as directed. Finish the batter by mixing in the drained sweet potato, plus 1½ oz chopped kale (use only the leafy parts and pat them dry before cutting into pieces no bigger than the potato), ¼ tsp sugar, ⅛ tsp salt, ⅛ tsp black pepper, and two sheets nori, quartered and cut into 1-inch-wide strips (use scissors). Stir well until the mixture coheres and collapses by roughly half the original volume. Fry for 2 to 3 minutes per side.

Rice-Paper Roll BASICS

I used to translate *gỏi cuốn* as "salad rolls" because the filling components often mirror what are in classic Viet salads called gỏi, but "rolled-up salad" sounds awkward. Gỏi cuốn are enjoyed year-round, so "spring rolls" or "summer rolls" is misleading. ("Fresh" spring rolls never made sense to me—are some old and tired?) Given all this, I now refer to them as "rice-paper rolls," or gỏi cuốn.

How to choose bánh tráng (rice paper)? Rice papers vary in thickness. For good flavor and easy manipulation, select sturdy rice paper that is approximately 8½ inches wide, which is typically labeled in metric as measuring 22cm; the 6-inch-wide papers are for extra-dexterous pros. See page 10 for bánh tráng shopping tips.

How do you best wet rice paper? Choose a dipping vessel wider than the paper, such as a shallow bowl or casserole dish. Fill it 1 to 2 inches deep with very warm water (slightly hotter than bathwater; replenish if the water turns cold as you work). If you're using a rice-paper water bowl (called tô nhúng bánh tráng and sold at Little Saigon markets and online), fill it three-fourths full.

Rice paper needs minimal moisture to rehydrate. Aim to wet, not soak; oversoaked rice paper turns opaque white and slides around rather than sticking to itself to seal and hold the roll's shape.

Wet a rice paper by holding it by its edge, sliding it partway into the water, and then immediately rotating through the water to wet it all over. Wetting rice paper takes seconds, and the paper remains stiff when you lift it from the water. Shake off excess water and then lay the paper down (I prefer smooth-side down) on your work surface. After about 1 minute, when the paper softens and turns tacky like a sticky note, it's ready to be filled.

How to make pretty rolls? Start by placing the filling components in the lower third of the rice paper. Lettuce typically goes down first to establish a bed, followed by other items arranged flat so that each bite contains everything. If you want to showcase blingy ingredients (such as mushrooms, tofu, or shrimp), don't add them to the first layer of filling.

Bring up the bottom edge of the rice paper to cover the filling, then roll upward once (so the lettuce faces you) and tuck the rice-paper edge under the filling to keep it in place. Now lay down the bling. Fold both side flaps inward (if you overfilled or want to serve with one end open for show, fold in only one side), then finish by rolling upward to close. The blingy items should be visible through the layers of rice paper. Rice paper is self-sealing, but place the roll on a plate seam-side down to make sure it stays closed. If you like, loosely cover the finished rolls with a dish towel to prevent them from drying out.

How to store the finished rolls? To keep gỏi cuốn for up to 4 hours, arrange the rolls side by side and weave a strip of wax paper or parchment paper between them to prevent sticking. Cover the rolls with plastic wrap (or use an inverted roasting pan) and keep them at room temperature. Refrigerated rolls lose their tender chew, turn dry, and may fall apart, so resist chilling them.

How to eat a roll? I bite off a bit of one end, drizzle in the sauce, and then make my way to the other end before repeating. Dipping the roll into the sauce risks the filling falling out.

Host a roll-your own party. Set out work surfaces, communal water-dipping vessels, fillings, dinner plates, and dipping sauces—and this book, open to this page!—and get to work.

Fillings You can roll up practically anything in rice paper as long as it is soft and thin. However, overly wet ingredients can make rolls bust as they sit—spin or pat excess moisture from lettuce and herbs!

Sauces Gỏi cuốn are typically served with nước chấm (see page 32—it makes a great complement for delicate ingredients such as mango) or a nutty hoisin sauce (see page 42—it's terrific for rich, salty-sweet gravitas). Don't know what sauce to pick? Start with super-versatile nước chấm.

Rice-Paper Rolls IN SIX STEPS

Slide the rice paper into the water and quickly rotate to wet without oversoaking.

Place the filling, then lift up the paper's edge, roll once, and tuck under.

Arrange filling bling snugly.

Fold in the sides.

Roll up to close.

Success!

8 oz mung bean sprouts

1 medium carrot, peeled and cut into bean sprout–size matchsticks

1½ Tbsp neutral oil (such as canola or peanut)

8 oz large fresh shiitake mushrooms, stems trimmed, cut as ¼-inch-thick slices

Fine sea salt

1 tsp soy sauce

1½ cups baby lettuce, thinly sliced lettuce (any kind), or sliced cabbage (napa or green)

1 cup mixed herb leaves (such as cilantro, mint, basil, dill, and shiso; choose 2 or 3), hand-torn if big

6 pieces Pan-Fried Tofu Slabs (page 52), each cut into 8 planks

12 (22-cm-diameter) rice-paper rounds (preferably Three Ladies or Tufoco Bamboo Tree brand)

1¼ cups Peanut-Hoisin Sauce (page 42)

Gỏi Cuốn Nấm Hương

Seared Shiitake and Tofu Rice-Paper Rolls

Allow vegetables to shine extra-bright in these rice-paper rolls by replacing the rice noodles with blanched bean sprouts. You'll benefit from the sprouts' crunch and have a low-carb version of the classic rolls. Seared fresh shiitake mushrooms and pan-fried tofu stand in for the shrimp and pork that are typically in Viet rice-paper rolls. Since you can make the sauce and most of the filling days in advance, gỏi cuốn nấm hương are wonderful for parties and impromptu snacking. Select big, thick-capped shiitakes for the most wow. See page 96 for rice-paper roll pointers.

Ready the filling

Bring a kettle of water to a boil.

Put the bean sprouts and carrot in two separate bowls and then pour the hot water over each vegetable to cover. Let sit for several minutes, until you can bend a sprout or piece of carrot and the ends touch. Drain well (if you like, reserve some of the mild "cooking" liquid for the sauce), let cool, and then combine the vegetables in one bowl.

Set a 12-inch nonstick or carbon-steel skillet over medium-high heat and add the neutral oil. When the oil ripples, add the mushrooms, stir to coat with oil, and then season with ¼ tsp salt. Spread out the pieces to sear for 1 to 2 minutes, until just softened and glistening, then swiftly stir again and drizzle in the soy sauce for deeper flavor and color. Keep cooking until no liquid is visible. Transfer the mushrooms to a plate and set aside to cool.

Wrap, roll, and serve

Prepare a dry, flat work surface and fill a large shallow bowl (or rice-paper water bowl) with very warm water for dipping. Set the mushrooms, lettuce, and herbs nearby. Lightly season the tofu, bean sprouts, and carrots with salt and place with the vegetables.

Partly slide a rice paper into the water and rotate to wet both sides for a few seconds. Shake off the excess water and place the paper on your work surface. When the paper is tacky, position 2 Tbsp lettuce in the lower-third portion of the rice-paper round, arranging it in a rectangle approximately 4 by 2 inches. Top with 3 Tbsp bean sprouts and carrot. Bring up the lower edge of the rice paper to cover the filling. Roll it upward once, like a cigar, and tuck the rice-paper edge under the filling to keep it in place.

On the unrolled portion of the rice paper, arrange the mushroom slices on a slant like a chorus line (how many depends on their size); let them touch the partially finished roll. Top with a layer of herbs, with their best-looking sides facedown. Now, add four tofu planks as two side-by-side rows that are parallel to the cylinder (the mushroom and herbs will now be mostly covered). Fold the sides of the rice paper inward (they likely won't meet in the center). Finish by rolling upward, jelly roll–style, to create a snug cylinder—the rice paper is self-sealing. Place the finished roll, with the mushroom-herb side faceup, on a serving platter. Repeat to make twelve rolls total. (If you're not serving these immediately, see page 96 for storage tips.)

Present the rolls whole (or halved crosswise with a sharp knife) with the sauce, and invite diners to spoon sauce into their rolls with each bite.

Notes

Timing The sprouts, carrot, and mushrooms may be prepped and chilled up to 2 days ahead.

Variations Instead of fresh shiitake, use big cremini or white button mushrooms. Store-bought baked tofu may replace the pan-fried tofu. To use noodles instead of bean sprouts, see the shrimp and mango rolls on page 100 for cooking guidance.

3 to 4 oz dried small round rice noodles (bún or maifun), or 5 to 6 oz dried rice capellini

18 medium-large (36/40 count) shrimp, peeled and deveined

1½ Tbsp neutral oil (such as canola or peanut)

Fine sea salt

1 lb unripe green mango, peeled, pitted, and cut into thin ½-inch-wide strips

2 Persian cucumbers, halved lengthwise, seeded, and cut diagonally into thin strips

1½ cups baby lettuce, thinly sliced lettuce (any kind), or sliced cabbage (napa or green)

1 cup mixed herb leaves (such as cilantro, mint, basil, and shiso; choose 2 or 3), hand-torn if large

12 (22-cm-diameter) rice-paper rounds (preferably Three Ladies or Tufoco Bamboo Tree brand)

1 cup Nước Chấm Dipping Sauce (page 32)

Gỏi Cuốn Tôm Xoài

Grilled Shrimp and Mango Rice-Paper Rolls

Checking off the salty, sweet, sour, and spicy flavor boxes, these tropical rice-paper rolls (pictured on page 11) signal warm-weather fun. Buy an unripe, rock-hard green mango (they're regularly eaten in salads too) and keep it chilled for up to 1 week, until you're ready to prep it. Shrimp are often poached for these rolls, but grilling them adds extra dimension. If you don't have a grill, sear the shrimp in a cast-iron or carbon-steel skillet; a griddle would work too. Check page 96 for rice-paper roll tips.

Ready the filling

Bring a 3-qt pot of unsalted water to a boil over high heat. Add the noodles and cook until tender-firm (the cooking time depends on the noodle and brand, so test to verify doneness). Drain the noodles in a colander, dump them back into the pot, and add cold water to cover. Swish for 30 to 60 seconds to quickly cool and release their starch, then re-drain. Set aside to cool to room temperature (they'll naturally get sticky).

In a large bowl, toss the shrimp with 1 Tbsp of the neutral oil and season with ¼ tsp salt. Set a cast-iron stovetop grill pan over high heat and brush with the remaining 1½ tsp neutral oil. When the pan is hot (water flicked onto its surface should evaporate within seconds), add the shrimp and grill them for 2 to 3 minutes, turning once or twice, until they have curled up and are mostly opaque at the thickest part (they'll finish cooking while cooling). Transfer to a plate and let cool to room temperature. (Without a grill, sear the shrimp in a hot skillet, using a little less time.)

Halve each shrimp by laying flat on a cutting board and then, using your index and middle fingers of one hand to steady, horizontally wield a knife (the blade parallel to the cutting board) in a sawing motion with your other hand. Set the halves on a plate.

When shrimp count per pound isn't available, look for ones about ⅝ inch wide at their thickest segment.

Splitting the shrimp symmetrically makes them more bendable for rolling up in rice paper.

Wrap, roll, and serve

Ready a dry, flat work surface, plus a large shallow bowl (or a rice-paper water bowl) filled with very warm water for dipping. Season the mango with 2 pinches of salt and add to the shrimp plate. Set the noodles, cucumber, lettuce, and herbs nearby. (If the noodles are too sticky to work with, briefly rinse them with water and drain well. Divide into twelve portions.)

Partly slide a rice paper into the water and rotate to wet both sides for a few seconds. Shake off the excess water, and then place the paper on your work surface. When the paper is tacky, position 2 Tbsp lettuce in the lower-third portion of the rice-paper round, arranging it in a rectangle approximately 4 by 2 inches. Put an egg-size mound of noodles atop the lettuce, spreading it into a rectangle. Arrange some cucumber and mango on top, and sprinkle some herb leaves over them. Bring up the lower edge of the rice paper to cover the filling. Roll it upward once, like a cigar, so the lettuce faces you, and tuck the rice-paper edge under the filling to keep it in place.

Add three shrimp halves, cut-side up, to the unrolled portion of the rice paper; let them touch the partially finished roll. Fold the sides of the rice paper inward (they likely won't meet in the center). Finish by rolling upward, jelly roll–style, to create a snug cylinder—the rice paper is self-sealing. Place the finished roll, shrimp-side up, on a serving platter. (If you're not serving these immediately, see page 96 for storage tips.)

Serve the rolls whole (or halved crosswise with a sharp knife) with the sauce, and invite diners to spoon sauce into their rolls as they eat them.

Note

Timing If you cook the noodles a day ahead, microwave them briefly to refresh and soften. The shrimp may be cooked and cut up to 2 days in advance. Refrigerate in separate containers.

FILLING

1 (2-oz) bundle dried glass noodles (saifun or bean threads; see page 9)

¾ cup canned chickpeas, well drained

1 oz dried shiitake mushrooms, soaked in water to cover for 6 hours, firmly squeezed, and caps and stems chopped

Brimming ¼ cup dried wood ear or black fungus mushrooms, softened in hot water for 15 minutes, drained, and cut into thin 1-inch-strips

¾ cup coarsely grated carrot (use the largest holes on a box grater)

4 oz super-firm tofu, patted dry and coarsely grated (use the largest holes on a box grater)

½ cup chopped green onions, white and green parts

2 sheets nori, snipped into strips ¾ inch wide by 1½ inches long (optional, for a briny touch)

1 Tbsp potato starch, or 1½ Tbsp cornstarch (potato starch yields slightly firmer texture)

1 tsp granulated sugar, plus more as needed

Fine sea salt

Recently ground black pepper

1 Tbsp plus 1 tsp soy sauce

MSG or Asian mushroom seasoning for balancing flavor (optional)

Chả Giò Chay

Oven-Fried Crispy Shiitake Imperial Rolls

Among the signature foods of Vietnam, chả giò signal celebration and comfort. The fried rolls are found on restaurant menus as a nosh, and they're made by doting grandmas, moms, and wives. Encased in rice paper and traditionally deep-fried, chả giò are cut into bite-size pieces and eaten as lettuce-and-herb wraps that are dunked in nước chấm. Traditional chả giò that are wrapped in rice paper are a feat of derring-do because the finicky rolls blister and may burst during frying if too tightly or loosely made, or if the oil isn't at an optimal temp. Many modern cooks make the rolls with easy-to-manage wheat-based wrappers. Wanting to preserve the superior flavor of rice-paper-wrapped chả giò and avoid fussy deep-frying, I experimented with hacks sourced from family, books, and online until I found an easy, healthful path to shatteringly crispy ones: blasting them with heat in the oven or an air fryer.

Like applying butter to phyllo, brushing seasoned coconut cream on the rice papers enriches and hydrates them just enough so they'll seal up and brown to a crisp. There's minimal drama involved as you efficiently bake batches. The formed and uncooked rolls freeze beautifully, so you may trot them out to create an impressive meal or add to bún rice noodle bowls (see page 256).

Using durable rice paper and making a low-moisture filling are the keys to this recipe. Along with the brand suggestions in the Notes, see page 10 for sourcing tips. Pat the wood ear mushrooms, carrot, tofu, and green onions dry with paper towels before chopping or grating (repeat blotting dry after prep if things still seem wet). Canned chickpeas stand in for the small amount of scratch-cooked mung beans that is required for binding. This is project cooking. Before diving in, review the instructions and plan ahead (for instance, the shiitakes need to be soaked for at least 6 hours!).

Prepare and portion the filling

To make the filling: Soak the noodles in hot water, messing them around for 30 to 45 seconds, just until they untangle and soften. Drain well and let them sit

(CONTINUED)

¾ cup coconut cream
(if the cream is hard, warm
in a small pan over low
heat or microwave for 10 to
15 seconds), plus more
as needed

2¼ tsp distilled white vinegar

Brimming ½ tsp dark
molasses

16 (22-cm-diameter)
sturdy rice-paper rounds
(preferably Three Ladies or
Tufoco Bamboo Tree brand)

1 cup Nước Chấm Dipping
Sauce (page 32, made with
garlic)

1½ cups drained Đồ Chua
Pickle (page 56; optional)

2 heads soft-leaf lettuce
(such as butter or red- or
green-leaf), separated
into leaves

1 small handful
cilantro sprigs

1 small handful mint sprigs

1 small handful Vietnamese
shiso or basil (any kind)
sprigs (optional)

for 5 to 10 minutes to further soften and whiten. While the noodles rest, put the chickpeas in a large bowl and, using a potato masher, render them into a mush. Using a cleaver, chef's knife, or scissors, cut and chop the noodles into pieces no longer than 1 inch.

In a large bowl, combine the noodles, chickpeas, shiitakes, wood ears, carrot, tofu, green onions, nori, potato starch, sugar, ½ tsp salt, and ½ tsp pepper and thoroughly mix (I use my hand for efficiency). Drizzle in the soy sauce and vigorously mix well (it's okay to gently squeeze). The filling should gradually compact and moisten. If it's too dry to come together, wet your hands under the faucet and then mix the filling again to gently moisten it. If you would like to check the flavor, microwave 1 tsp filling for about 10 seconds and taste. If needed, add salt, pepper, or sugar. You may also season with MSG, ⅛ tsp at a time, or mushroom seasoning, ¼ tsp at a time.

Firmly and evenly press the filling into a 9 by 13-inch baking pan or a small baking sheet. Using a knife or a metal bench scraper, divide the filling into sixteen portions (quarter, then quarter again). If you're not filling the rolls soon, loosely cover the pan to prevent the filling from drying out.

Fill the rolls

In a small bowl or liquid measuring cup, stir together the coconut cream, vinegar, and molasses. Select a large brush (silicone works well), a roomy work surface (such as a large cutting board), and a platter or a baking sheet to hold the finished rolls.

Working with three or four rice papers at a time, paint the coconut cream mixture in quick, broad strokes all over the smooth side of each rice paper (including the edges!). Flip the paper and repeat on the rougher side. Repeat with another two or three rice papers, setting them atop one another so they partially overlap like you're dealing out playing cards. The overlapping helps them stay put, moisten, and soften. Expect this to look artfully messy.

Using a dinner knife or offset spatula, transfer a portion of filling to the lower-third section of the top rice paper. Use your fingers to mold it into a 4-inch-long log; include any renegade bits. Lift the bottom edge of the rice paper up and over the log and tuck it under the filling, avoiding wrinkles or air bubbles. Using firm yet gentle pressure, neatly roll the filling twice until only the upper third of the rice paper remains. Press the paper down on the ends of the log, fold the side flaps inward over the top of the log, press to secure, and then roll the log the rest of the way to seal. If the rice paper isn't tacky on the sealed edge, dab on some coconut cream to glue it in place. Place the finished roll on the baking sheet. Repeat to make sixteen rolls total. Loosely cover the rolls. (If not cooking within an hour, see the Notes for freezing tips.)

Oven-fry the rolls

Position a rack in the upper third of the oven and preheat to 425°F. (If your oven has convection capability, select it for even crisper results; use 400°F if your oven does not automatically convert the temperature for convection cooking.) Line a rimmed baking sheet with parchment paper. Set a wire cooling rack in the baking sheet. (For maximum air circulation, select a rack that sits nearly level with the rim.) Put the rolls on the rack, seam-side down and spaced about 1 inch apart, transfer to the oven, and cook for 8 to 10 minutes. Rotate the rolls until they're seam-side up (some rolls won't behave, so do your best), and cook 6 to 8 minutes longer, until browned and crispy-crunchy.

Cut and serve

Let the rolls rest for about 2 minutes, until just cool enough to handle, and then, using kitchen scissors, cut each roll crosswise into three or four pieces. Loosely pile the pieces on one or two platters. If needed, let them sit for about 5 minutes to further cool.

Enjoy the rolls warm or at room temperature with the dipping sauce, pickle (if using), lettuce, cilantro, mint, and shiso (if using). Invite diners to wrap chả giò chunks along with the herbs in palm-size pieces of lettuce, dunk their creations in the sauce, and munch, nibbling on a pickle on the side (or adding it to the wrap).

Notes

Equipment Pressing the filling into a pan or a baking sheet makes portioning and placing easier; otherwise, use a ¼-cup measure to portion and place the filling.

If you're cooking in an air fryer (because air fryers differ), initially cook one roll to test temperature and timing. Arrange as many rolls as can fit into the tray, spacing them about ¾ inch apart, and air-fry at 375°F for 12 to 15 minutes. Rotate them after 6 to 8 minutes and continue to cook until they turn brown and very crispy. Repeat with any remaining rolls. As needed, re-crisp earlier batches by air-frying them again for a few minutes.

Lifespan The formed rolls freeze beautifully in an airtight container with plastic wrap, parchment paper, or wax paper between the layers. Let the rolls partially thaw while the oven preheats to 450°F (in an air fryer, put frozen rolls in at 375°F); the cooking time will be 2 to 5 minutes longer than for fresh, whether in the oven or an air fryer.

Cooked rolls soften slightly if left to sit around for too long. You can cook them up to several hours in advance and then re-crisp in a 425°F oven for 4 to 6 minutes, or in a 350°F air fryer for 3 to 4 minutes. Monitor the rolls because they change color fast.

FILLING

1 (2-oz) bundle dried glass noodles (saifun or bean threads, see page 9)

10 oz medium (41/50) shrimp, peeled and deveined

6 oz super-firm tofu, patted dry and coarsely grated (use the largest holes on a box grater)

1 cup coarsely grated carrot (use the largest holes on a box grater)

¼ cup finely chopped shallots or red onion

¼ cup packed chopped cilantro, stems included

1½ Tbsp fish sauce (store-bought or vegan version, page 29)

2 tsp potato starch, or 1 Tbsp cornstarch (potato starch yields slightly firmer texture)

½ tsp granulated sugar

½ tsp fine sea salt

Generous ½ tsp recently ground black pepper

——

¾ cup coconut cream (if the cream is hard, warm in a small pan over low heat or microwave for 10 to 15 seconds), plus more as needed

2¼ tsp distilled white vinegar

Brimming ½ tsp dark molasses

16 (22-cm-diameter) sturdy rice-paper rounds (preferably Three Ladies or Tufoco Bamboo Tree brand)

Chả Giò Tôm

Oven-Fried Crispy Shrimp Imperial Rolls

If you enjoy seafood, this recipe is for you. Compared with fancy chả giò made with shrimp, crab, and ground pork, these are equally wonderful, yet lighter because the filling features shrimp and tofu that are seasoned with cilantro, black pepper, and fish sauce to yield a crablike flavor. Oven-frying or air-frying imperial rolls produces crispy results with less hassle than traditional deep-frying. This recipe shares techniques with the shiitake chả giò recipe on page 103; those freezing and reheating techniques apply here too.

Hydrate the noodles

To make the filling: Soak the noodles in hot water, messing them around for 30 to 45 seconds, just until they untangle and soften. Drain well and let them sit for 5 to 10 minutes to further soften and whiten. Using a cleaver, chef's knife, or scissors, cut and chop the noodles into pieces no longer than 1 inch. Transfer to a large bowl.

Mix and portion the filling

Using a paper towel, pat the shrimp dry. Cut the shrimp into blueberry-size nuggets. Add the shrimp to the noodles, along with the tofu, carrot, shallots, cilantro, fish sauce, potato starch, sugar, salt, and pepper. Mix everything well (I use my hand for efficiency), aiming to create a compact mixture. Firmly and evenly press the filling into a 9 by 13-inch baking pan or a small baking sheet. Using a knife or a metal bench scraper, divide the filling into sixteen portions (quarter, then quarter again). If you're not filling the rolls soon, loosely cover the pan to prevent the filling from drying out.

Fill the rolls

In a small bowl or liquid measuring cup, stir together the coconut cream, vinegar, and molasses. Select a large brush (silicone works well), a roomy work surface (such as a large cutting board), and a platter or a baking sheet to hold the finished rolls.

1 cup Nước Chấm Dipping Sauce (page 32, made with garlic)

1½ cups drained Đồ Chua Pickle (page 56; optional)

2 heads soft-leaf lettuce (such as butter or red- or green-leaf), separated into leaves

1 small handful cilantro sprigs

1 small handful mint sprigs

1 small handful Vietnamese shiso or basil (any kind) sprigs (optional)

Using sturdy rice paper is key. See page 10 for selection and sourcing tips.

To minimize moisture in the filling, use paper towels to pat dry the shrimp, tofu, carrot, and cilantro; repeat blotting after prep if things still seem wet.

Working with three or four rice papers at a time, paint the coconut cream mixture in quick, broad strokes all over the smooth side of each rice paper (including the edges!). Flip the paper and repeat on the rougher side. Repeat with another two or three rice papers, setting them atop one another so they partially overlap like you're dealing out playing cards. The overlapping helps them stay put, moisten, and soften. Expect this to look artfully messy.

Using a dinner knife or offset spatula, transfer a portion of filling to the lower-third section of the top rice paper. Use your fingers to mold it into a 4-inch-long log; include any renegade bits. Lift the bottom edge of the rice paper up and over the log and tuck it under the filling, avoiding wrinkles or air bubbles. Using firm yet gentle pressure, neatly roll the filling twice until only the upper third of the rice paper remains. Press the paper down on the ends of the log, fold the side flaps inward over the top of the log, press to secure, and then roll the log the rest of the way to seal. If the rice paper isn't tacky on the sealed edge, dab on some coconut cream to glue it in place. Place the finished roll on the baking sheet. Repeat to make sixteen rolls total. Loosely cover the rolls.

Oven-fry the rolls

Position a rack in the upper third of the oven and preheat to 425°F. (If your oven has convection capability, select it for even crisper results; use 400°F if your oven does not automatically convert the temperature for convection cooking.) Line a rimmed baking sheet with parchment paper. Set a wire cooling rack in the baking sheet. (For maximum air circulation, select a rack that sits nearly level with the rim.) Put the rolls on the rack, seam-side down and spaced about 1 inch apart, transfer to the oven, and cook for 8 to 10 minutes. Rotate the rolls until they're seam-side up (some rolls won't behave, so do your best), and cook 6 to 8 minutes longer, until browned and crispy-crunchy.

Cut and serve

Let the rolls rest and cool for about 2 minutes, then snip each into three or four pieces. Pile onto platters, and, if needed, let cool further before serving.

Enjoy the rolls warm or at room temperature with the dipping sauce, pickle (if using), lettuce, cilantro, mint, and shiso (if using). Invite diners to wrap chả giò chunks along with the herbs in palm-size pieces of lettuce, dunk their creations in the sauce, and munch, nibbling on a pickle on the side (or adding it to the wrap).

Note

Ingredients Medium shrimp measure about ½ inch at the thickest segment. Shell-on shrimp taste best but to save time, opt for 8 oz peeled shrimp.

BRIGHT GREEN ONION OIL

Mounded ½ cup chopped green onions, green and white parts

¼ tsp fine sea salt

1 pinch baking soda (optional, for preserving the bright color)

3 Tbsp neutral oil (such as canola or peanut)

———

½ petite baguette or bolillo roll, or 1 slice white sandwich bread

2 Tbsp neutral oil (such as canola or peanut)

4 oz fresh mushrooms (such as cremini, shiitake, or oyster)

Fine sea salt

1 large egg

1 cup spicy microgreens (such as daikon or arugula), ½ cup coarsely chopped fresh herbs (such as cilantro, mint, or basil), or a combination

8 (22-cm-diameter) sturdy rice-paper rounds (preferably Three Ladies or Tufoco Bamboo Tree brand)

Viet Chile Sauce (page 39), Vegan Sate Sauce (page 40), or sriracha for serving

¼ cup Umami Q.P. Mayonnaise (page 48), Umami Sriracha Mayonnaise (see variation, page 48), or plain mayonnaise

Bánh Tráng Nướng

Grilled Rice-Paper "Pizzas"

This Viet street food isn't "pizza" per se, but that's how people have described these crisp, chewy grilled rice-paper platforms, which are topped with a mixture of eggy green onion oil and a choice of savory, crunchy, unctuous, spicy add-ons. The snack is a hit with schoolkids, I was told by a street vendor in Danang as I sat on a low stool waiting for her to craft my order on a coal-fired brazier. Among her toppings was a hot, salty-sweet sauce reminiscent of beef jerky and canned shoestring potato sticks. Her riotous combo of textures and flavors was superb. My travel buddy ate so many that she got a stomachache.

Because rice paper sold in the United States is thinner than what's used in Vietnam, replicating bánh tráng nướng here requires gluing pairs of relatively thick rice paper together with water, a key tip from Brooklyn chefs Dennis Ngo and Jerald Head. You just need a hot surface to grill the rice paper, and a stovetop cast-iron grill pan does the job well. Be patient because this is an unusual way to manipulate rice paper. Personalize your Viet pizza via the toppings. The croutons stand in for cracklings (a tip shared by a Saigon home cook), and the seared mushrooms lend earthy richness. See the Notes for additional ideas. Just as with Italian pizza, some topping and sauce choices require advance prep. Plan ahead. These pizzas are a fun group activity, too; see the timing tip in the Notes.

Prepare the green onion oil

To make the Bright Green Onion Oil: In a small, microwavable bowl, stir together the green onions, salt, baking soda (if using), and neutral oil. Microwave on high power for 45 to 60 seconds, until the mixture turns bubbly, steamy, and fragrant. (Alternatively, heat the neutral oil in a 1- to 1½-qt saucepan over medium heat until a green onion piece gently sizzles upon contact, and then add the remaining green onions, salt, and baking soda and stir for 30 seconds, until things soften.) Let cool to room temperature.

(CONTINUED)

Using strong rice paper is crucial here. See page 10 for sourcing tips.

Make the croutons and mushrooms

Preheat the oven or toaster oven to 350°F. Using a serrated knife, trim the crust from the bread and then tear or cut the bread into pieces no bigger than ½ inch. Put them into a bowl and toss with 1½ Tbsp of the neutral oil. Spread the bread pieces on a baking sheet and bake for 10 to 15 minutes, stirring two or three times, until golden brown and crisp on all sides. Set these croutons aside to cool completely.

If you're using cremini or shiitake mushrooms, slice them into pieces ¼ inch thick (including the stems); if you're using oyster mushrooms, tear them into bite-size pieces. Put the mushrooms in a medium bowl and season with 2 big pinches of salt and the remaining 1½ tsp neutral oil.

Set a 10-inch nonstick skillet over medium-high heat. When the skillet is hot (water flicked onto its surface should evaporate within seconds), add the mushrooms, spreading them out to sear, and leave undisturbed for about 1 minute, until they're moist and slightly softened. Stir and turn them to sear on the other side, 1 minute longer, or until just cooked through. Let cool completely.

Get organized like a street-food vendor

Set a large cutting board (or similar work surface), a small bowl filled with water, a pastry brush, a flexible spatula, and a cooling rack near the stove. In a small bowl, beat the egg with the green onion oil to combine well. Place near the stove, along with the croutons, mushrooms, microgreens, rice paper, and chile sauce. Put the mayonnaise in a small ziplock bag and then snip a small hole in the corner to pipe it out (if the room is warm, keep the mayo chilled until garnishing time).

Assemble the pizza bases

Set a stovetop cast-iron grill pan over medium heat. Meanwhile, put a rice paper on the cutting board and liberally brush with water, working from the center to the edges. Position another rice paper on top of the first one and press them firmly together. Brush a little additional water on edges that don't stick together. (Although it doesn't seem to matter which sides face outward, I typically put the two smoother sides facing each other.) Repeat to make another three pizza bases, and set them aside with minimal overlap.

Grill the pizza

When the grill pan is sufficiently hot (water flicked onto its surface should evaporate within seconds), add one of the pizza bases. Immediately press the base with a flexible spatula to ensure maximum contact with the pan's ridges and exposure to the radiant heat; aim to minimize the eventual air bubbles.

Press all over, rotating the rice paper in the pan to strategic hot spots so the rim crisps too. Flip frequently as opaque white areas appear; giant bubbles subside if you keep pressing. (If the cooking seems out of control at any time, slightly lower the heat. If the heat is too low, increase it. Experiment.)

After about 1 minute, when most of the rice paper has crisped up and is whitish, you have two options.

If you plan to finish the pizzas later, remove the pizza base from the grill, set on a baking sheet, and repeat to cook the remaining bases. (See the Note for advance prep details and how to reheat the bases before continuing.)

Or, keep the pizza base on the grill and add toppings. Spoon 2 Tbsp eggy green onion oil onto the paper. Using the back of the spoon, spread the oil, leaving a 1-inch border at the edges. Scatter one-fourth of the croutons and mushrooms over each rice paper and cook for 2 to 3 minutes, until the egg is opaque yellow and, maybe, gently sizzling. The toppings will stick to the egg mixture.

Finish with sauce and greenery

When the egg is done, transfer each pizza to the cooling rack. Let cool for about 1 minute and then squiggle some chile sauce and mayonnaise (or plop sate sauce) over the pizza. Finish with a sprinkling of microgreens, herbs, or both. Using scissors, snip the pizzas into quarters; or, if you don't want to share, fold the pizza in half like a quesadilla. Eat up your creations!

Notes

Equipment If a grill pan isn't available, use a cast-iron griddle or a large cast-iron or carbon-steel skillet. With more direct surface contact, the rice paper crisps faster, so apply lower heat as needed.

Timing Make the green onion oil, croutons, and seared mushrooms up to 2 days ahead. Refrigerate them separately and return to room temperature before using.

For a group event, grill all the pizza bases in advance and set the stack aside (uncovered and overlapping is fine) for up to 6 hours. To finish the pizzas, reheat the grill to medium and add a previously grilled base. Gently press and turn it for about 20 seconds, until reheated and re-flattened. Add the eggy green onion oil and toppings and then cook and garnish as directed. Demo one and then invite diners to create their own.

Variations Instead of the croutons, use 3 to 4 Tbsp fried onions or shallots (see page 46), or ½ cup shoestring potato sticks or coarsely crushed potato chips. The mushroom topping may be replaced by ½ cup Umami Tofu Crumbles (page 50) or diced Peppery Vegan Bologna (page 53). Dream up your own toppings (try previously cooked leftovers cut into small pieces), but always keep the eggy green onion oil to ensure that the toppings adhere to the rice-paper base.

CHINESE STEAMER GUIDE

A collapsible metal steamer works for certain recipes in this book, but you need a Chinese steamer for this chapter's bao recipes. Shop for one at East and Southeast Asian markets or online. Both bamboo and metal options steam well, but bamboo looks great at the table. However, bamboo can warp or fall apart over time—wash gently and dry well before storing! A stainless-steel steamer is less handsome but easy to clean and will last many years.

Regardless of the material, a 10-inch-wide steamer (measured edge to edge, excluding any handles) is the equivalent of the versatile 10-inch skillet. It is easy to store and good for households of up to four people. Go for a 12-inch steamer if you regularly feed up to six people or do large-scale cooking. Resist cutie small steamers, like the ones used at dim sum restaurants, because they don't hold much food.

When buying a bamboo steamer, get two or three trays (baskets), one lid, and a metal steamer ring, which resembles a ring-shaped Frisbee. The ring sits on the rim of a pot of water and the trays are placed on the ring, creating an efficient seal for conducting strong steam heat. Not using the ring can lead to weak steaming (your buns won't properly puff). A stainless-steel steamer consists of three tiers: a bottom pot to hold water, two trays, and a lid. Having a Chinese steamer on hand may lead to cooking other foods, such as dumplings and tamales.

SHIITAKE-VEGGIE FILLING

1 oz dried shiitake mushrooms, soaked in 1 cup water for 6 hours

2 cups packed thinly sliced green cabbage, kale, or other low-moisture leafy greens

⅓ cup small diced or coarsely grated carrot

1½ tsp granulated sugar

Fine sea salt

½ tsp recently ground white or black pepper

1 Tbsp soy sauce

2 tsp fish sauce (store-bought or vegan version, page 29), plus more as needed

1 tsp toasted sesame oil

2½ tsp cornstarch

2 Tbsp neutral oil (such as canola or peanut)

¼ cup finely chopped shallots or yellow onion

¾ cup Umami Tofu Crumbles (page 50)

———

1 batch Bao Dough (see page 117)

2 hard-cooked eggs, at room temperature, quartered

Bánh Bao Hấp

Steamed Shiitake-Veggie Bao

A filling of vegetables and pork defines many Viet-style steamed buns (bao), but when I cut out the pork for these bodacious, softball-size beauties, I didn't miss the meat. The filling comprises a treasure trove of ingredients—woodsy shiitake mushrooms anchor the vegetable medley, while tofu crumbles contribute protein and extra umami. A pop of egg lends a fun note. Encased in fluffy steamed dough, these are great for breakfast, lunch, or a snack. Add a salty, spicy jolt by dipping your bao in a pool of Maggi Seasoning sauce (or soy sauce) and black pepper (that's how I eat them). For best flavor, remember to rehydrate the shiitakes for at least 6 hours (I do it overnight). Also, make the tofu crumbles ahead. Check the Notes for variations to further your bao adventure.

Prepare the filling

To make the Shiitake-Veggie Filling: Gently squeeze the softened shiitake mushrooms, reserving their soaking liquid. Chop the mushroom caps and stems, then combine them in a bowl with the cabbage and carrot.

In a small bowl, stir together 2 Tbsp of the shiitake soaking liquid, the sugar, ¼ tsp salt, pepper, soy sauce, fish sauce, and sesame oil. Set this flavoring sauce near the stove.

In another small bowl, combine 1 Tbsp shiitake soaking liquid and the cornstarch and stir until fully dissolved. (Refrigerate the rest of the soaking liquid for another use.)

Set a 12-inch skillet over medium heat and add the neutral oil. When the oil ripples, add the shallots and cook, stirring frequently for 2 minutes, until fragrant with some golden bits. Add the vegetable mixture, stir to combine, and then pour in the flavoring sauce. Cook, stirring for 2 to 4 minutes, until the carrot is just tender and a small amount of liquid remains. Give the cornstarch mixture a stir, pour it into the pan, and cook, stirring for 20 seconds, to lightly bind everything. Remove from the heat and let sit, uncovered, for 5 minutes.

(CONTINUED)

Gently mix in the tofu crumbles. Taste, and if needed, add 1 tsp fish sauce or pinches of salt for a strong savory finish. Cover this filling and set aside at room temperature, or chill in the fridge until you're ready to assemble the buns.

Prepare to steam and assemble the buns

While the bao dough is rising, cut eight parchment paper squares, each about 3 inches wide. Return the filling to room temperature, if necessary.

You shouldn't need to flour your work surface, but if the dough seems sticky, very lightly dust the surface with flour before transferring the risen dough to it. Shape the dough into a thick log, then, using a knife, cut it crosswise into eight equal pieces. Using a light touch, roll each piece into a ball. Now, smack each ball with the palm (or heel) of your hand into a 4-inch-wide disk.

Imagine a 2-inch-wide center, or "belly," to help evenly distribute the dough as the bun is shaped. Using a rolling pin, roll away from the belly toward the edge. Roll mostly on the 1-inch perimeter and rotate the wrapper to prevent sticking. Aim for a 5-inch-wide wrapper that resembles a giant fried egg. Repeat to make seven more wrappers, setting them aside without overlapping.

Fill and shape the buns

Because this dough is very soft, the big wrapper may seem unwieldy. If you're an ace at filling and shaping Chinese-style buns while holding the wrapper in the air, do it! Otherwise, keep the wrapper on your work surface. Center 2 Tbsp filling on the wrapper, add an egg wedge, and then mound another 2 Tbsp filling on top. Try to keep a ¾-inch border clear of filling. The wrapper will seem very full.

Using the thumb and index finger of your dominant hand, gently pull up the edges of the wrapper and pinch them together to make a 1-inch-wide pleat. Keep pleating and pinching counterclockwise (clockwise for left-handers) to gather up the wrapper rim like you're cinching up a drawstring bag. The thumb and index finger of your other hand naturally work to pass dough to the pleating fingers. Partway through, the "bag" will seem secure enough to gently rotate so you can comfortably keep pleating and gathering. If needed, use a thumb to keep the filling inside the wrapper. Toward the end, feel free to pick up the shaped bun as you pinch and twist the wrapper rim closed.

Place each bun on a paper square; pleat-side up if you're confident of your seal, or pleat-side down for a domed finish and to hedge on the seal. Put the bun in a steamer tray, away from the steamer wall and spaced about 1 inch from other buns (it's okay if the paper overlaps). Repeat with the remaining dough and filling to make eight buns total, putting overflow buns on a baking sheet after the steamer trays fill up.

Because you have the Chinese steamer handy, steam the eggs instead of hard-boiling them. Set up a Chinese steamer with water and bring to a boil. Pull the eggs straight from the fridge, place them on the steamer tray, cover, and steam for 12 to 13 minutes. When done, transfer the eggs to an ice bath, let cool for 15 minutes, and then drain. Peel the eggs, then cover and set aside at room temperature, or refrigerate until bun assembly time. More about steaming eggs is on page 218.

Be sure to review the bao dough instructions so you can plan accordingly.

New to shaping and filling bao? Watch the how-to video plus extra tips at Vietworldkitchen .com/evergreentips.

Let rise, steam, and serve

Cover the buns with a dry dish towel to prevent them from drying out. Let them rise in a draft-free, warm spot for 20 to 30 minutes, until they look roughly one-fourth bigger. Meanwhile, set up a wire cooling rack near the steamer. About 10 minutes before the rising time is over, fill the steamer pan or pot halfway with water and bring to a rolling boil over high heat. Lower the heat slightly until you are ready to steam.

Steam the buns over the boiling water, one or two trays at a time, for 10 to 12 minutes, until they're puffy and dry-looking. Turn off the heat and wait for the steam to subside before lifting the lid, tilting it away from you to avoid condensation dripping onto the buns or hot steam hitting your face.

Remove the trays and, using a metal spatula, transfer the buns, still on their parchment paper, to the cooling rack for 5 minutes. Loosely cover the cooked buns to keep them from drying out. If needed, wipe the moisture from the steamer tray before repeating to steam the remaining buns.

Arrange the buns, still on their parchment paper, on a platter or two serving plates. Serve immediately. Remove the parchment before eating these buns out of hand.

Notes

Equipment See page 112 if you need guidance on Chinese steamers.

Ingredients Cut the prep time by using 6 oz coleslaw mix instead of the sliced cabbage and carrot; if the coleslaw is in ribbons, chop it a few times.

Instead of chicken eggs, use eight whole quail eggs. Many Viet cooks employ canned, precooked quail eggs sold at Asian markets.

Lifespan The filling may be prepared up to 2 days ahead and refrigerated in an airtight container. Steamed bao may be refrigerated for 1 week. The egg turns rubbery when frozen, so if you want bao that freeze well for 3 months, make the following vegan variations or omit the egg. Regardless, return the bao to room temperature, then re-steam for about 5 minutes for best texture and flavor. Or, cover them with a damp dish towel and microwave in 30-second blasts.

Variations For a nonvegetarian version, omit the tofu crumbles, add 5 oz ground pork (or ground chicken or turkey dark meat) after cooking the shallots. Stir and mash the meat into small pieces, and after 1 minute, or when it is halfway cooked, add the vegetables. Continue cooking and bind as directed. (If you skip the egg, cook 8 oz ground meat.)

To make Steamed Vegan Bao, replace the boiled egg with an additional ⅓ cup tofu crumbles (or use ⅓ cup thawed frozen petite peas, adding them with the tofu to preserve their bright color). For Steamed Char Siu Pulled-Jackfruit Bao, use the filling in the baked bao recipe on page 121.

BAO DOUGH

⅓ cup lukewarm water

2 tsp rapid-rise (instant) dry yeast

3 Tbsp granulated sugar

½ cup lukewarm whole milk or oat milk

2 Tbsp neutral oil (such as canola or peanut)

2½ cups all-purpose flour (bleached or unbleached), plus more for dusting

1½ tsp baking powder

___

2 tsp neutral oil (such as canola or peanut)

¼ cup Thai sweet chile sauce

3 Tbsp hoisin sauce

1½ Tbsp unseasoned rice vinegar

2 tsp soy sauce

½ to 1 Tbsp Viet Chile Sauce (page 39) or sriracha

1 lb Char Siu Roasted Cauliflower (page 227), still warm and cut into bun-size wedges

3 green onions, green parts only, thinly sliced on the diagonal into 2-inch-long pieces

1 Persian cucumber, thinly sliced (optional)

Bánh Bao Kẹp Chay

Char Siu Cauliflower Bao Sliders

Small, fluffy steamed buns (bao) have long been enjoyed in Vietnam with morsels of Cantonese-style barbecue; but in recent years, people have been making bigger buns for sandwich-like Taiwanese-style guà bāo. Filling options include braised pork belly, American-style barbecued pulled pork, and fried chicken. These savory-sweet stuffed buns are rich mini meals. For a lighter vegan version, I've taken to sliding my char siu–roasted cauliflower wedges into the soft rolls. This roasted vegetable takes the sauce beautifully and has a meaty quality; the pulled jackfruit on page 229 would work too. If you like, include lettuce, pickled veggies, cilantro, and crushed peanuts, like some cooks do in Vietnam. Regardless of which version you try, assemble the buns or lay out all the components as a snack board and invite diners to build their own mini sandwiches. Made from everyday ingredients at hand, this bao dough comes together quickly for this recipe as well as the stuffed vegetable bao on page 113. See page 112 if you need guidance on Chinese steamers, and the Notes for making bao in advance.

Prepare the dough

To make the Bao Dough: Lightly oil a medium bowl.

Put the water in a small bowl, sprinkle with the yeast, and let sit for 1 minute to soften the yeast. Stir in the sugar, milk, and neutral oil until the yeast and sugar dissolve.

To make with a stand mixer—In the mixer bowl, combine the flour and baking powder and stir together. Make a well in the center and pour in the yeasty liquid. Stir with a spatula to form a ragged dough that mostly cleans the bowl. Let sit, uncovered, for about 3 minutes to further hydrate.

Attach the dough hook and run the mixer on medium speed. After 1 minute, when a ball forms around the hook, let the machine run for another 30 seconds, until the dough is relatively smooth and elastic, but sticky.

(CONTINUED)

For bright-looking bao, use bleached all-purpose flour. For deeper flavor and a tad more chew, choose unbleached flour. For best results, weigh the flour; it should be 355g.

Lightly dust a work surface with flour. Using a flexible dough scraper, transfer the dough onto the surface, flipping and lightly coating the dough in flour to make it easier to handle. Gently knead for about 30 seconds to form a smooth, roundish shape. Press your finger into the soft, slightly tacky dough (like a sticky note); the dough should spring back, leaving a faint indentation.

To make by hand—In a large bowl, combine the flour and baking powder and stir together. Make a well in the center and pour in the yeasty liquid. Stir with a spatula to form a ragged dough that mostly cleans the bowl. Let sit, uncovered, for about 3 minutes to further hydrate. Gather the dough into a ball, transfer to a work surface, and knead for about 4 minutes, dusting minimally with flour until a soft, smooth dough forms. If the dough feels dry, work in lukewarm water by the teaspoon.

Put the machine-made or handmade dough into the prepared bowl, rotating to coat with oil. Cover with plastic wrap and then set in a warm, draft-free place for 1 hour, or until it has nearly doubled. (Alternatively, cover tightly and let rise in the refrigerator overnight; return the dough to room temperature before continuing.)

Shape and steam the buns

While the dough rises, cut twelve parchment paper squares, each about 3 inches wide. Ready your Chinese steamer setup (a water-filled pot, two or three trays, plus a lid), the 2 tsp neutral oil, and a pastry brush.

You shouldn't need to flour your work surface, but if the dough seems sticky, very lightly dust the surface with flour before transferring the risen dough to it. Shape the dough into a thick log. Using a knife, cut it crosswise into twelve equal pieces. Using a light touch, roll each piece into a ball. Now, smack each ball with the palm (or heel) of your hand into a 3-inch-wide disk.

Using a rolling pin, roll a dough piece into a thin oval that measures about 5 by 3 inches. Roll from the top down, or from the midline to the edge, rotating the dough often to prevent sticking. Brush a little of the neutral oil on half of the oval, then fold it over. Place the shaped bun on a paper square and set in a steamer tray, away from the steamer wall and spaced about 1 inch from other buns (it's okay if the paper overlaps). Repeat with the remaining dough to make twelve buns total, putting overflow buns on a baking sheet after the steamer trays fill up.

Loosely cover the shaped buns with a dry dish towel to prevent them from drying out. Let rise in a draft-free, warm spot for 20 to 30 minutes, until they've nearly doubled in size. Meanwhile, set up a wire cooling rack near the steamer. About 10 minutes before the rising time is over, fill the steamer pan or pot halfway with water and bring to a rolling boil over high heat. Lower the heat slightly to steady the steam.

Steam the buns over the boiling water, one or two trays at a time, for 6 to 8 minutes, until they're puffy and dry-looking. Turn off the heat and wait for the steam to subside before lifting the lid, tilting it away from you to avoid condensation dripping onto the buns or hot steam hitting your face.

Remove the trays and, using a metal spatula, transfer the cooked buns, still on their parchment paper, to the cooling rack for 5 minutes. Loosely cover them to keep from drying out. If needed, wipe the moisture from the steamer tray before repeating to steam the remaining buns. Once all the buns are cooked, return them to the steamer trays, arranging them standing up if you're tight on space. Cover with the steamer lid so they will stay soft—perfect for serving.

Make the sauce, assemble, and serve

In a small bowl, stir together the Thai sweet chile sauce, hoisin sauce, rice vinegar, and soy sauce. Spike it with the hot Viet chile sauce for an edge of fire.

Open the buns and moisten the top and bottom with 2 tsp of the spicy sauce. Slide in a wedge of warm cauliflower and sprinkle with green onions. Serve the bao with additional sauce on the side for anyone who wants to drizzle in more. If desired, nibble on the cucumber to refresh the palate or slide it into the bun.

Notes

Ingredients If hoisin sauce is unavailable, mix together 3 Tbsp dark miso (such as red miso), 1 Tbsp agave syrup or mild honey, ½ tsp toasted sesame oil, and 1 pinch Chinese five-spice powder as a substitute.

Timing While the dough rises, roast the cauliflower, if you have not already done so. By assembly time, if needed, warm the cauliflower in a 375°F oven or toaster oven for about 5 minutes, or until it gently sizzles.

Lifespan Steamed buns may be completely cooled and then frozen for up to 1 month; thaw and re-steam them for about 3 minutes to refresh, or cover with a damp dish towel and microwave in 30-second blasts.

BAKED BAO DOUGH

10 Tbsp lukewarm water, plus more as needed

2 tsp rapid-rise (instant) dry yeast

1½ Tbsp granulated sugar

Mounded ½ tsp fine sea salt

½ cup sweetened condensed milk (coconut, if preferred)

2⅓ cups bread flour, plus more for dusting

CHAR SIU PULLED-JACKFRUIT FILLING

1½ cups packed Char Siu Pulled Jackfruit (page 229), coarsely chopped

2 green onions, green and white parts, finely chopped

2 Tbsp brown sugar (light or dark), agave syrup, or mild honey

⅛ tsp Chinese five-spice powder

2 Tbsp ketchup

1½ Tbsp soy sauce

1 tsp toasted sesame oil (optional, for aroma)

2 tsp cornstarch

────

1 Tbsp sweetened condensed milk (coconut, if preferred)

2½ tsp water

Bánh Bao Xá Xíu Chay Nướng

Baked Char Siu Pulled-Jackfruit Bao

After years of trying to make a very fluffy, not-too-sweet bao dough that recalls Chinese milk bread and Portuguese and Hawaiian sweet bread, I found the simple solution in sweetened condensed milk and bread flour. It took too many rounds to count but the result is a simple dough that bakes beautifully, whether you use standard condensed milk or a coconut one. Diluted condensed milk also glazes the buns before and after baking to add shine and an extra-sweet touch. These bao are filled with pulled jackfruit that has been seasoned like Cantonese-style char siu pork. They are incredibly fun to make and eat.

Prepare the dough

To make the Baked Bao Dough: Lightly oil a medium bowl.

To make with a stand mixer—Pour the water into the mixer bowl, sprinkle with the yeast, and let sit for 1 minute to soften. Stir in the sugar, salt, and ½ cup condensed milk. Add the flour; stir thoroughly with a spatula to form a ragged dough. Let it sit, uncovered, for about 3 minutes to further hydrate.

Attach the dough hook, then run the mixer on medium speed for 2 to 3 minutes, until the dough is relatively smooth and elastic, but sticky.

Flour a work surface. Using a flexible dough scraper, transfer the dough onto the surface, flipping and lightly coating the dough in flour to make it easier to handle. Gently knead for about 30 seconds to form a smooth, roundish shape. Press your finger into the soft, slightly tacky dough (like a sticky note); the dough should spring back, leaving a faint indentation.

To make by hand—Pour the water into a large bowl, sprinkle with the yeast, and let sit for 1 minute to soften. Stir in the sugar, salt, and ½ cup condensed milk. Add the flour; stir thoroughly with a spatula to form a ragged dough. Let it sit, uncovered, for about 3 minutes to further hydrate.

(CONTINUED)

Use precise measures when preparing the dough; weigh the water (142g), condensed milk (156g, excluding the 1 Tbsp for glazing), and flour (332g). For vegan dough, use sweetened condensed coconut milk.

For the filling, make a half batch of the Char Siu Pulled Jackfruit, then measure (1½ packed cups weighs 285g).

Need a bao shaping assist? There's a how-to video at Vietworldkitchen.com/evergreentips.

Flour a work surface. Gather the dough into a ball, transfer to the surface, and knead swiftly for about 5 minutes, dusting minimally with flour until a soft, smooth dough forms. If the dough feels dry, work in lukewarm water by the teaspoon.

Put the machine-made or handmade dough into the prepared bowl, rotating to coat with oil all over. Cover with plastic wrap, then set in a warm, draft-free place to rise for 1½ hours, or until it has nearly doubled in size. (Alternatively, cover tightly and let rise in the refrigerator overnight; return the dough to room temperature before using.)

Prepare the filling

To make the Char Siu Pulled-Jackfruit Filling: In a medium bowl, combine the jackfruit, green onions, brown sugar, five-spice powder, ketchup, soy sauce, sesame oil (if using), and cornstarch and stir to incorporate. Cover, if not using within 30 minutes.

Shape and bake the buns and serve

Lightly flour a work surface. Line a large baking pan with a silicone mat or parchment paper. Divide the filling into eight equal portions (about 3 Tbsp each).

Remove the plastic wrap from the dough bowl, lightly oil one side of the plastic, and set aside. Punch down the dough, turn it out onto the prepared work surface, and shape it into a thick log. Cut the log crosswise into eight equal pieces. Separate the slightly sticky pieces. Using your hands (minimally flour them, if needed), roll the dough into rough balls.

Because the dough can be unwieldy, fill and shape each bun separately (instead of prepping all the dough wrappers). Press a dough ball with the palm (or heel) of your hand until ½ inch thick. Pat with your fingertips, like you're playing the bongos, working from the center to edges to form an approximately 4½-inch round. Turn and flip once or twice to very lightly coat with flour and prevent sticking. Make the edges thinner than the center to evenly distribute the dough.

If you're adept at filling and shaping bao while holding the wrapper in midair, do it! Otherwise, keep the wrapper on your work surface. Center a portion of filling on the wrapper, flattening it slightly and keeping a ¾-inch border of dough clear.

Using the thumb and index finger of your dominant hand, gently pull up the edge of the wrapper and pinch together a 1-inch-wide pleat. Keep pleating and pinching counterclockwise (clockwise for left-handers) to gather up the wrapper rim like you are cinching up a drawstring bag. The thumb and index finger of the other hand naturally work to pass dough to the pleating fingers. Partway through, the "bag" will seem secure enough to gently rotate so you can comfortably keep pleating and gathering. If needed, use a thumb to keep filling inside the wrapper. Toward the end, feel free to pick up the bun as you pinch and twist the wrapper rim closed. Flip the bun onto your work surface and rotate between cupped hands to round it. Place on the prepared baking sheet and repeat to make eight buns total.

Loosely cover the shaped buns with the reserved plastic wrap, oiled-side down, to prevent sticking. Let rise in a warm spot for 1 hour, or until nearly doubled in size. About 15 minutes before the buns have sufficiently risen, position a rack in the middle of the oven and preheat to 350°F.

In a small bowl, combine the 1 Tbsp condensed milk and 2½ tsp water. Brush the risen buns with half of this glaze.

Bake the buns for 16 to 18 minutes, rotating the pan at about 10 minutes, or when the buns are lightly golden; continue to bake until richly browned.

Transfer the buns to a wire rack (or set the baking sheet on the rack) and let cool for 3 minutes, then brush the tops with the remaining glaze. Let the buns rest for 10 minutes before eating. Enjoy warm or at room temperature.

Note

Lifespan Refrigerate leftovers for up to 5 days, or freeze for 3 months. Thaw at room temperature. To refresh, using a spray bottle, lightly spritz them with water and reheat on a baking sheet in a 350°F oven (or a toaster oven) for 8 minutes, until warm and softened. If you like, re-glaze with a spoonful of sweetened condensed milk diluted with a spoonful of water before serving.

Banh Mi Possibilities

SAY "BANH MI" AND MOST PEOPLE THINK OF the quotidian Vietnamese sandwich. This tour de force is ubiquitous in Vietnam as well as outside of the country in Little Saigon enclaves. As a remarkably good, endlessly customizable sandwich, it enjoys a far-reaching fan base all over the world. It's one of the three gateway foods that get people excited about Vietnamese cuisine.

I love banh mi for its synergy as well as for the story it tells. French colonials, who officially controlled Vietnam from 1883 to 1954, introduced the light, crisp baguette to Vietnam around the turn of the twentieth century. In this tropical, humid country, where rice—not wheat—culture was traditional, bakers managed to fashion lofty loaves. According to a northern Vietnamese foodways book published in Hanoi, the bread was initially called bánh Tây ("Western bread" or "French bread"; bánh generically describes foods primarily made with various flours, starches, and legumes).

My maternal grandfather's breakfast ritual included a round, fist-size baguette-style roll, sweetened condensed milk, and coffee. My parents, born during the 1930s in northern Vietnam, recalled bread vendors who strategically positioned themselves near schools to attract kids. "Young people, not adults, ate street food," Dad told me. "My parents gave me a small allowance and if I had only one penny, I could buy a freshly baked roll with a sprinkling of salt and pepper. If I had two cents and wanted a splurge, I would add a smearing of pork liver pâté. It was heavenly."

By 1945, wheat-based bread was no longer foreign food. The baguette had infiltrated the culture enough for people to drop Tây and simply call it bánh mì (bread made from wheat). Viet people had taken ownership of the bread. In the early 1940s, entrepreneurial Saigon vendors began crafting cross-cultural sandwiches composed of a length of baguette lined with French (canned) salted butter or freshly made mayonnaise, various cold cuts, pickled veggies, cucumber, cilantro, and chile. A drizzle of Maggi Seasoning sauce lent savory-salty notes to help define the sandwich's flavor.

The banh mi blueprint on page 128, along with the vegetarian sausage, Kewpie mayonnaise dupes, pickles, and pâté elsewhere in this book, equip you to create your own sensational sandwiches. Banh mi is about options and creativity. With the ideas contained here, you'll easily unify vegetarians, vegans, and omnivores.

But banh mi can be more than just a sandwich. Under the 1954 Geneva accords that split Vietnam into two countries, my mother's family migrated from northern Vietnam to the more-promising city of Saigon. Not only did they experience the bountiful joys of new-fangled banh mi but they also learned about steamed banh mi, a delicious snack of stale baguettes rendered soft and warm in the steamer and topped with green onion oil. That simple preparation has since evolved into a more complex but deliciously fun lettuce-wrap dish, which inspired my recipe on page 135. In Vietnam, stale bread may also be rolled out and baked into a different banh mi snack that's delightfully crunchy and spicy; my take on bánh mì nướng muối ớt on page 132 skips the rolling and offers a method for creating your own.

My parents raised us in Saigon, but I didn't know about Bánh Mì Hòa Mã, a beloved local restaurant in operation since 1958, until 2014 when writer Robyn Eckhardt and I spoke to the owner for a *Wall Street Journal* story. The hẻm (alleyway) establishment serves a sit-down banh mi breakfast. It's a riff on the old-school Viet approach of serving banh mi in the French casse-croûte manner: a plate of ham, cold cuts, pâté, cheese, and butter with bread on the side. Use the recipe on page 130 to make a vegetarian version for a splendid DIY brunch, lunch, or dinner.

For a different style of deconstructed banh mi, try the meatless meatball banh mi on page 137, which combines sandwiches with dim sum! Recipe tester Terri Tanaka reported that her meat-loving husband approved, even tucking some of the meatballs into a roll for a simple sandwich.

Banh mi or *bánh mì? Pho* or *phở?* The Vietnamese words for the culture's iconic sandwich and soup are listed in the Oxford and Merriam-Webster English dictionaries, so they are no longer considered foreign terms requiring accent marks. Crossing that threshold also reflects how much people living outside of Vietnam have embraced the foods of Vietnamese culture.

While banh mi signals the legacy of French and Chinese colonialism, it also embodies Vietnamese self-determination. Taken in totality, the bread and sandwich in all their varied incarnations represent how Viet people have appropriated foreign ideas to create a unique Vietnamese experience. It's our delectable strategy for cultural survival and evolution. Join us!

Banh Mi BLUEPRINT

Like iconic rice-paper rolls and pho, Vietnam's signature sandwich is highly personalizable. As long as you maintain the framework of crisp bread, succulent filling, tangy pickled vegetables, chile slices, cucumber, and herbs, you can feature practically anything else in it. (Pulled jackfruit is in the banh mi pictured opposite.) Follow these instructions and use the recipes in this book to create your own masterpiece.

INGREDIENTS FOR ONE SANDWICH

Bread (choose one)

The best banh mi bread isn't fancy or rustic. It feels light, has a thin crust, possesses an airy, cottony interior, tastes faintly sweet, and is affordable. To source the bread, mine the supermarket's bakery section (especially the bulk area), bodegas, delis, and Asian grocers. Viet banh mi shops may sell bread too. Go standard or gluten-free.

> 1 petite baguette
>
> 1 bolillo roll
>
> 1 Kaiser roll
>
> 6-inch-section French-style baguette
>
> 2 sandwich bread slices

Fat (choose one)

Rich, fatty elements prevent dry banh mi.

> Mayonnaise (plain, umami, sriracha, or vegan mayo; see pages 48 and 49)
>
> Salted European-style or cultured butter (regular or dairy-free)
>
> Thin avocado slices

Seasoning (choose at least one)

Maggi Seasoning sauce is part of the signature banh mi flavor, but Bragg Liquid Aminos is very similar. Or opt for something else to lend umami pop or zippy pungency.

> Maggi Seasoning sauce, Bragg Liquid Aminos, or soy sauce
>
> Fine sea salt
>
> Recently ground black pepper

Featured Filling (choose one or two)

Vary the featured filling according to mood and what's available. Cook, cut, reheat, sear, or return the main filling to room temperature.

> 2 to 3 Tbsp Five-Spice Mushroom-Walnut Pâté (page 92)
>
> 3 to 4 oz Pan-Fried Tofu Slabs (page 52), Peppery Vegan Bologna (page 53), Grilled Eggplant with Garlicky Green Onion Sizzle (page 212), Spicy Oyster Mushroom and Lemongrass Stir-Fry (page 221), Char Siu Roasted Cauliflower (page 227), Char Siu Pulled Jackfruit (page 229), Beef and Tofu Lá Lốt Rolls (page 259)
>
> 2 fried eggs (see page 130)
>
> 2-egg omelet

Vegetable Add-Ons (choose all, some, or none)

Have these prepped before you assemble the sandwich. A handful of ribbons of crisp iceberg or romaine lettuce may stand in for the cucumber.

> ¼ cup Đồ Chua Pickle (page 56), Pickled Bean Sprout Salad (page 172), or Racy Pickled Fennel (page 58), drained
>
> 3 or 4 thin slices medium-hot chile (such as jalapeño or Fresno)
>
> 4 to 6 cucumber strips, rounds, or ovals, cut as scant ¼-inch-thick pieces
>
> 1 to 2 Tbsp coarsely chopped or hand-torn cilantro sprigs, mint leaves, basil leaves, or a combo

HOW TO ASSEMBLE BANH MI

Do not overstuff banh mi with protein. A well-balanced banh mi resembles a salad in a sandwich. Visualize a ratio of 1-to-1 or 1-to-2 of main filling to vegetables.

Prep the Bread

As needed, re-crisp the roll or baguette in a toaster oven or regular oven. If the crust is soft or the bread seems stale, revive it by lightly misting or rubbing the exterior with wet hands before baking at 350°F for about 7 minutes; the heat and moisture will soften the crumb and crisp up the crust. Otherwise, slide the bread into a 325°F oven for 3 to 6 minutes. (If using sliced bread, lightly toast it.)

Let the bread cool briefly to avoid melting the mayo. Using a serrated knife, slit the bread lengthwise, maintaining a hinge, if possible. Hollow out some of the insides to make room for the filling.

Flavor the Insides

Spread your chosen fat on the two cut sides of bread, covering all the way to the edge. If you're using avocado, lay down thin slices and mash them so they adhere to the bread. Season by drizzling in Maggi or another liquid condiment or sprinkling with salt and pepper.

Add the Filling

Working from the bottom up, layer the filling, pickle, chile, cucumber, and herbs. Close the sandwich. Serve whole or cut in half crosswise.

4 petite baguettes or bolillo rolls, 1 French-style baguette, or other bread suitable for banh mi

1 cup drained Đồ Chua Pickle (page 56)

2 small Persian cucumbers, thickly sliced

12 to 16 cherry tomatoes, halved, or 2 tomatoes, halved and thickly sliced

1 small handful cilantro sprigs, kept whole or coarsely chopped (optional)

⅔ cup Five-Spice Mushroom-Walnut Pâté (page 92)

⅓ cup Umami Q.P. Mayonnaise (page 48), or 4 thick pats butter (preferably salted)

¼ cup neutral oil (such as canola or peanut), plus more as needed

4 to 8 large eggs (depending on how egg-loving diners are)

4 slices onion (any kind), each ¼ inch thick

12 slices Peppery Vegan Bologna (page 53), each a scant ¼ inch thick and halved crosswise

Recently ground black pepper

Maggi Seasoning sauce (excellent on fried eggs!), Bragg Liquid Aminos, or soy sauce for drizzling

Viet Chile Sauce (page 39) or sriracha for drizzling

Banh mi bread pointers are on page 128.

Bánh Mì Chảo

Grand Slam Banh Mi Breakfast Combo

Banh mi is great for on-the-go eating but there is also a glorious sit-down, deconstructed version called bánh mì chảo. I adore the one at Hoà Mã in Saigon but, with two sunny-side-up eggs, thick slices of Viet bologna, Spam, pâté, butter (or mayonnaise), and pickles, it's a gut buster akin to Denny's Original Grand Slam breakfast platter. My lighter take is equally satisfying. Set out everything and let diners fashion their own banh mi bites.

Prep the bread and set up the plates

As needed, re-crisp or toast the bread in the oven. When done, set the oven to its warm setting. Arrange the pickle, cucumbers, tomatoes, cilantro (if using), pâté, and mayonnaise on serving dishes for sharing. Set at the table.

Fry, assemble, and serve

If you favor a method for frying eggs, go for it. Vietnamese cooks often fry eggs to tender softness, not with crisp edges. Set a 12-inch nonstick or carbon-steel skillet over medium-low heat and add about 1½ Tbsp of the neutral oil to film the bottom. When the oil ripples, crack in three or four eggs, depending on how many will fit comfortably. Cover, slightly lower the heat, and cook for about 2 minutes, or until there's a thin opaque rim of white around the yolks. Slide the pan off the heat and let the egg finish cooking for 30 seconds (or leave the pan on the heat for firmer yolks, although a thin film of white may mask the runnier yolks). If you want over-easy eggs, use a thin spatula to turn the eggs and cook them on the other side for about 10 seconds. Transfer to a platter and slide them into the warm oven. Fry the other eggs, adding oil as needed.

Reheat the skillet over medium-high heat and swirl in 1 Tbsp neutral oil. Add the onion slices and sauté for about 2 minutes, until they turn soft with some browning, then transfer to a plate. Add the bologna and sear for 30 to 60 seconds per side to warm and brown slightly; add it to the onion plate if you like. Sprinkle pepper on the bologna and egg, if desired. Present at the table with Maggi and chile sauce to drizzle over everything.

BUTTERY GREEN ONION OIL

Mounded ½ cup chopped green onions, green parts only

1½ Tbsp finely chopped garlic

⅛ tsp fine sea salt

1 pinch baking soda (optional, for preserving the bright color)

2 Tbsp neutral oil (such as canola or peanut)

1½ Tbsp unsalted butter (nondairy, if preferred), cut into 3 or 4 chunks

___

2 bolillo rolls, petite baguettes, or other bread suitable for banh mi

2 Tbsp Vegan Sate Sauce (page 40; optional, for extra umami hit)

½ cup Five-Spice Mushroom-Walnut Pâté (page 92)

2 batches Fast-Fried Shallots (page 46), or ⅓ cup store-bought fried shallots or onions

2 to 3 Tbsp Viet Chile Sauce (page 39), Thai sweet chile sauce, or sriracha

¼ cup Umami Q.P. Mayonnaise (page 48), Umami Sriracha Mayonnaise (see variation, page 48), or plain mayonnaise

¼ cup coarsely chopped cilantro (optional)

Bánh Mì Nướng Muối Ớt

Crunchy Spicy Garlic Bread

Not all bread in Vietnam is destined for sandwiches. Softened days-old baguettes are repurposed for snacks such as the lettuce wraps on page 135 and for treats like this one, which is best described as a Viet-style loaded-up garlic bread. The highly customizable bánh mì nướng muối ớt is a savory, spicy, rich newcomer from southwestern Vietnam (some specify Chau Doc, a lively city that borders Cambodia).

In Vietnam, cooks flatten squishy day-old rolls with rolling pins before brushing on margarine spiked with briny-savory sate sauce, chile, and garlic for a muối ớt (salt chile) experience; pâté or cheese may be stuffed into a pocket that's been cut into the roll. The bread gets grilled to a crisp and then, perhaps, topped with pork floss, sliced hot dogs, Viet bologna, fried shallots, sweetish chile sauce, and ketchup. Regardless, mỡ hành (green onion oil) and Kewpie-style mayo are always included. In San Jose, California, I tried a version that sported cheddar cheese. It's a fun snack that's easy to make. Here's a vegetarian take for you to whip up in the oven with American supermarket bread, which doesn't require flattening to bake to a crunch.

Prepare the green onion oil

To make the Buttery Green Onion Oil: In a small microwavable bowl, stir together the green onions, garlic, salt, baking soda (if using), and neutral oil. Put the butter on top and then microwave on high power for 45 to 60 seconds, until the mixture bubbles and the onions just soften. (Alternatively, combine the oil and butter in a 1- to 1½-qt saucepan and set over medium heat until an onion piece gently sizzles upon contact; then stir in the remaining green onions, garlic, salt, and baking soda and cook for 30 seconds until things soften.) Let cool to room temperature.

See bread-buying tips on page 128.

Bake to a crunch and serve

Meanwhile, preheat the oven (or a toaster oven) to 350°F.

Fully split the rolls lengthwise into four pieces. Lightly mist or brush water all over the bread pieces. Bake them on the oven rack, cut-side up, for 5 minutes, or until crisp all over. If using the sate sauce, smear it on here and there, or spoon on a bit of the oil and butter from the green onion mixture. Spread with the pâté, then divide the garlicky green onion pulp (plus any remaining oil and butter) on top.

Return the bread to the oven and bake 1 to 2 minutes to further crisp it and warm the topping. Switch to broil mode for about 45 seconds to lightly brown the edges for good looks and extra crunch. Transfer to a cutting board, let cool briefly, and then cut each crosswise into three or four pieces. Arrange tightly on a plate or keep on the board. Sprinkle the fried shallots on the bread pieces and then add drizzles of chile sauce and squiggles of mayonnaise. Finish with cilantro, if desired. These are best eaten soon after baking.

Notes

Ingredients Instead of the rolls, use half of a French-style baguette, splitting it into two. In lieu of pâté, sprinkle with ¾ cup shredded melty cheese, such as Colby Jack. Bake for the same amount of time until the cheese has melted.

Technique To make mayonnaise squiggles, put the mayo in a small ziplock bag and then snip a small hole from a corner; squeeze to pipe out the mayo.

It is easier to garnish the bread pieces with the shallots, chile sauce, and mayo after baking, but then cutting them when fully loaded can be messy. In that case, cut fewer pieces or serve uncut, if you like.

SESAME GREEN ONION OIL

1 cup chopped green onions, white and green parts

⅛ tsp fine sea salt

1 pinch baking soda (optional, for preserving the bright color)

3 Tbsp neutral oil (such as canola or peanut)

1 to 2 tsp toasted sesame oil (use the maximum amount for a toasty flavor hit)

———

1 Tbsp neutral oil (such as canola or peanut)

2 Tbsp chopped shallots or yellow onion

1½ cups chopped shiitake, cremini, or white mushrooms, stems included

¾ cup Umami Tofu Crumbles (page 50) or diced jicama, carrot, or sweet potato

⅛ tsp recently ground black pepper

1½ tsp Maggi Seasoning sauce, Bragg Liquid Aminos, soy sauce, or fish sauce (store-bought or vegan version, page 29)

Fine sea salt

2 petite baguettes or bolillo rolls, ½ French-style baguette, or other bread suitable for banh mi

⅓ cup unsalted roasted peanuts or cashews, chopped or crushed

3 Tbsp Fast-Fried Shallots (page 46) or store-bought fried shallots or onions

Bánh Mì Hấp Nhân Chay

Steamed Banh Mi Lettuce Wraps

In Vietnam, baguettes are baked and eaten within 24 hours. After my mom migrated to Saigon in 1954 from Hai Duong in northern Vietnam, her family lived in a home tucked down a winding alleyway off a busy street. Every evening, a neighbor came home with a load of long baguettes, which were bent over from the tropical humidity. By the next morning, she'd have transformed the sad bread into a popular breakfast snack to sell at the open-air market. She cut thick slices, steamed them into pillowy-chewy softness, and topped them with green onion oil for humble bánh mì hấp, which simply means "steamed bread."

My mom replicated it for us in America, and I adored the slightly squishy bread and rich pungent garnish. Nowadays, bánh mì hấp is fanciful, topped with a jicama-meat mixture and other goodies and served with nước chấm, lettuce, and herbs for making wraps. You don't need meat for bánh mì hấp to be exciting. It's a deliciously thrilling way to use days-old bread.

Prepare the green onion oil

To make the Sesame Green Onion Oil: In a small microwavable bowl, stir together the green onions, salt, baking soda (if using), neutral oil, and sesame oil. Microwave on high power for 45 to 60 seconds, until the mixture bubbles and the onions just soften. (Alternatively, combine the neutral oil and sesame oil in a 1- to 1½-qt saucepan and set over medium heat until an onion piece gently sizzles upon contact; then stir in the remaining green onions, salt, and baking soda and cook for 30 seconds until things soften.) Let cool to room temperature.

Cook the topping

Set a 10-inch nonstick skillet over medium heat and add the 1 Tbsp neutral oil. When the oil nearly ripples, add the shallots and cook, stirring for 1 to 2 minutes, until they turn soft and sweetly fragrant. Add the shiitake mushrooms, tofu crumbles, pepper, and Maggi, then continue sautéing for about 3 minutes, until the shiitakes are soft and just cooked through. (If you're using diced vegetables

(CONTINUED)

Leaves from 1 head of soft-leaf lettuce (such as butter or red- or green-leaf)

1 small handful mint, basil, shiso, or other soft-leaf fresh herbs other than cilantro

1 small handful cilantro sprigs

1 cup Nước Chấm Dipping Sauce (page 32)

instead of tofu, splash in 2 Tbsp water and steam-sauté, covered, for about 5 minutes until they're nearly done, then uncover toward the end to finish cooking and concentrate flavor.) Let cool for 5 to 10 minutes. Season with salt.

Steam the bread

Fill a wide pot, such as a 6-qt Dutch oven, with water to about ½ inch deep and set a collapsible metal steamer inside. (Or, set up a Chinese steamer, filling the bottom pot halfway with water.) Bring to a boil over high heat, then slightly lower the heat to steady the steam. Meanwhile, cut the bread crosswise into scant ¾-inch-thick slices. In batches, steam the bread, cut-sides down, for 3 to 5 minutes, until soft and warm; transfer the steamed bread to a platter and cover with a dish towel to keep warm. (If you're using a collapsible steamer, position the bread on the upward-sloping side to keep it from touching the water.)

Assemble and serve

Divide the green onions and their oil among the slices of bread, crown the bread with the shiitake topping, and sprinkle with the nuts and fried shallots. Arrange the lettuce and herbs on a platter and the sauce in a communal bowl for guests to portion out for themselves (or put the sauce in individual rice bowls or bigger dipping-sauce bowls). Tuck a piece of bread and its topping inside a lettuce leaf and add some herbs. Bundle it up, dunk in the sauce, and munch away.

Check out page 128 for a bread-buying guide.

Note

Timing Prep the green onion oil and shiitake mixture up to 3 days ahead. Refrigerate them separately and return to room temperature before using.

MEATBALLS

¾ cup finely chopped yellow onion

Chubby 1¼-inch section fresh ginger, peeled and minced

2 large garlic cloves, minced

2 Tbsp toasted sesame oil

6 oz fresh shiitake or cremini mushrooms, chopped no bigger than a corn kernel (include stems)

1 (8-oz) can sliced water chestnuts, drained, patted dry, and chopped

1½ Tbsp fish sauce (store-bought or vegan version, page 29)

1 tsp granulated sugar

½ tsp recently ground white pepper

Neutral oil (such as canola or peanut) for brushing

1 cup canned chickpeas, drained well

1⅓ cups cooked rice, cold or at room temperature

Mounded ¼ tsp MSG, or ¾ tsp Asian mushroom seasoning (optional)

Fine sea salt

1½ Tbsp potato starch or 2 Tbsp cornstarch

Bánh Mì Xíu Mại Chay

Deconstructed Vegan Meatball Banh Mi

When it comes to borrowing the best from other cuisines, Vietnamese cooks never shy away from getting creative. Take xíu mại, which are named after shumai, a dim sum classic, but instead of a dumpling, you get tender pork meatballs presented in broth or a light tomato sauce with bread, cucumber, chile, and herbs for dipping and fashioning open-faced, sandwich-y bites. The dish is about off-road cooking and freestyle eating. It's wonderful.

I anchor this tasty vegan version with a mushroom-y base studded with crunchy bits of water chestnut. Rice and chickpeas lend texture and protein, while starch holds things together. The meatballs bake up efficiently and can be stored for days (make a double batch to enjoy during the week!) before getting sauced and devoured as a tapas-like snack or light lunch.

Prepare the meatball mixture

To make the meatballs: In a small bowl, combine the onion, ginger, and garlic and mix to incorporate. Set aside ¼ cup of this mixture in another small bowl for the sauce.

Set a 12-inch nonstick skillet over medium heat and add the sesame oil. When the oil barely ripples, add the onion mixture and cook for about 2 minutes, stirring occasionally, until it turns fragrant and is no longer raw-smelling.

Add the mushrooms, water chestnuts, fish sauce, sugar, and pepper to the skillet; turn the heat to high; and cook for 8 to 10 minutes, stirring frequently and spreading the mixture out to evenly cook, until it compacts to nearly one-third of its original volume (expect some browning). Remove from the heat and let sit, uncovered, for about 5 minutes to cool and further concentrate the flavor.

Meanwhile, preheat the oven to 400°F. Line a large rimmed baking sheet with parchment paper and brush with a light film of neutral oil.

(CONTINUED)

SAUCE

1½ Tbsp neutral oil (such as canola or peanut)

¼ cup onion mixture (reserved from the meatballs)

1 cup canned crushed tomatoes

¾ cup water, plus 1½ tsp

1 Tbsp fish sauce (store-bought or vegan version, page 29)

2 tsp granulated sugar

¾ tsp potato starch

——

3 petite baguettes, bolillo rolls, or other bread suitable for banh mi

1 small English or 2 Persian cucumbers, sliced into scant ¼-inch-thick pieces

⅔ cup coarsely chopped cilantro, mint, or basil leaves

1 large Fresno or jalapeño chile, sliced

> Hand-chopping the vegetables yields meatballs with nice chunky texture. Chopping via a food processor is easier, but the ingredients can easily get over-chopped and wet, which makes the meatballs softer.
>
> Brown rice or dryish rice (what's used for fried rice) yields firmer meatballs.

In a small or full-size food processor, pulse the chickpeas eight to ten times into a coarse, crumbly texture (a few remaining whole ones are okay). Scrape into a medium bowl. Add the rice to the processor and pulse three to seven times to break up the grains a bit. Add the rice to the chickpeas along with the shiitake mixture. Combine and taste; if oomph is required, add the MSG or big pinches of salt. Add the potato starch and use one hand to work it in, gently kneading everything into a slightly sticky mixture that can be easily shaped.

Shape and bake the meatballs

Shape the chickpea mixture into sixteen balls (about 2 Tbsp each) and put on the prepared baking sheet, rolling to coat with oil.

Bake the meatballs for 20 to 25 minutes, until slightly darkened on the outside, dry to the touch, and browned on the bottom (pick up one to check). Remove from the oven and let cool for 5 minutes to dry their exteriors.

Cook the sauce

To make the sauce: While the meatballs bake, set a 12-inch nonstick skillet over medium heat and add the neutral oil. When the oil begins to ripple, add the reserved onion mixture and cook 3 to 4 minutes, until some bits turn golden. Add the tomatoes, ¾ cup water, fish sauce, and sugar; turn the heat to medium-high; and bring to a gentle boil. Then turn the heat to medium-low and let the sauce steadily percolate for 2 to 3 minutes to develop flavor. In a small bowl, dilute the potato starch with the remaining 1½ tsp water. Pour this slurry into the pan and stir for about 30 seconds, until the sauce slightly thickens. Remove from the heat and partially cover if the meatballs are not done.

Assemble and serve

If needed, re-crisp the bread in the still-hot oven (see page 129). Slice it thickly (or keep whole) and set on the table. Return the sauce to a gentle simmer and add the warm meatballs, carefully turning them to coat in the sauce. Cook for about 1 minute, spooning sauce onto the meatballs to lightly cloak them.

Serve the sauced meatballs immediately in a shallow dish along with the bread, cucumber, cilantro, and chile. Invite diners to halve each meatball before putting it on a slice or hunk of bread with sauce, herbs, and chile. Finish with a cucumber slice, or eat it on the side for refreshing crunch.

———

Note

Lifespan Make the meatballs and sauce up to 5 days in advance and refrigerate separately. Microwave the meatballs in 30-second blasts to warm, then add to the sauce.

Soup Celebrations

CONSIDER VIETNAM'S LENGTHY COASTLINE, natural lakes, mighty rivers, and productive rice paddies and it's easy to understand why water influences Viet foodways. In fact, soups are all categorized as món nước (water dish). There are so many kinds that you may eat soup for breakfast, brunch, lunch, or dinner.

I love the comforts and thrills of a cozy bowl of soup. It's a mild obsession. My husband jokes that I'm always eyeing his dinner for a future noodle-soup lunch. My simple strategy is this: Extend a leftover stir-fry or curry with water, broth, or stock; re-season it with salt or fish sauce; and then add two bundles of soaked glass noodles (see page 9). It's re-purposeful cooking that effectively deals with lingering food in the fridge. He always enthusiastically slurps it all up.

I also save vegetable scraps in a container that I keep refrigerated or frozen. When it's full, I make stock, adding water and salt, plus a knob of ginger, some onion, and maybe a few dried shiitake mushrooms for Asian impressions. The result is a great water replacer for stir-fries, instant-noodle soups, and the like. Such imprecise stocks are adventures in cooking. They're not always great, but they're good enough; they help me better understand how to use vegetables to build flavor. Plus, the stocks make maximum usage of well-cultivated ingredients.

The recipes here offer more-formalized concepts, but they contain plenty of versatility too. A trio of easy everyday soups open this chapter. None of them requires make-ahead stock. You'll simply use water and vegetables (use water that you like to drink because it's a critical ingredient). Some are categorically called canh (everyday quick soups), but there's also a fancy-ish asparagus súp (based on French soupe) that you may present for a special meal. If you hanker for creamy cháo (porridge) with little hassle, there's a blender method that I adore. When there's more time, make dumplings and serve them in broth; or pan-fry them and serve the soup on the side!

Three regional noodle soups fill the rest of this section. Originating in northern Vietnam, the seat of Viet culture in many respects, pho appears delicate, yet its flavors are deep and strong, just like the region itself. But similar to many Viet things, as pho spread elsewhere, it deliciously morphed at the hands of creative cooks. Gauge the elasticity and parameters of Vietnam's iconic dish by cooking up a trio of pho—a quickie, a deluxe vegan, and a chicken-vegetable iteration.

Feisty bún bò Huế, a spicy beef-and-pork rice-noodle soup, defines the geographically narrow and immensely resourceful central region of Vietnam. This soup is a very hearty, meat-laden affair. My vegan recipe is an exciting brow-wiper that won't weigh you down like the traditional rendition does.

Kaleidoscopic hủ tiếu belongs to southern Vietnam, where people are not afraid to mix and match and to create, cook, and eat as they please. Slightly sweet and as spicy as you want, hủ tiếu is the ultimate have-it-your-way Viet noodle soup.

Don't be daunted by the long noodle-soup recipes. You're simply pressure-cooking, simmering, or boiling ingredients. The recipes are doable with readily available produce, seasonings, and accoutrements.

1½ cups drained Pickled Mustard Greens (page 60), plus about 1 cup brine

1 Tbsp neutral oil (such as canola or peanut)

½ medium yellow onion, thinly sliced

6 oz large white, cremini, or shiitake mushrooms (or a combination), quartered through the stems

Fine sea salt

4 cups water

1 Tbsp fish sauce (store-bought or vegan version, page 29), plus more as needed

8 oz ripe tomatoes, quartered and kept unseeded

2 tsp minced peeled ginger

Canh Dưa Cải

Pickled Mustard Greens Soup

Keeping pickled mustard greens in the fridge equals easy meals. Aside from just eating the tasty crisp pickle as is, I make the most of its tangy umami-ness by employing both the pickle and brine for this light, satisfying soup. Mushrooms stand in for the pork rib nuggets used in the traditional version.

Prep the pickle and simmer the soup

Cut the mustard greens into bite-size pieces and set aside with the brine. Include any green onion sections that may have been in the measure, halving them crosswise if they appear too awkward to chew. If you used garlic in the pickle, chop one or two halves to include with the mustard and green onion.

Set a 3-qt saucepan over medium heat and add the neutral oil. When the oil barely ripples, add the onion and cook, stirring frequently for about 3 minutes, until it turns soft and fragrant. Add the mushrooms and ¼ tsp salt, then continue cooking for about 2 minutes, until the mushrooms glisten. Stir in the pickled mustard greens, 1 cup brine, the water, and fish sauce. Turn the heat to high, bring to a boil, and then turn the heat to medium-low and let simmer vigorously for 5 minutes.

Finish with tang and zip

Add the tomatoes to the pan and, once the soup returns to a simmer, turn off the heat. Let the soup sit, uncovered, for 5 to 10 minutes, then add the ginger for zing. Taste the broth and add more salt, fish sauce, or brine for savoriness (or splash in some water if it's too strong). Serve in a communal bowl or individual bowls.

Note

Ingredients Replace the mushrooms with 6 oz cooked ground pork or chicken. Or, add 6 oz cooked shrimp or mild white fish fillet (such as barramundi, tilapia, or sablefish) along with the tomato. Recipe tester Rosemary Metzger kept the mushrooms and added the seafood. You can't go wrong.

1 (14- or 16-oz) package tofu (silken, medium, medium-firm, or firm)

1½ Tbsp neutral oil (such as canola or peanut)

1 small yellow onion, or 1 shallot, halved and thinly sliced

12 oz ripe tomatoes, cored and coarsely chopped

Fine sea salt

6 oz fresh mushrooms (shiitake, cremini, or white), thickly sliced through the stems

1½ Tbsp fish sauce (store-bought or vegan version, page 29), plus more as needed

4 cups water

2 Tbsp chopped fresh herbs (such as dill, cilantro, Vietnamese shiso, any kind of basil, or garlic chives)

Recently ground black pepper, or 1 Thai or small serrano chile, sliced

Before coring, peel the tomato (use a serrated peeler) if floating skin bits do not appeal.

If possible, give this soup and others a rest before adding final garnishes. Even 15 minutes will allow the flavors to settle, meld, and concentrate. (There's a reason that day-after soup rocks.)

Canh Đậu Hũ

Tofu-Tomato Soup

When I think of a vegetarian quickie soup on a weeknight, my mind goes to this recipe. There's tofu, tomato, and mushroom for umami, plus herbs to refresh at the end. You can riff on this recipe blueprint, as suggested in the Note, to create other soups. Tomato, called cà chua ("sour eggplant," because the two fruit-vegetables are kin), also lends bright tang and color. That said, when fresh tomatoes were lousy, tester Cate McGuire used a drained 14-ounce can of diced tomato and adjusted the cooking time as needed, with good results.

Drain the tofu and build the soup foundation

Pour out any liquid from the tofu tub. Cut the tofu into cubes, each about ¾ inch big. Set aside.

Set a 3- to 4-qt saucepan over medium heat and add the neutral oil. When the oil barely ripples, add the onion and cook, stirring occasionally, for about 3 minutes, or until it turns fragrant and soft. Add the tomatoes and ¾ tsp salt, cover, and cook for 4 to 6 minutes, until the tomatoes collapse. Stir occasionally and, if necessary, lower the heat to prevent them from sticking or scorching.

Uncover the pan and add the mushrooms and fish sauce. Let cook, stirring, for a few minutes to draw out umami goodness, then add the water. Turn the heat to high, bring to a boil, and skim off and discard any scum that rises to the surface.

Add the tofu, simmer, and serve

Pour off any water that has drained from the tofu and add the tofu to the soup. Turn the heat to a simmer and cook, uncovered, for about 5 minutes to develop and concentrate the flavors. If you are not serving the soup right away, turn off the heat and cover.

Just before serving, return the soup to a simmer. Taste and add salt or fish sauce, if necessary. Remove from the heat. Stir in the herbs and transfer the soup to a serving bowl. Garnish with a healthy sprinkling of pepper and serve.

Note

Variations For Seaweed-Tofu Soup, omit the mushrooms and add 2 Tbsp dried wakame along with the water. Drop in a handful of shrimp toward the end, if you want seafood bling.

For Tofu and Pork Soup, swap out the mushrooms for 3 to 4 oz ground pork and add with the fish sauce. Poke and mush the meat into small pieces; once the rawness disappears, add the water and continue as directed. If you want a brothier result, add 8 to 12 oz of tofu instead of the full amount.

Instead of pork, you can use an equal amount of ground chicken or turkey.

POINTERS FOR EXCELLENT SOUP INGREDIENTS AND TOOLS

The recipes in this chapter benefit greatly from certain ingredients and pieces of equipment. Of note, seaweed builds savory depth, briny flavor, and a rich round mouthfeel that is akin to well-constructed meaty stocks and broths. Unfamiliar with kombu, nori, and wakame? Check page 19 for sourcing tips. Flavor enhancers play pivotal roles in certain broth recipes to send the results over the top; page 20 offers details.

When making vegetarian noodle soups from scratch, weigh the vegetables (including ginger!) for stellar, consistent broth. Bones and meat are typically weighed, so why not treat veggies similarly? Use a pressure cooker (a stovetop model or an electric multicooker, like an Instant Pot) because that appliance extracts flavor from vegetables really well and quickly. You don't achieve the same depth of flavor with a stovetop simmer, but the recipes do include that option.

However the broth may be brewed, employ something strong to strain the results and squeeze out as much liquid as possible from the solids. Cheesecloth isn't as sturdy as lightweight unbleached muslin, which washes up easily and is reusable for years. (At a fabric store, shop for the type of muslin that may be used to line quilts or a face mask; tear it into 18- to 24-inch-square pieces and wash, preferably with fragrance-free soap, before the first use and after each use.) A non-terry dish towel or nut milk bag works too.

6 by 6-inch piece kombu, snipped into quarters

½ oz dried shiitake mushrooms

1-inch section fresh ginger, peeled, cut into thick coins, and smashed with the flat side of a knife

6 cups water, plus 3 Tbsp

12 oz asparagus

1½ Tbsp neutral oil (such as canola or peanut)

½ cup thinly sliced shallots or yellow onion

Fine sea salt

1 large egg, plus 1 egg yolk

1 tsp fish sauce (store-bought or vegan version, page 29), plus more as needed

¼ tsp recently ground black pepper

2 Tbsp cornstarch

MSG or Asian mushroom seasoning for balancing flavor (optional)

Súp Măng Tây Nấm Hương

Silky Asparagus-Shiitake Soup

When Viet people plan a fancy meal, they often think of asparagus-and-crab soup, a luxurious marriage of land and sea. Old-fashioned cooks, like my mom, used canned asparagus (it's what they had access to), but I prefer fresh spears. To create a deeply savory vegetarian version, I use a triple whammy of kombu, shiitake, and asparagus. There's little waste, as the woody ends of the asparagus add umami to the broth, and the rehydrated kombu and shiitake contribute texture and flavor to the final soup. The egg, mixed with fish sauce and black pepper, mimics crab butter.

Build the broth

Put the kombu, shiitake mushrooms, ginger, and 6 cups water in a 4-qt sauce-pan. Let soak and hydrate for at least 30 minutes, or overnight for best flavor. When ready to cook the broth, trim and coarsely chop the woody ends from the asparagus and add them to the pan. Partially cover the saucepan, set over medium heat, and bring to a boil. Then lower the heat to maintain a simmer and cook, uncovered, for 15 minutes.

Meanwhile, cut the remaining asparagus stalks on a steep diagonal into 2-inch-long pieces. Separate the tender tips to add toward the end of cooking for a bright green finish. Set the stalks and tips aside.

When the broth finishes cooking, turn off the heat and let rest for 5 minutes. Using tongs, retrieve the kombu and shiitakes, giving each mushroom a squeeze to expel its liquid back into the pot; set aside. Strain the broth into another pan or large bowl, discarding the solids. Thinly slice the shiitake caps, discarding the stems or saving for another use. Trim the kombu, which may be slippery and viscous, of jagged edges and thin patches that may break apart in the soup, then cut into 2-inch-long strips, about ¼ inch wide. Add the shiitakes and kombu to the asparagus stalks.

Make the soup and serve

Return the saucepan to medium-high heat and add the neutral oil. When the oil barely ripples, add the shallots and 1 pinch salt and cook, stirring, for about 3 minutes, until soft and fragrant; a few golden edges are fine. Add the shiitakes, kombu, and asparagus stalk pieces and stir to combine. Sprinkle with ¾ tsp salt and then add the broth. Partially cover and bring to a boil. Turn the heat to a simmer and cook, still partly covered, for 15 minutes; midway through, add the reserved asparagus tips. Meanwhile, in a small bowl, combine the egg, egg yolk, fish sauce, and pepper; beat with a fork; and set aside.

In a separate small bowl, mix the cornstarch and remaining 3 Tbsp water to make a slurry. Uncover the saucepan, turn the heat to medium and, after bubbling action resumes, gradually stir in the slurry. You may not need the entire amount to create a thick, silky texture. Continue stirring for about 30 seconds, or until the soup thickens. Turn off the heat.

Pour the egg mixture into the soup in a wide circle, wait about 5 seconds for it to start setting, and then stir gently to break it up. Taste and season with additional salt and fish sauce, or MSG, if needed. Partially cover and let rest for 5 to 10 minutes to further develop the flavor. Ladle into individual bowls and serve immediately.

Note

Timing When making this soup several hours in advance, you will need to pause the cooking before adding the asparagus tips. Just remove the pan from the heat and partly cover. When ready to finish, reheat to a simmer and add the asparagus tips, cornstarch, and egg.

1 cup raw white or brown jasmine rice

8 cups lightly salted broth, stock, or bouillon (any kind), plus more as needed

1½-inch section fresh ginger, peeled, split lengthwise, and smashed with the flat side of a knife

2 green onions

Fine sea salt

Leftovers from any main dish in this book (see Note)

Vegan Sate Sauce (page 40), for drizzling

3 Tbsp Fast-Fried Shallots (page 46) or store-bought fried shallots or onions

Chopped cilantro or green onions, or both, for serving

Cháo

Blender Rice Porridge

Unattended cooking is the best cooking. When I wake up wanting a cozy bowl of rice porridge for lunch, I don't go through the traditional process of carefully simmering the grains until they expand and nearly disintegrate to release all their starches, creating a creamy soup. I simply do a fast boil and then leave the pot alone for an hour or longer. The rice grains soften, sometimes splitting and blooming at the ends like flowers. Close to lunchtime, I blend the rice to break up the grains and then warm it over medium heat to allow the rice starch to finish thickening and become creamy cháo. As a blank canvas, this porridge may be adorned by a zillion savory toppings, including leftovers (a personal favorite). It's versatile, adaptable, and customizable.

Boil and rest the rice

Rinse the rice once to remove its surface starch, then add to a 4-qt saucepan with the broth, ginger, and green onions, folding them to fit in the pot and for easy retrieval later. Set over high heat and bring to a boil. As needed, adjust the heat to maintain a steady boil for 3 to 5 minutes (use the longer time for brown rice), until the grains have plumped up and are slightly chewy. Turn off the heat and cover tightly. Let sit for at least 1 hour so the grains continue to cook as they cool. (I have let it sit for as long as 4 hours!)

Blend the porridge

Uncover the pot and, using tongs, retrieve and discard the ginger and green onions. Using an immersion blender or countertop blender, puree the porridge. The consistency will be watery with tons of teeny-tiny rice bits. It's not pretty at this point.

Reheat, taste, and serve

Close to serving time, ready your accompaniments by warming and refreshing things as needed. Concurrently, reheat the porridge over medium heat, stirring now and then.

Use your everyday rice. Mine is jasmine, although I've also made excellent cháo with broken rice, short- and medium-grain white rice, and sticky (glutinous) rice.

By the time the porridge starts simmering, it should be creamy and thick from the rice's natural starches having been released. If the porridge is too thick, add water or additional broth. If it's too grainy for your liking, lower the heat and let simmer gently for about 5 minutes more to further develop the rice starch; as needed, add liquid to facilitate cooking and avoid scorching.

When you're satisfied with the texture, taste and add more salt, if needed. Divide the porridge among individual bowls and top with a leftover and a drizzle of sate sauce, followed by the fried shallots, cilantro, or green onions. Enjoy your masterpiece.

Notes

Ingredients The cooking liquid can be as simple as store-bought broth or bouillon (if you use Better Than Bouillon, dilute it to half-strength so its flavor does not dominate). However, homemade broth will add extra dimension, as would any noodle-soup broth from this chapter.

Other easy topping ideas include fried or boiled eggs, sliced Pan-Fried Tofu Slabs (page 52), chopped Pickled Mustard Greens (page 60), or chopped Peppery Vegan Bologna (page 53). A sprinkling of Nori Dust (page 27) adds a briny touch too.

Lifespan Refrigerate leftovers for up to 5 days and reheat over medium-low heat, adding a splash of water to loosen.

Variation For Blender Multigrain Porridge, use ⅔ cup rice and ⅓ cup quinoa, teff, or millet.

5 by 10-inch piece kombu

1 oz dried shiitake mushrooms

8 cups water

6 oz napa or green cabbage, sliced into ½-inch-wide pieces

6 oz carrot; finely diced to yield ½ cup for the filling, the remainder sliced ¼ inch thick for the soup

½ small yellow onion, thinly sliced

Chubby ¾-inch section fresh ginger, peeled, cut as 3 slices, and smashed with the flat side of a knife

Fine sea salt

Brimming 1 cup canned chickpeas, plus 1½ Tbsp canning liquid

2 green onions; whites and green parts finely chopped to yield ¼ cup, the remainder thinly sliced

1 Tbsp plus 1 tsp soy sauce, plus more as needed

2 tsp toasted sesame oil, plus more for serving

¾ tsp granulated sugar

¼ tsp recently ground white or black pepper

1 Tbsp Nori Dust (page 27; optional, for extra-savory depth)

28 to 32 round pot sticker (gyoza) or sue gow wrappers

1½ Tbsp fish sauce (store-bought or vegan version, page 29), plus more as needed

1 large handful baby spinach, kale, or power greens mix (optional, for deep-green bling)

Canh Sủi Cảo

Shiitake Dumplings Soup

With plump mushroom-y dumplings, seaweed, and cabbage ribbons swimming in a gentle, soothing broth, this soup is perfect for whenever you want a wonderfully light one-dish meal. The star is sủi cảo, which in Vietnamese denotes Chinese-style dumplings that may be poached, steamed, or fried, even though the Viet term is borrowed from the Chinese shuǐ jiǎo, which technically means "poached dumplings." To coax the best flavors and textures from dried shiitakes and kombu, rehydrate them overnight or during the day while you're doing other things. Either way, you'll be effortlessly building the foundations for the dumpling filling and broth (the kelp gets sliced into short noodle-like pieces and included in the soup). For a vegan sủi cảo filling, Viet cooks often use mashed, cooked mung beans to bind the chopped vegetables, but I take a shortcut with canned chickpeas and its viscous cooking liquid (aquafaba). Some ingredients do double duty here, so prep them once to employ them twice. The Notes offer a meaty swap and options for taking this recipe in different directions.

Start the soup

Snip or tear the kombu into six to eight pieces, dropping them into a 4-qt saucepan. Add the mushrooms and water. Cover and rehydrate at room temperature for at least 6 hours or up to overnight.

Retrieve the soaked shiitakes, firmly squeezing each one above the pot to expel excess liquid, and then set aside. Remove the kombu (expect the pieces to be slippery and viscous), trim off any jagged edges and thin patches that may break apart in the soup, and then cut into 2-inch-long strips, each about ¼ inch wide. Return the kombu to the pot and add the cabbage, sliced carrot, onion, ginger, and ½ tsp salt. Set over medium heat and bring to a gentle boil. Let cook, uncovered, for about 5 minutes, or until the carrot is tender. Turn off the heat and cover.

(CONTINUED)

> To avoid clouding up the broth with starchiness, cook the dumplings separately.

Make the dumplings

While the soup cooks, put the chickpeas and their 1½ Tbsp liquid in a medium bowl. Using a potato masher, mash them into a cohesive firm-ish mixture. Finely chop the shiitake caps and stems. Add them to the chickpeas, along with the diced carrot, finely chopped green onions, soy sauce, sesame oil, sugar, pepper, and nori dust (if using). Mix well with a spatula or your hand. Taste and, if a strong, savory flavor is needed, mix in more soy sauce, ½ tsp at a time, or add salt by the pinch.

Line a baking sheet with parchment paper and lightly flour.

Working in batches of four to six wrappers, arrange them on your work surface. Using a pastry brush, paint a wide border of water on the wrappers. Place a scant 1 Tbsp filling off-center on each wrapper. If you have a favorite shape, go with it. Otherwise, fold the wrapper in half and seal well to create a half-moon. Press from the filling mound's edge to the wrapper rim to remove air bubbles; make a few pleats if you like. Set the dumplings on the prepared baking sheet. Repeat to use all the filling. Loosely cover your dumpling beauties to prevent them from drying out.

Finish the soup and poach the dumplings

Uncover the soup pot, then remove and discard the ginger. Add the fish sauce, taste, and, if needed, add more salt and fish sauce for savory oomph. Return the soup to a slow simmer. Cover to keep hot.

Fill a 5- or 6-qt pot halfway with water, set over high heat on your biggest burner, and bring to a boil. Add the dumplings, stirring and nudging them to avoid sticking. As the dumplings float to the top, adjust the heat as needed to gently cook them (a rolling boil may bust the skins) for a few minutes more, until they look glossy, maybe puffy, and a bit translucent. Using a skimmer or a slotted spoon, scoop the dumplings from the pot, pausing above it to let excess water drip back down, and then divide among four soup bowls.

Return the soup to a swift simmer. Add the spinach (if using), and when it softens, turn off the heat. Divide the broth and vegetables among the bowls, then finish with a few drops of sesame oil and a sprinkle of sliced green onions. Serve immediately with chopsticks and spoons for a two-handed eating experience.

Notes

Technique If your soup pot is table-ready, serve from it. Instead of dividing the dumplings among individual bowls, add them to the soup after the vegetables have softened. Turn off the heat, finish with the sesame oil and green onions, and then bring to the table. You may also serve the soup and dumplings from an impressive tureen or very large bowl.

Timing The soup and dumplings may be made a day ahead. Cover and refrigerate separately. Cook the dumplings straight from the fridge.

Variations Instead of chickpeas and their cooking liquid, use 7 oz raw ground pork or chicken or turkey dark meat. The seasoning remains the same, although the nori dust isn't needed. If you're subbing square wonton skins, you may need more than thirty-two wrappers because they are sometimes smaller than pot sticker wrappers; adjust the amount of filling for each dumpling.

Instead of poaching the dumplings, pan-fry them into pot stickers, called sủi cảo chiên, in Vietnamese. Set a 12-inch nonstick or carbon-steel skillet over medium-high heat and add a generous splash of neutral oil. When the oil ripples, add the dumplings, sealed edges facing up and crowded in (it's okay to let them touch), and briefly fry to brown the bottoms. Turn the heat to medium, add about ⅓ cup water so it bubbles halfway up the sides of the dumplings, and cover to steam-cook for about 6 minutes, until the wrappers are translucent and the water has disappeared. Carefully uncover and fry gently for about 1 minute to crisp the bottoms. Serve them, crisp bottoms-up, with soy sauce and vinegar as a dip and the soup as an accompaniment.

To serve just the soup with other dishes, skip the dumpling-making and slice the soaked shiitakes to add with the other vegetables to cook in the soup. Flying solo, this soup is what I'd call Kombu Vegetable Soup. If you'd like to include protein, add 6 to 8 oz cubed tofu or a handful of peeled raw shrimp toward the end, letting it heat and cook through before adding the leafy greens. Taste to re-verify saltiness before serving.

5 oz dried narrow flat rice noodles (bánh phở or pad Thai noodles; see page 9)

1 star anise (8 robust points)

1-inch cinnamon stick

2 green onions; whites kept whole, greens thinly sliced

Chubby ¾-inch section fresh ginger, peeled and cut into matchsticks

1 Tbsp neutral oil (such as canola or peanut)

4 oz fresh mushrooms (such as shiitake, oyster, or cremini), sliced or torn into large bite-size pieces

4½ cups water

1 Tbsp vegetable bouillon base

2 small ribs celery, 1 carrot, 3-inch wedge cabbage (green, napa, or savoy), or a combo, sliced

4 pieces Pan-Fried Tofu Slabs (page 52), or 4 oz store-bought fried or baked tofu, sliced or cut into chopstick-able pieces

1½ Tbsp fish sauce (store-bought or vegan version, page 29)

¼ cup chopped cilantro

Recently ground black pepper

Optional add-ins: 2 handfuls raw or blanched mung bean sprouts, 1 sliced hot chile (Thai, serrano, jalapeño, or Fresno), 1 small handful herbs (mint, Thai basil, culantro, or rice paddy), 1 lime cut into wedges, hoisin sauce, sriracha, Vegan Sate Sauce (page 40), and Viet Chile Sauce (page 39)

Phở Chay Nhanh

Fast Vegetarian Pho

Yes, there are instant pho options out there; but honestly, I'm always doctoring them up. One day when I didn't have time to craft the deluxe pho on page 158, I made a quick pho using bouillon base and basic vegetables to add complexity and nutrition. It was super-flavorful, more satisfying than commercial instant pho, and took about 30 minutes. Since then, I've returned to this method, which offers nearly immediate gratification and lots of versatility (go ahead and play around with pho!).

For this shortcut pho, I soak dried bánh phở and let the partially hydrated noodles finish cooking in the pho-ish broth. That time-saving technique, plus the bouillon base, clouds up the broth a bit. The bowl assembly process doesn't align with the more nuanced, from-scratch pho recipes in this book. However, this fast pho is perfect for an easy-peasy meal.

Soak the noodles and make the broth

Put the noodles in a large bowl and add very hot water to cover.

Set a 3-qt saucepan over medium heat. When the pan is hot (water flicked onto its surface should evaporate within seconds), add the star anise and cinnamon, stirring to toast for about 1 minute, until they turn aromatic. Add the green onion whites and ginger and dry-sauté, stirring constantly for about 1 minute, until they become fragrant and maybe a little brown. Add the neutral oil and mushrooms, and swiftly stir for 1 minute, until glistening. Pour in the water, then stir in the bouillon base and celery.

Cover the pan, turn the heat to high, and bring to a boil. Uncover and lower the heat to boil gently for 5 minutes to cook the vegetables and develop the broth's flavor. Retrieve and discard the star anise and cinnamon. Add the tofu and let it warm through for about 1 minute. Using a spider or a slotted spoon, divide the vegetables and tofu between two noodle-soup bowls. (It is okay if you miss retrieving some from the pot.)

What are chopstick-able tofu pieces? For this and other noodle-soup recipes in this book, sharply angle your knife to slice tofu slabs into pieces about ¼ inch thick; their broadness offers a svelte texture that absorbs the broth well, evokes sliced meat, and is easily retrievable with chopsticks. If that cut seems challenging, aim for triangles or thick sticks for noodle soups.

One whole star anise has about eight seed pods (referred to as "points" in my recipes). If the points are not all big and robust, break off and add additional points to ensure good flavor. Using broken star anise is okay.

Finish the broth, add the noodles, then assemble

Season the broth with the fish sauce for an umami burst (add a little more if needed for a strong flavor). Return the broth to a strong boil. Drain and rinse the noodles well, snip them if the strands are long, and then add them to the broth. When they're just cooked through, about 1 minute, divide the noodles and broth between the bowls. Garnish with the reserved sliced green onions, cilantro, and a sprinkling of black pepper. Serve with all the add-ins you choose.

Note

Ingredients If whole spices are unavailable, use a brimming ¼ tsp Chinese five-spice powder. Add it along with the mushrooms. The broth will be murkier but still taste good. Instead of tofu, use leftover steak, chicken, shrimp, or fish.

Pho PRINCIPLES

Vietnam's most iconic dish, pho noodle soup, has been part of protest poetry, covert operations, and even romantic relationships (people joke that rice is your reliable wife and pho is your flirty mistress). Pho was created at the beginning of the twentieth century when Vietnamese, French, and Chinese cultures rubbed shoulders in the Hanoi area. Early versions were modest in size and spartan (broth, noodles, and sliced cooked meat), but as pho's popularity grew, beef pho begot a chicken version and then other renditions. After pho arrived in freewheeling Saigon, cooks sweetened the broth, served bigger portions, and added extra cuts of beef. A Hanoi- versus Saigon-style (north versus south) pho fight emerged. Vietnamese refugees and immigrants seeded pho culture wherever they resettled, and many others embraced it. Nowadays, there are pho-ish banh mi, pizza, and burritos, but this book focuses on vegetable-forward pho noodle soup. Here are relevant principles for your pho adventures.

PHO FLAVOR ELEMENTS

Creating pho noodle soup involves an umami-laden broth seasoned by a member of the onion family, warm spices, and ginger. The resulting aromatic broth is savory-sweet, somewhat rich-tasting, and ideally clear, although some cloudiness is okay. Bánh phở flat rice noodles (think pad Thai–size or narrower, see page 9 for buying tips) absorb and carry the broth flavors, as do the toppings. Garnishes in the bowl and add-ins at the table vary per the diner's preferences.

TECHNIQUES AND TWEAKS

Traditional, stovetop-simmered pho requires charring unpeeled onion (or shallots) and ginger, a process that cooks the aromatics to slightly mellow their harshness and create sweet compounds that lend complexity to the broth. When making pho broth in pressure cookers or from a bouillon base, the nuances from charring are missed. Dry-sautéing the aromatics is good enough, so you can skip the charring for the pho recipes in this book! And, here's an added bonus to letting vegetables drive the broth bus: No parboiling of bones is needed for clear, clean-tasting broth. Strain the broth well and always slightly overseason it for a bold flavor; the other components in the bowl are barely salted.

BOWL ASSEMBLY INSIGHTS

Be organized and prep ahead. Broth keeps well in the fridge and freezer. Ready the noodles, toppings, garnishes, and add-ins before, while, or after the broth cooks. As needed, return them to room temperature. While reheating the broth, set all your optional add-ins (bean sprouts, herbs, lime, and condiments) at the table.

Divide the noodles among individual bowls, spreading them out before arranging the toppings flat on top; if the ingredients are cold, pause to microwave each bowl in 30-second blasts. Finish with the garnishes. Re-taste the broth before ladling it into bowls in a circular pattern to efficiently heat everything.

VEGAN PHO BROTH

2 whole cloves

1½-inch cinnamon stick

2 star anise (16 robust points)

1½ tsp coriander seeds

1-oz section fresh ginger, peeled, thickly sliced, and smashed with the flat side of a knife

9 oz yellow onion, halved and thickly sliced

6 cups water

5 by 10-inch piece kombu, snipped into 6 to 8 pieces

1 Tbsp dried wakame

6 oz turnip or daikon, unpeeled, scrubbed, and cut into large chunks

3 oz celery stalk, coarsely chopped

10 oz napa or green cabbage, quartered lengthwise and cut crosswise into large pieces

8 oz mung bean sprouts

5 oz carrot, cut crosswise into 4 sections (add the peel to the broth, if you removed it)

Fine sea salt

½ tsp Marmite

½ to ¾ tsp MSG, or 1 to 1½ tsp Asian mushroom seasoning, plus more as needed

1 tsp agave syrup or granulated sugar (preferably organic)

___

10 oz dried narrow flat rice noodles (bánh phở or pad Thai noodles; see page 9)

1½ tsp neutral oil (such as canola or peanut)

Phở Chay Đặc Biệt
Deluxe Vegan Pho

I've written vegetarian pho recipes but, until now, have not given them enough attention. For this book, I aimed to craft a recipe that would stand shoulder to shoulder with its beefy kin. The broth relies on glutamate-rich vegetables from land and sea. In particular, kombu contributes a round mouthfeel like that of meat collagen, while wakame injects a briny back note like that of dried seafood employed in traditional northern Viet pho. Pressure cooking plus straining the solids through cloth render maximum flavor. To season the broth before serving, use Marmite, for beef-like flavor and color, plus MSG, a common pho seasoning that unifies and amplifies flavors. Some say pho isn't *pho* without a flavor enhancer, so don't be afraid to use one. Omit the sugar for a northern-Viet finish; add it for southern Viet–style pho.

For đặc biệt (special) bowls, get fancy with the add-ins, as shown on page 157 (with tofu skin). Use a combination of mushrooms to vary texture and flavor. Some are silky or meaty while others are crunchy or chewy—just like the different cuts of beef in a bowl. Absorbing broth flavors during a brief cooking, the tender tofu is terrific dipped in a combo of hoisin sauce and sriracha. See the Notes for bonus topping ideas.

Prepare the broth

To make the Vegan Pho Broth: In a 6-qt electric multicooker, combine the cloves, cinnamon stick, star anise, and coriander seeds. Program the cooker to sauté on moderate-high heat and toast the spices for several minutes, stirring until fragrant. Add the ginger and onion and stir for 45 to 60 seconds, until aromatic (browning is fine).

Add the water, kombu, wakame, turnip, celery, cabbage, bean sprouts, carrot, and 2 tsp salt to the cooker. (The carrots don't cook to a mush and are easily removed when layered on top.) Lock the cooker's lid in place, then program it to pressure-cook on high for 15 minutes. When it's done, unplug the cooker and let vent naturally for 20 minutes. Manually release any residual pressure. (With a stovetop pressure cooker, toast the spices over medium-high heat, add 6½ cups water, lock the lid, bring to high pressure, and cook for 15 minutes. Let the cooker depressurize naturally on a cool burner for 15 minutes.)

4 oz fresh mushrooms (such as shiitake, maitake, and oyster), sliced or torn into large bite-size pieces

Fine sea salt

12 pieces Pan-Fried Tofu Slabs (page 52), sliced or cut into chopstick-able pieces

2 oz yellow or red onion, thinly sliced

2 green onions, green parts only, thinly sliced

¼ cup chopped fresh cilantro, leafy tops only

Recently ground black pepper (optional)

Optional add-ins: 3 handfuls raw or blanched mung bean sprouts, 1 or 2 sliced hot chiles (serrano, jalapeño, Thai, or Fresno), 1 handful herbs (mint, Thai basil, culantro, or rice paddy), 2 limes cut as wedges, hoisin sauce, sriracha, Vegan Sate Sauce (page 40), and Viet Chile Sauce (page 39)

Carefully remove the lid, tilting it away from you to avoid the hot steam. If the carrot pieces are not too mushy, reserve them to use as a topping. Let the hot broth rest for about 5 minutes. Place a muslin-lined mesh strainer over a 3-qt saucepan. Strain the broth into the saucepan. Let the solids sit for 15 to 30 minutes, until they are cool enough to handle, before firmly twisting and pressing the muslin to yield more broth. Discard the solids. You should have about 8 cups; if your yield is way less or more, add water to dilute or boil the broth to concentrate it. Season with the Marmite for beefiness, MSG for savory depth, and agave syrup for a slightly sweet edge.

Prep and assemble the bowls

While the broth cooks, or about 30 minutes before serving, boil the noodles in a big pot of water until chewy-tender. Drain, rinse them well, and divide among four bowls.

Set a 10-inch nonstick skillet over medium heat and add the neutral oil. When the oil ripples, add the mushrooms and season with 2 big pinches of salt and cook for about 2 minutes, until the mushrooms turn soft and glistening. Set aside.

Set the broth over high heat, bring to a simmer, and then lower the heat to steady cooking. Cut any reserved carrot and add with the mushrooms and tofu to the broth; after a few minutes, when they are hot and refreshed, use a slotted spoon or spider to divide them between the bowls. If things feel cold, microwave each bowl in 30-second blasts to warm. Garnish with the yellow onion, green onions, and cilantro. Finish with black pepper, if desired.

Taste the broth to make sure it's robust; add MSG or salt as needed. Turn the heat to high and bring the broth to a boil. Ladle about 2 cups into each bowl. Serve immediately with any optional add-ins at the table.

Notes

Equipment To make the broth in a 6- to 8-qt stockpot, gather and ready the same broth ingredients. The difference is that you'll increase the water to 9 cups total. Toast the cloves, cinnamon, and star anise over medium heat; add the ginger and onion and aromatize; and then add the water, kombu, wakame, turnip, celery, cabbage, bean sprouts, carrot, and 2 tsp salt. Partially cover and bring to a boil. Lower the heat to maintain a simmer and cook, uncovered, for about 1 hour to yield a lightly salted broth. Strain and, before using, finish with the final seasoning. This broth is lighter in flavor than the pressure-cooker version, so you may need to add more salt, MSG, or a glug of fish sauce. Prep and assemble the bowls as directed.

Ingredients Instead of searing the mushrooms, poach the raw pieces in the reheating broth. They'll add more varied flavors and textures to your bowls but lack richness. You may opt to cook some and leave others raw.

(CONTINUED)

Don't want to use Marmite or MSG? Season with 1 Tbsp fish sauce (store-bought or vegan version, page 29), Maggi Seasoning sauce, Bragg Liquid Aminos, or soy sauce, plus an additional 1½ tsp salt. The broth will be good, but not great.

Unless you're on a special date, there's no need to soak the onion for these bowls; its pungency evokes the pho flavor experience.

Interested in slightly snappy vegan beef balls? Check Chinese and Viet markets, especially the frozen plant-based foods section. Halve four to six thawed meatballs and warm them in the broth for bowl assembly.

For woodsy complexity in the broth and chewy topping in the bowl, cook the broth with dried tofu-skin sticks, which look like nunchaku and are sold at Viet and Chinese markets in plastic bags, usually near dried mushrooms. Break two sticks (1.5 oz total) crosswise into four pieces and add them to the pot with the seaweed to ensure they're fully submerged and will rehydrate well. After cooking, reserve the tofu pieces along with the carrot. Cut the tofu pieces crosswise so they're easier to eat; reheat them in the broth with the other toppings. Use six to eight pieces of pan-fried tofu when including the tofu sticks.

Timing When cooking in advance, postpone seasoning the broth until bowl assembly. Partially cover the strained broth and let cool to room temperature.

Lifespan Store the broth in an airtight container in the refrigerator for up to 5 days, or freeze for up to 3 months.

The mushroom topping may be refrigerated for up to 5 days.

NOODLE-SOUP NAVIGATION GUIDE

Viet noodle soups are served with lots of optional add-ins and condiments that can confound. To enjoy every bowl, develop a strategic eating ritual. Apply a two-handed approach—chopsticks (or a fork) in one hand and a Chinese (or regular) soupspoon in the other hand—to gently stir the soup to distribute and combine the components. Then taste and adjust to create your tasty soup experience. For example:

- Add vegetables (such as sprouts, lettuce, or cabbage) for contrasting texture and flavor.

- Drop in chile slices for fresh vegetal heat, stir in sate sauce for spicy richness, or sprinkle on black pepper for pungent zip.

- Pluck herb leaves from their stems (set stems aside), tear up large leaves, and add them into your bowl. Herbs lose their punch in hot broth, so for peak flavor, add more as you eat.

- Squirt in lime juice to uplift and brighten flavors. Set the spent wedge aside, not in the bowl (it's noodle soup, not a cocktail).

- Sprinkle in fish sauce, MSG, or salt for extra savory oomph.

- Resist squirting hoisin or chile sauces into the bowl because they'll ruin good broth balance. Instead, put some in small dish (for pho, do a yin-yang-like combo of hoisin and chile sauces) and dip toppings in it before enjoying each mouthful.

- Slurp with gusto until the bowl is empty.

CHICKEN-VEGETABLE PHO BROTH

2 whole cloves

2 tsp coriander seeds

1½-oz section fresh ginger, peeled, cut into thick coins, and smashed with the flat side of a knife

8 oz yellow onion, halved and thickly sliced

7½ cups hot or just-boiled water

8 oz napa or green cabbage, cut through the core into 2 or 3 wedges

5 oz carrot, cut crosswise into 4 sections (add the peel to broth, if you removed it)

3 oz celery stalk, cut into 3-inch lengths

1 cup coarsely chopped cilantro sprigs

Fine sea salt

1¾ lb bone-in chicken parts, such as 1 breast and 1 whole leg

2 Tbsp fish sauce (store-bought or vegan version, page 29), plus more as needed

1 tsp agave syrup or granulated sugar (optional; preferably organic)

———

10 oz dried narrow flat rice noodles (bánh phở or pad Thai noodles; see page 9)

2 oz yellow or red onion, thinly sliced, soaked in water for 10 minutes, and drained

2 green onions, green parts only, thinly sliced

Phở Gà Rau Củ

Chicken-Vegetable Pho

After spotting Instagram photos of cooks adding vegetables beyond bean sprouts to my pressure-cooker chicken pho recipe, I decided to create a recipe with the vegetables built into the broth. It turned out wonderful, lighter than the original but equally satisfying. The spices and vegetables complement and supplement the chicken-y flavor, which is sourced from chicken parts (more convenient than a whole chicken). I enjoy adding the soft, cooked vegetables from the broth to my bowls, but you may discard them and opt for leafy greens, as suggested in the Notes. Recipe testers Candy and Doug Grover cooked fresh carrot coins and celery sticks in the finished broth as it reheated. If you don't have a pressure cooker, see the Notes for a stovetop simmer method.

Prepare the broth

To make the Chicken-Vegetable Pho Broth: In a 6-qt electric multicooker, combine the cloves and coriander seeds. Program the cooker to sauté on moderate-high heat and toast the spices for several minutes, stirring until fragrant. Add the ginger and onion and stir for 45 to 60 seconds, until aromatic (some browning is okay).

Add the hot water, cabbage, carrot, celery, cilantro, and 2 tsp salt to the cooker. Arrange the chicken parts on top. Lock the multicooker's lid in place, then program to pressure-cook on low for 15 minutes. When it's done, unplug the cooker and let it vent naturally for 15 minutes. Manually release any residual pressure. (With a stovetop pressure cooker, toast the spices over medium-high heat, add 8 cups water, lock the lid, bring to low pressure, and cook for 15 minutes. Let the cooker depressurize naturally on a cool burner for 12 minutes.)

Carefully remove the lid, tilting it away from you to avoid the hot steam. Let the hot broth rest for 5 minutes. Using tongs, transfer the chicken to a bowl. Add water to cover the chicken, let soak for 5 minutes to cool and prevent drying, and then discard the water. Partially cover the chicken and set aside to cool.

If you like, retrieve the carrot and celery from the broth, and keep them on a plate or add to the chicken. If the cabbage isn't too soft to hold together, retrieve

(CONTINUED)

¼ cup chopped fresh cilantro, leafy tops only

Recently ground black pepper (optional)

Optional add-ins: 3 handfuls raw or blanched mung bean sprouts, 1 or 2 sliced hot chiles (serrano, jalapeño, Thai, or Fresno), 1 handful herbs (mint, Thai basil, culantro, or rice paddy), 2 limes cut as wedges, 1 batch Ginger Dipping Sauce (see variation, page 33)

it too. Place a muslin-lined mesh strainer over a 3-qt saucepan. Strain the broth into the saucepan. Let the solids sit for 15 to 30 minutes, until they are cool enough to handle, before firmly twisting and pressing the muslin to yield more broth. Discard the solids. You should have about 8 cups; if your yield is way less or more, add water to dilute or boil the broth to concentrate it. Leave the bit of fat for good flavor. Finish the broth by seasoning with the fish sauce and agave syrup, if needed, for a savory-sweet taste.

Prep and assemble the bowls

While the broth cooks, or about 30 minutes before serving, boil the noodles until chewy-tender. Drain, rinse them well, and divide among four bowls.

Set the broth over medium heat and bring to a simmer, then lower the heat to maintain the simmer. Cut or tear the cooled chicken into bite-size pieces about ¼ inch thick; include the skin, if you like. Cut any of the reserved veggies and reheat in the broth. Use a slotted spoon or spider to retrieve and divide among the bowls. Add chicken to each bowl too. If things feel cold, microwave each bowl in 30-second blasts. Garnish with the yellow onion, green onions, cilantro, and black pepper.

Taste the broth to ensure it's robust; add fish sauce or salt as needed. Raise the heat and bring it to a boil. Ladle about 2 cups of broth into each bowl. Serve with any optional add-ins at the table. The ginger sauce is for dipping the chicken, although some people add it to their bowls.

Notes

Equipment To make the broth in a 6- to 8-qt stockpot, toast the spices and then sear the ginger and onion over medium heat. When everything is very aromatic (a little browning is okay), add 10 cups hot water, then the cabbage, carrot, celery, cilantro, and 2 tsp salt. Arrange the chicken parts on top. Partially cover and bring to a simmer over high heat. Uncover and skim off and discard any scum. Lower the heat to maintain a gentle simmer and cook, uncovered, for 1 hour, until the broth is heady and savory-sweet. Proceed as directed.

Timing If you're cooking in advance, postpone seasoning the broth until bowl assembly. Partially cover the strained broth and let cool before storing.

Lifespan The broth, chicken, and vegetables can be kept in separate airtight containers and refrigerated for up to 3 days. The broth and uncut chicken freeze well for 3 months, but the veggies won't.

Variation For Extra-Green Chicken Pho, add 8 oz chopped kale, chard, spinach, or cabbage as the noodles finish boiling. Divide the greens among the bowls along with the noodles. (Or, cook the greens separately with a splash of broth, and use as a topping.)

Kick-starting the broth with hot water and placing the chicken atop the other ingredients ensures that its flesh won't overcook.

The broth emphasizes coriander to reflect northern Viet–style chicken pho, which is soothing and tonic-like.

BÚN BÒ HUẾ BROTH

9 oz yellow onion, halved and thickly sliced

5 oz lemongrass stalks, untrimmed, cut into 3-inch lengths and bruised with a meat mallet or a heavy saucepan (see page 44 for tips)

5 by 10-inch piece kombu, snipped with scissors into 6 to 8 pieces

3 Tbsp dried wakame

10 oz napa or green cabbage, quartered lengthwise and cut crosswise into large pieces

8 oz mung bean sprouts

8 oz turnip or daikon, unpeeled, scrubbed, and cut into large chunks

3 oz celery stalk, coarsely chopped

Fine sea salt

½ tsp paprika or ground annatto (achiote)

6½ cups water

1 tsp Marmite

¾ tsp MSG, or 1½ tsp Asian mushroom seasoning, plus more as needed

2 to 3 Tbsp Vegan Sate Sauce (page 40), plus more as needed

1 tsp agave syrup or granulated sugar (optional; preferably organic)

—

12 oz large or extra-large dried round rice noodles (see Note) or rice spaghetti

4 to 6 oz fresh mushrooms (such as oyster, shiitake, or king trumpet, or a mixture), sliced or torn into large bite-size pieces

Bún Bò Huế Chay

Vegan Spicy Huế Noodle Soup

Vietnamese food aficionados love to discuss which is better: Northern pho or central bún bò Huế (aka BBH). They're wonderfully different noodle soups and both deserve space in your Viet cooking. Pho is nuanced and delicate. BBH is fiery and gutsy. Both reflect the topography and cultures of their regions. The people of central Vietnam, especially in and around the historic capital of the Nguyễn dynasty, are resourceful and determined. Tourism guides may boast about the area's delicate imperial court food, but I favor its funky, rustic, soulful dishes; like this noodle soup, which is conventionally made with tough beef and pork cuts, and punctuated with fermented shrimp paste, lemongrass, and chiles.

To craft a respectable vegan broth, I apply my playbook of pressure-cooking vegetables and seaweed, adding additional wakame to mimic the umami brininess of fermented shrimp paste, which would be stirred into standard versions. You must finish the broth with the Vegan Sate Sauce or it won't conjure the BBH brow-wiping experience. If you haven't made the craveable condiment, this is your excuse to prepare a batch.

Prepare the broth

To make the Bún Bò Huế Broth: In a 6-qt electric multicooker, combine the onion, lemongrass, kombu, wakame, cabbage, bean sprouts, turnip, celery, 2 tsp salt, paprika, and water. Lock the lid in place, then program the cooker to pressure-cook on high for 15 minutes. When it's done, unplug the cooker and let vent naturally for 20 minutes. Manually release any residual pressure. (With a stovetop pressure cooker, add 7 cups water, lock the lid, bring to high pressure, and cook for 15 minutes. Let the cooker depressurize naturally on a cool burner for 15 minutes.)

Carefully remove the lid, tilting it away from you to avoid the hot steam. Let the hot broth rest for about 5 minutes. Place a muslin-lined mesh strainer over a 3-qt saucepan. Strain the broth into the saucepan. Let the solids sit for

(CONTINUED)

8 to 12 pieces Pan-Fried Tofu Slabs (page 52), sliced or cut into chopstick-able pieces

4 to 6 slices Peppery Vegan Bologna (page 53; optional), each halved

2 oz yellow or red onion, thinly sliced, soaked in water for 10 minutes, and drained

2 green onions, green parts only, thinly sliced

¼ cup coarsely chopped fresh cilantro, Vietnamese coriander, or a combo

Optional add-ins: 3 cups thinly sliced romaine lettuce or shaved cabbage (red or green), 3 handfuls raw mung bean sprouts, 1 or 2 sliced hot chiles (Thai, serrano, jalapeño, or Fresno), 1 handful fresh herbs (mint, Thai basil, or Vietnamese shiso), 2 limes cut as wedges, and Vegan Sate Sauce (page 40)

15 to 30 minutes, until they are cool enough to handle, before firmly twisting and pressing the muslin to yield more broth. Discard the solids. You should have about 8 cups; if your yield is way less or more, add water to dilute or boil the broth to concentrate it. Season the broth with the Marmite for beefiness, MSG for savory depth, and sate sauce for spicy brininess. For a sweet edge, add the agave syrup.

Prep and assemble the bowls

While the broth cooks, or about 30 minutes before serving, boil the noodles until chewy-tender. Drain, rinse them well, and divide among four bowls.

Set the broth over high heat and bring to a simmer, then lower the heat to maintain the simmer. Add the mushrooms and tofu, and when they are hot and supple, add the bologna (if using) and let it warm for 1 minute (it clouds the broth if left too long in the pot). Using a slotted spoon or spider, divide among the bowls. If things feel cold, microwave each bowl in 30-second blasts to warm. Garnish with the yellow onion, green onions, and cilantro.

Taste the broth and, as desired, add MSG, salt, or sate sauce for a salty, spicy finish. Raise the heat and bring the broth to a boil. Ladle about 2 cups into each bowl. Serve immediately with any optional add-ins at the table. The produce lends texture, lime and mint brighten, and the sate sauce further spices things up.

Notes

Equipment To make the broth in a 6- to 8-qt stockpot, gather and ready the same broth ingredients. The difference is that you'll increase the water to 10 cups total. Partially cover and bring to a boil. Lower the heat to a simmer and cook, uncovered, for about 1 hour to yield a lightly salted broth. Strain and, before using, finish with the final seasoning. This broth is lighter in flavor than the pressure-cooker version, so you may need to add more salt, MSG, or even a glug of fish sauce. Prep and assemble the bowls as directed.

Ingredients BBH requires super-thick rice noodles, which are often identified as "XL" bún bò Huế Giang Tây or Jiangxi rice sticks. Look for the dried noodles at Chinese or Southeast Asian markets. If they're unavailable, substitute rice-based spaghetti, sold in the gluten-free section of mainstream supermarkets.

Lifespan If you're cooking in advance, make the broth but keep it unseasoned and refrigerate in an airtight container for up to 5 days, or freeze for up to 3 months. Season before using.

Variation Like with the Deluxe Vegan Pho on page 158, you can change up the toppings with dried tofu-skin sticks and vegan meatballs (see Note, page 160). They'll add variety to your bún bò Huế chay. Back off the other add-ins to avoid overwhelming the bowl.

2 Tbsp fresh lime juice

1½ to 2 Tbsp granulated sugar, agave syrup, or mild honey

1½ to 2 Tbsp fish sauce (store-bought or vegan version, page 29)

1 small garlic clove, minced and mashed or put through a garlic press

1 Thai or small serrano chile, finely chopped

12 oz beets

1⅓ lb unripe green mango

¼ cup packed coarsely chopped fresh mint or basil (any kind)

⅓ cup finely chopped or pounded unsalted roasted peanuts or cashews

Gỏi Xoài Xanh

Green Mango, Beet, and Herb Salad

Vibrant colors, varied textures, and lively flavors mark many Vietnamese dishes, and this fuchsia-hued take on popular green mango salad delivers. I've paired the tropical fruit with jicama for gỏi xoài xanh, but why not swap in beet since it's also a root vegetable used in Viet cooking? Beets are usually cooked in Viet recipes, but in raw form, as used in this salad, they retain their earthy flavor and slight crunch—a lovely contrast to the mango. Tart and assertive, green mango's flesh sweetens and softens once the salad is tossed.

Make the dressing

In a large bowl, stir together the lime juice, 1½ Tbsp of the sugar, and 1½ Tbsp of the fish sauce. Taste and season with up to 1½ tsp each of the remaining sugar and fish sauce to create a strong, tart-sweet-salty finish (in that order of flavor hits). Stir in the garlic and chile. Set this dressing aside.

Prep the beets and mango

Peel the beets and cut into sticks about the size of a bean sprout. Add to the dressing and toss well. Let marinate and soften, about 5 minutes, depending on the size of the sticks you just cut.

Meanwhile, peel the mango, cut off its thick, fleshy "cheeks," and then cut those into sticks about three times thicker than the beet sticks. Cut around the pit to harvest any lingering flesh.

Assemble, toss, and serve

Add the mango, herbs, and nuts to the beets. Toss well, then transfer to a serving bowl or plate, leaving the excess dressing behind. Serve immediately.

Note

Timing Up to 2 days ahead, make the dressing and cut the beet and mango. Keep the three items separate and refrigerate. Return the beet to room temperature before marinating.

Select a rock-hard green mango (a bit of red on the skin is fine); refrigerate the unpeeled mango for up to 2 weeks.

4 oz oyster mushrooms

1½ tsp neutral oil (such as canola or peanut)

Fine sea salt

1 lb red grapefruit

5 oz Persian cucumbers

¼ tsp granulated sugar, plus 1½ Tbsp

2 Tbsp fresh lime juice

1½ tsp fresh Meyer lemon juice, or 1 tsp unfiltered apple cider vinegar

1½ tsp fresh tangerine juice or orange juice

1 small Fresno or jalapeño chile, halved lengthwise, seeded, and thinly sliced

2 Tbsp hand-torn mint leaves

Gỏi Bưởi

Grapefruit, Mushroom, and Cucumber Salad

Simple, gorgeous, and refreshingly delicious, this is a casual, meatless take on a Viet special-occasion salad featuring pomelo. Gỏi bưởi often includes shrimp and chicken, but you don't need animal protein to celebrate. This version highlights citrus season with grapefruit as the main star. Seared oyster mushrooms and cucumber contribute texture, flavor, and color contrast. The dressing is great when made with calamansi (trái tắc) juice; because this distinctively tart fruit is hard to come by, blending citrus juices is my workaround. The only challenge to this salad is peeling the grapefruit segments. Choose citrus with smooth, taut skin, and its juice sacs will be on the firm side and hold together for this salad. If available, use a pomelo or the Oroblanco variety of grapefruit. Otherwise, the common Ruby Red grapefruit variety is perfect.

Cook the mushrooms and prep the grapefruit

Tear medium or large oyster mushrooms into bite-size pieces no wider than 2 inches at their fan-like caps; keep in mind that they will shrink a fair amount during cooking. It's fine to keep clusters of smaller mushrooms intact.

Set a 10-inch nonstick or carbon-steel skillet over high heat and add the neutral oil. When the oil ripples, add the mushrooms, season with ⅛ tsp salt, and cook for 2 minutes, or until the mushrooms are soft and shrunken to about one-third of their original volume. Remove from the heat and let cool completely. Coarsely chop the mushrooms if the pieces are overly gangly and won't distribute well when later mixed with the other veggies.

Peel the grapefruit and separate into halves. Working over a large bowl to catch any juices, with one half, one segment at a time, using your fingers (and, if needed, a paring knife), peel back the membrane to release the segment; do your best to not break many juice sacs and release liquid. As you work, gently break each segment into bite-size pieces, dropping them into the bowl.

HỦ TIẾU BROTH

¾-oz section fresh ginger, peeled, cut into thick coins, and smashed with the flat side of a knife

9 oz yellow onion, halved and thickly sliced

5 by 10-inch piece kombu, snipped with scissors into 6 to 8 pieces

3 Tbsp dried wakame

12 oz napa or green cabbage, quartered lengthwise, then cut crosswise into large pieces

6 oz white mushrooms, stems included, coarsely chopped

6 oz Fuji apple, peeled, cored, and coarsely chopped

5 oz carrot, sliced

4 oz celery stalk, coarsely chopped

Fine sea salt

6½ cups water

¾ tsp MSG, or 1½ tsp Asian mushroom seasoning, plus more as needed

1 tsp agave syrup or granulated sugar (optional; preferably organic)

FRIED GARLIC

1½ Tbsp chopped garlic

1½ Tbsp neutral oil (such as canola or peanut)

HỦ TIẾU SAUCE

Garlic oil for frying (reserved from Fried Garlic)

½ cup hủ tiếu broth (from above), plus 2 Tbsp

3 Tbsp soy sauce

2 Tbsp granulated sugar (preferably organic)

Hủ Tiếu Khô Chay

Vegan Chiu Chow Rice Noodles

Northern pho is reserved and central bún bò Huế is bold, but hủ tiếu is varied, flamboyant, and shape shifting—the spiritual embodiment of freewheeling southern Vietnam. There are loose parameters for crafting the popular noodle dish, which belongs to the Chiu Chow (Teochew), a migratory people from coastal southeast China who are masters at making flat rice noodles that are the same as those used for pho but are called hủ tiếu. Confusingly, that same term applies to a rice noodle preparation defined by a sweet-savory broth that is often made with pork and dried seafood.

Wherever the Chiu Chow settled in Southeast Asia, they nimbly adapted their foodways. That's why in Vietnam, hủ tiếu expresses itself in a Chinese/Cambodian/Viet style, with many iterations created across the porous borders. The result is the ultimate have-it-your-way soup experience: Choose a noodle type (mix them if you like) and then select preferred toppings, add-ins, and condiments. You may enjoy a salad-ish "dry" hủ tiếu seasoned by a dark, savory-sweet sauce with the broth on the side for sipping; or slurp hủ tiếu as a spectacular brothy noodle soup. No matter how I have hủ tiếu, it's a synergistic marriage of components that never fails to blow me away.

Get ready to create your own vegan version! You can't go wrong because it is highly customizable. The main recipe is for the dry version and the variation that follows offers the soupier version. Lessen the pressure by making everything in advance. Review this recipe to create a prep plan that fits hủ tiếu into your life.

Prepare the broth

To make the Hủ Tiếu Broth: In a 6-qt electric multicooker, combine the ginger, onion, kombu, wakame, cabbage, mushrooms, apple, carrot, celery, 2 tsp salt, and water. Lock the lid in place and then program the cooker to pressure-cook on high for 15 minutes. When it's done, unplug the cooker and let vent naturally for 20 minutes. Manually release any residual pressure. (With a stovetop

(CONTINUED)

1 tsp fish sauce (store-bought or vegan version, page 29)

1 Tbsp cornstarch

———

1½ tsp neutral oil or Fast-Fried Shallots oil (see page 46)

5 oz fresh mushrooms (such as shiitake, oyster, or king trumpet), sliced or torn into large bite-size pieces

Fine sea salt

12 oz dried medium-size flat rice noodles (see page 9) or dried tapioca stick noodles (see Note)

8 to 12 pieces Pan-Fried Tofu Slabs (page 52), sliced or cut into chopstick-able pieces

¾ cup Umami Tofu Crumbles (page 50), at room temperature

3 Tbsp Fast-Fried Shallots (page 46) or store-bought fried shallots or onions

⅓ cup chopped fresh cilantro or thinly sliced green onions

Optional add-ins: 2 handfuls blanched mung bean sprouts, 2 cups raw tender greens (chrysanthemum, baby arugula, coarsely chopped Chinese celery or regular celery leaves, or a combo), ¼ cup garlic chives cut into 1½-inch-long pieces, 2 limes cut as wedges, 1 sliced hot chile (Thai, serrano, jalapeño, or Fresno), Vegan Sate Sauce (page 40), Viet Chile Sauce (page 39) or sriracha

pressure cooker, add 7 cups water, lock the lid, bring to high pressure, and cook for 15 minutes. Let the cooker depressurize naturally on a cool burner for 15 minutes.)

Carefully remove the lid, tilting it away from you to avoid the hot steam. Let the hot broth rest for about 5 minutes. Place a muslin-lined mesh strainer over a 3-qt saucepan. Strain the broth into the saucepan. Let the solids sit for 15 to 30 minutes, until they are cool enough to handle, before firmly twisting and pressing the muslin to yield more broth. Discard the solids. You should have about 8 cups; if your yield is way less or more, add water to dilute or boil the broth to concentrate it. Season with the MSG for umami depth, agave syrup for a sweeter edge, or salt, ¼ tsp at a time, for savory depth.

Prepare the fried garlic and sauce

To make the Fried Garlic: In a 1- to 1½-qt saucepan over medium-low heat, combine the garlic and neutral oil. After they start sizzling, let the garlic cook gently for 2 to 3 minutes, stirring frequently, until it turns mostly golden. Pull the pan off the heat, let the garlic cook for 1 minute longer, until it turns crisp, and then, using a slotted spoon, transfer to a ramekin or small bowl, leaving the oil behind. Set aside to cool and reserve to use as a topping.

To make the Hủ Tiếu Sauce: In the same pan with the garlic oil, combine the ½ cup hủ tiếu broth, soy sauce, sugar, and fish sauce. Set over medium-high heat and bring to a boil. In a separate small bowl, combine the cornstarch and remaining 2 Tbsp hủ tiếu broth to make a slurry; then stir the slurry into the pan. Once the sauce has thickened, let cool completely before using or storing.

Ready other toppings and garnishes

Set a 10-inch nonstick skillet over high heat and add the 1½ tsp neutral oil. When the oil ripples, add the mushrooms, season with 2 pinches of salt, and cook for about 2 minutes, stirring, until the mushrooms are soft and glistening. Set aside.

Prep and assemble the bowls

While the broth cooks or about 30 minutes before serving, boil the noodles until chewy-tender, usually 3 to 4 minutes for rice noodles and 5 to 7 minutes for tapioca stick noodles. Drain, rinse well, and let cool. (To prevent tapioca noodles from sticking, leave them in cool water, then drain before using.)

Reheat 4 cups of the broth and have four rice bowls ready for serving.

Meanwhile, divide the sauce among four soup bowls, then top with the noodles. If you like, toss the noodles with the sauce, or leave them pristine-looking. Arrange the mushrooms, pan-fried tofu, and tofu crumbles atop the noodles. Crown with the shallots, fried garlic, and cilantro.

Taste the broth and, as needed, add MSG or salt for savory depth. Ladle the hot broth into the rice bowls and serve immediately along with the noodle bowls and any optional add-ins at the table. Invite diners to mix up all the ingredients, adding vegetables, lime, sliced chile, and sate and chile sauces to personalize their experience; if things seem too thick or heavy, mix in spoonfuls of broth. They should sip on the broth to refresh the palate too.

Notes

Equipment To make the broth in a 6- to 8-qt stockpot, gather and ready the broth ingredients. The difference is that you'll increase the water to 10 cups total. Partially cover and bring to a boil. Lower the heat to a simmer and cook, uncovered, for about 1 hour to yield a lightly salted broth. Strain and, before using, finish with the final seasoning. This broth is lighter in flavor than the pressure-cooker version, so you may need to add more salt or MSG. Prep and assemble the bowls as directed.

Ingredients In Vietnamese, tapioca stick noodles are called hủ tiếu bột lọc (tapioca noodles) and hủ tiếu dai (chewy noodles); ones labeled hủ tiếu Sa Đéc or hủ tiếu Mỹ Tho signal that they contain a special chewy rice from Mekong Delta locations renowned for the noodles. Typically sold at hard-core Viet markets, the noodles cook up relatively clear and chewy. In a pinch, boil Korean sweet potato starch noodles (dangmyeon) for 6 to 8 minutes, until chewy-tender. Drain and snip them into 8-inch lengths.

You may also use shirataki noodles sold at health-food stores; they're pricey, so consider mixing them with the flat rice noodles. Wheat-based Chinese-style noodles or ramen are an option too.

Lifespan If you're cooking in advance, make the broth, skip seasoning it, refrigerate for up to 5 days (or freeze up to 3 months), and season just before using.

Up to 3 days ahead, make the fried garlic and sauce and refrigerate them separately; return them to room temperature to use.

The mushroom topping may be refrigerated for up to 5 days.

Leftovers Extra broth from the dry version may be used for a half-batch of hủ tiếu noodle soup (see Variation) or as a stock in other recipes in this book.

Variations For Vegan Chiu Chow Noodle Soup, called hủ tiếu chay, in Vietnamese, prepare the main recipe but skip making the sauce. If you like a fried garlic hit, fry 1½ Tbsp chopped garlic in 1½ Tbsp neutral oil as directed. Use the leftover oil for one of the tofu toppings.

Like with Deluxe Vegan Pho (page 158), you may cook the mushrooms in a skillet or let them poach in the broth. Either way, prepare four noodle-soup bowls and adorn the noodles with pan-fried tofu, tofu crumbles, mushrooms, fried shallots, fried garlic (if desired), and any green garnish. Heat the 8 cups broth to a boil, then ladle into the bowls. Serve with any optional add-ins.

Refreshing Salads

MULTIHUED SUMPTUOUS SALADS MARK many Viet celebrations. People love them so much that there are Viet-language cookbooks devoted to gỏi, the southern term for such salads; northerners refer to their creations as nộm. Regardless of regional differences, the salads typically signal project cooking because it's assumed that you'll be prepping and assembling lots of ingredients for wow factor. They're usually presented as a "ta-da!" first course. And although vegetables, herbs, seeds, and nuts are involved, it's traditionally the proteins (usually poached seafood and matchstick-cut pork or chicken) that lend an air of luxury to the salads. Understandably, in a country where animal protein is highly valued, cooks splurge for pricey, rich ingredients when making something special.

When I began making Vietnamese salads without or with less animal protein, the salads naturally lightened up, yet they remained hấp dẫn (exciting)—a must-have characteristic. For example, there are plenty of intriguing color, texture, and flavor contrasts in this chapter's grapefruit, oyster mushroom, and cucumber salad. The cabbage slaw and young jackfruit salad also benefit from cooked mushrooms along with lots of herbs and a lively fish sauce–based dressing. Spicy-sweet cashews add bling to the cucumber and kale gỏi, while soy sauce–seared tofu lends umami richness to the kohlrabi salad, which includes wood ear mushrooms as a veggie stand-in for slivers of pork ears.

Tang, crunch, and color govern the green mango and beet salad as well as the broccoli slaw, which is made in a flash with the addition of đồ chua daikon and carrot pickle, a Viet kitchen stalwart. The more traditional bean sprout salad is also super-easy to make and is fantastic served alongside other dishes (or even tucked into a sandwich!).

Vietnam's interactions with the West means that Western-style salads are also part of the repertoire. Instead of presenting an old-school vinaigrette composition, I created a grilled romaine salad adorned by a creamy fermented-tofu dressing and fried shallot.

However, liberating yourself from the constraints of traditional cooking doesn't mean abandoning khéo (thoughtful) cooking concepts. One of the recurring techniques in many Viet salads is extracting moisture from wet vegetables to render them crisp and thirsty for absorbing dressing. In recipes such as the green papaya nộm (a restaurant and street-food favorite), you'll toss the prepped veggies with sugar and salt to soften and release their natural liquid before squeezing them to a dryish state. After being squeezed, the vegetables can be refrigerated for days—perfect for easy weekday meals or entertaining.

You don't have to follow traditions to stay true to Viet foodways. These modern recipes elevate vegetables but also employ time-honored ideas. They are easygoing and pair well with other dishes (casually serve them as part of the main meal instead of a separate course). In other words, they fit today's lifestyles. I hope these salads unleash your creativity and you enjoy them often, any time you desire.

⅔ cup granulated sugar

1½ tsp fine sea salt

1 cup distilled white vinegar

1 cup water

1 lb mung bean sprouts

4 oz carrot (see Note), peeled and cut into matchsticks

¾-inch-thick bunch garlic chives, or 5 slender green onions, green parts only, cut into 1½-inch lengths

Dưa Giá
Pickled Bean Sprout Salad

Delicately crunchy and pleasantly bright, this easygoing southern Vietnamese favorite is technically a pickle because the vegetables steep in brine, but it's eaten in large amounts like a salad, usually in bright contrast with kho, intensely flavored dishes cooked with savory caramel sauce. The vegetables are terrific with dumplings or sandwiches. Mung bean sprouts and carrot are typically combined with hẹ (garlic chives, see page 15), but tender green onions work well too.

Make the brine
In a 4-qt saucepan, combine the sugar, salt, vinegar, and water. Set over medium heat and stir occasionally until the sugar and salt dissolve. Remove from the heat and let this brine cool completely.

Steep and toss the vegetables
Wash the bean sprouts and let drain well. At least 40 minutes or up to 2 hours before serving, add the bean sprouts, carrot, and garlic chives to the brine and gently toss. (I use my hands to easily manage the large amount of veggies without crushing them.) Set aside at room temperature for 30 minutes, turning the vegetables two or three times to expose them evenly to the brine. At first, they won't be covered by the brine, but they will shrink in volume and become more covered. They're ready when they taste pleasantly tangy and are a mix of crunchy and soft. If needed, let them sit for 10 minutes longer.

Drain and serve
Using a strainer or colander, strain the vegetables, saving the brine to reuse, if you like (see Note). Pile the vegetables high on a plate. Serve at room temperature within 2 hours to enjoy them at their peak.

Notes

Ingredients Use different-colored carrots for extra interest. The pickle shown in the photo on page 219 included purple carrots.

Lifespan Reuse the brine right away or refrigerate for up to 3 days for another batch.

If halving this recipe, use a wide 2-qt pot or a bowl of similar size.

1 (12-oz) package broccoli slaw (see Note)

1⅓ cups drained Đồ Chua Pickle (page 56), plus ⅓ cup pickle brine

3 to 4 Tbsp fresh lime juice

Fine sea salt, or 1 Tbsp fish sauce (store-bought or vegan version, page 29)

2 tsp chile-garlic sauce (see page 37), plus more as needed

⅓ cup unsalted roasted peanuts or cashews (optional)

½ cup lightly packed, coarsely chopped fresh basil (any kind)

Gỏi Bông Cải Xanh

Confetti Broccoli and Herb Slaw

Vietnamese broccoli salads often feature boiled mini-treelike crowns but I prefer the faster approach of using packaged broccoli slaw, which is simply the peeled pale-green stems that have been cut into matchsticks and mixed with similarly cut carrot pieces. Toss the slaw with lots of daikon and carrot pickle (including its tangy brine) along with a few other staples and let the mixture sit for up to 2 hours before finishing with herbs for fresh pungency and nuts for richness. That's it!

The light and crunchy salad is a perfect counterpoint to other bold dishes. Recipe tester Cate McGuire put this on burgers and fish sandwiches too. For a richer finish, she suggests mixing in some umami mayo (see pages 48 and 49).

Season and soften the slaw

In a large mixing bowl, combine the broccoli slaw, pickle, brine, 1½ Tbsp of the lime juice, ¾ tsp salt, and chile-garlic sauce. Toss well and let sit, uncovered, for 5 to 10 minutes to slightly soften the slaw (you should easily bend a long piece of the broccoli). Feel free to toss the vegetables two or three times as they sit.

Pound the nuts, assemble, and serve

If including the peanuts, use a mortar and pestle to pound them to a coarse texture. (Alternatively, chop with a knife.)

Add the nuts and basil to the slaw, toss well, and then taste. Add the remaining 1½ to 2½ Tbsp lime juice for brightness, pinches of salt for savoriness, or an additional plop of chile-garlic sauce for pungent heat. Transfer to a shallow platter or bowl, leaving the excess liquid behind. Serve immediately.

Note

Ingredients Avoid broccoli slaw packages in which the broccoli is cut on the thick side, like a sturdy skewer, because it won't soften nicely. Look for slaw that has been rendered as slender matchsticks resembling skinny, elegant bean sprouts. If broccoli slaw is unavailable, try a multicolor coleslaw mix.

1 Thai or small serrano chile, chopped

½ garlic clove

Fine sea salt

½ tsp granulated sugar

3½ Tbsp unseasoned rice vinegar, plus more as needed

1 to 1½ Tbsp fish sauce (store-bought or vegan version, page 29), plus more as needed

¼ cup thinly sliced red onion or shallot

3 Tbsp unsalted roasted peanuts or cashews

1 Tbsp neutral oil (such as canola or peanut)

6 oz king trumpet mushrooms, halved lengthwise and cut diagonally into 2-inch-long pieces, each about ¼ inch thick

2 cups packed thinly sliced green cabbage

1 small carrot, cut into thin matchsticks or shredded (on the largest holes of a box grater)

¼ cup chopped mint, cilantro, or Vietnamese coriander leaves, or a combo

3 Tbsp Fast-Fried Shallots (page 46) or store-bought fried shallots or onions

When making Viet salads, prep the veggies to be more or less of similar size. Each eventual mouthful ideally contains pops of all the textures, flavor, and color.

Gỏi Bắp Cải Gà Chay

Spicy Mushroom and Cabbage Slaw

Offering bright zippy flavors and textural pops, gỏi bắp cải gà chay represents a fabulous meatless version of Vietnamese chicken salad, which typically includes poached chicken breast. For an apt substitute, I cook king trumpet mushrooms (called nấm dùi gà, which translates to "chicken leg mushroom") in a hot skillet where they turn slithery rich and mimic poultry well.

Make the dressing and pound the peanuts

Using a mortar and pestle, swirl and mash the chile, garlic, 1 pinch of salt, and sugar into a fragrant, slightly sticky paste; or use a knife to mash and crush the ingredients. Transfer to a small bowl and stir in the vinegar and season with up to 1½ Tbsp of the fish sauce to create a pungent, tangy, salty dressing. Rinse the onion in a strainer under cold running water for about 10 seconds. Shake the strainer to drain well, then add the onion to the dressing.

Without washing the mortar and pestle, use them to pound the peanuts to a coarse, crushed state; or chop the peanuts with a knife.

Cook the mushrooms and assemble the veggies

Set a 10-inch nonstick skillet over medium heat and add the neutral oil. When the oil ripples, add the mushrooms, season with 2 pinches of salt, and cook, stirring, for about 3 minutes, until soft. Transfer to a large bowl and let cool completely, about 10 minutes. Add the cabbage, carrot, mint, and peanuts.

Toss and serve

Pour the dressing over the salad and toss. The cabbage should soften slightly. Taste and, if needed, add a splash of vinegar or gentle glug of fish sauce. Heap onto a serving dish, garnish with the fried shallots, and serve.

Note

Timing Prep the dressing and veggies hours ahead. Cover and refrigerate separately; return to room temperature to toss and serve.

Cut the cucumber and combine the vegetables

Halve the cucumbers lengthwise and cut each half into triangular pieces about 1 inch wide, so the pieces sort of match the shape of the grapefruit pieces. Put into a bowl and toss with the ¼ tsp sugar and ⅛ tsp salt. Set aside for 10 minutes, until a small pool of water appears in the bottom of the bowl. Rinse the cucumber briefly and, standing over the sink, use your hands to gently squeeze it by the handful to expel additional moisture. Add the cucumber and the mushrooms to the grapefruit.

Make the dressing, toss, and serve

In a small bowl, stir together the remaining 1½ Tbsp sugar, ½ tsp salt, lime juice, lemon juice, and tangerine juice. Add the chile and let sit for 5 to 10 minutes to let the flavors of this dressing bloom.

If the bowl of grapefruit and veggies contains a lot of liquid at the bottom, pour it off. Add the mint, then pour in the dressing. Toss very gently with two spoons. Transfer to a shallow bowl and serve immediately.

Note

Timing The combined grapefruit and vegetables can be refrigerated for up to 4 hours before tossing.

1½ Tbsp granulated sugar, plus ¾ tsp

3 Tbsp fresh lime juice, plus more as needed

2 Tbsp fish sauce (store-bought or vegan version, page 29)

1 Tbsp neutral oil (such as canola or peanut), plus 1 tsp

1 tsp chile-garlic sauce (see page 37), or 1 Thai chile, thinly sliced

⅔ cup raw cashew halves and pieces (see Note)

1½ Tbsp pure maple syrup (see Note)

⅛ tsp cayenne pepper or recently ground black pepper

Fine sea salt

1 large English cucumber, or 1 lb Japanese or Chinese cucumbers

1 small carrot

3 to 4 cups hand-torn curly kale leaves (see Note; aim for bite-size pieces when tearing from the stems)

1 cup hand-torn mix of tender herbs (such as mint, shiso, and any kind of basil)

Gỏi Dưa Leo Chay

Cucumber, Kale, and Spiced Cashew Salad

Crisp gỏi dưa leo is a classic Viet salad often served as an appetizer with fried shrimp chips for scooping. To lighten the knife workload on weeknights and turn it into a side salad to accompany other dishes, I add kale for texture and a bunch of fresh herbs for punchy notes. Make sure the kale plays well with the other veggies and tastes good when raw by selecting curly kale with frilly, tender leaves resembling a swirly skirt, not a stiff scratchy tutu. A generous amount of spicy-sweet candied nuts stands in for the meat that's typically found in this salad. In Vietnamese, cucumbers go by two charming names, dưa leo ("climbing squash" in southern Vietnam) and dưa chuột ("mouse squash" in northern Vietnam), so this salad may also be called gỏi dưa chuột. Around my house, we regularly have this salad and call it the 3C gỏi (cucumber + carrots + cashews).

Make the dressing

In a small bowl, whisk together the 1½ Tbsp sugar, lime juice, fish sauce, 1 Tbsp neutral oil, and chile-garlic sauce to combine well. Knowing that the candied cashews will bring extra sweetness later, taste and add lime juice ½ tsp at a time for a tangy finish. Set this dressing aside.

Candy the cashews

Place a piece of parchment paper near the stove. In a 10-inch nonstick skillet, combine the cashews, maple syrup, remaining 1 tsp neutral oil, cayenne, and 1 big pinch of salt, stirring to coat well. Set over medium heat. After gentle bubbling begins, lower the heat slightly and cook for about 5 minutes, stirring frequently, to toast and coat the cashews in crystalline bits of maple sugar and spice. Turn the heat to medium-low to slow the cooking. When you see a whisper of smoke, pull the pan off the burner. Stir the cashews for 20 seconds to coax deeper flavor and then dump them onto the parchment paper, spreading them out in one layer to cool. Before using, coarsely chop if there are many large pieces.

(CONTINUED)

Made with or without cayenne, the candied nuts are a great stand-alone snack.

Prep the vegetables

Trim the ends from the cucumber and halve it crosswise and then lengthwise. Use a teaspoon to scrape out the seeds. With the cut side down, thinly slice each piece on a steep diagonal. Transfer to a large bowl. Peel the carrot, cut into thin matchsticks, and add to the cucumber. Toss the veggies with ¾ tsp salt and the remaining ¾ tsp sugar. Massage gently for about 2 minutes to quickly release water; if you're not in a hurry, let them sit for about 20 minutes to weep moisture.

Once a healthy pool of liquid gathers in the bowl, drain the veggies in a mesh strainer. Give the mixture a quick rinse under water, then press the veggies against the mesh with your hand to expel lingering water. Dry the bowl and return the veggies to it.

Assemble and serve

Add the kale, candied cashews, and herbs to the cucumber and carrot and then toss to combine. Pour the dressing over the salad and toss again. Transfer to a serving bowl, leaving any unabsorbed dressing behind, and serve.

Notes

Ingredients Coarsely chopped whole cashews can be used instead of halves and pieces. Instead of cashews, you may candy walnuts or pecans.

No maple syrup on hand? You could replace it with 1 Tbsp mild honey, but the cashews will stick together as little clumps instead of finishing as individual nuggets of sweet nuttiness.

Instead of kale, try escarole, which is also grown and eaten in Vietnam.

Timing Up to 3 days in advance, prep the dressing and vegetables. Put the cucumber, carrot, and kale in a bowl and keep them covered in the fridge. Before tossing, pour out any accumulated water, then add the remaining ingredients to finish. Scale this down to a jar or plastic container to make a portable salad for on-the-go eating.

Variation For a Viet-style Seaweed Salad, combine ¼ cup soaked and drained wakame with the prepped cucumber, carrot, and kale. The herbs are optional. The nuts are not necessary, so make the vinaigrette with about 2 Tbsp sugar; toss as directed to serve. This is a great way to use the seaweed left over from making Vegan Fish Sauce.

1 batch Lemongrass Fermented-Tofu Sauce (see page 88)

2 romaine hearts, halved lengthwise through the root end

1½ Tbsp neutral oil (such as canola or peanut) or Fast-Fried Shallot oil (see page 46)

Fine sea salt

Recently ground black pepper

3 Tbsp Fast-Fried Shallots (page 46) or store-bought fried shallots or onions

Xà Lách Romaine Nướng Trộn Chao

Grilled Romaine with Spicy Fermented-Tofu Sauce

At the Vietnamese table, lettuce often takes a backseat as a filler in rice-paper rolls or a casing for wraps. But cooks also use lettuce, called rau xà lách (salad vegetable), in Western-style tossed salads. While I was growing up, a green salad dressed in an oil-and-vinegar vinaigrette regularly appeared at dinnertime. Cooking and eating between cultures led me to dream up this modern Vietnamese salad, which borrows from both East and West: Hearty, crisp romaine hearts get a quick searing on a hot grill (a stovetop grill pan makes the job fast and easy) and then they're adorned with a creamy fermented-tofu sauce spiked by lemongrass, chile, and lime. On page 88, that sauce is served with crudités, but like many crudité dips, the sauce can be a salad dressing too. Caramelized fried shallots accent the lettuce and sauce with fatty, savory goodness; for extra flavor, use the leftover shallot oil for grilling the lettuce.

Season the lettuce

Let the sauce come to room temperature, about 10 minutes. Meanwhile, blot away any lingering water from the romaine. Brush or drizzle the neutral oil onto the cut sides of the romaine hearts, followed by a light seasoning of salt and pepper.

Grill, assemble, and serve

Set a cast-iron stovetop grill pan (or a griddle or a heavy skillet) over high heat. When the pan is hot (water flicked onto its surface should evaporate within seconds), add the lettuce cut-side down and grill for 20 to 30 seconds to sear with grill marks and add a touch of flavor. Do this in batches as needed, and gently press the stem ends down on the pan to ensure maximum contact (it's okay if some soft leafy parts get seared too). As you work, transfer the seared lettuce to four individual plates or a serving platter.

Pour about 2 Tbsp sauce over each romaine heart, then sprinkle with the fried shallots. Serve immediately, inviting diners to cut the halves crosswise in several places and toss with the sauce and shallots.

Instead of romaine hearts, use four Little Gem lettuce heads, dressing each grilled half with roughly 1 Tbsp sauce.

2 lb green papaya (see Note)

Fine sea salt

1 tsp granulated sugar (see Note), plus 2 Tbsp, plus more as needed

3 to 4 oz jerky (beef or vegan)

3 Tbsp unfiltered apple cider vinegar or fresh lime juice, plus more as needed

2½ Tbsp fish sauce (store-bought or vegan version, page 29), plus more as needed

2 to 4 tsp chile-garlic sauce (see page 37), plus more as needed

⅓ cup unsalted roasted peanuts or cashews, pounded or chopped to a coarse texture

⅔ cup hand-torn Vietnamese balm, Thai basil, cilantro, mint, or Vietnamese coriander leaves

Nộm Đu Đủ

Green Papaya Salad with Jerky

Papaya grows easily in tropical Southeast Asia, so much so that it's eaten when the flesh matures to a tender sweetness as well as when it's still young, firm, and mild-tasting. Unripe, rock-hard green papaya is often rendered into thin strips for crunchy, chewy salads, like this spunky northern Viet version that includes beef jerky, punchy herbs, and a tart-salty-sweet-spicy dressing. Choose bold-tasting jerky, such as grass-fed beef jerky or a spicy vegan jerky; alternatively, opt for unsweetened dried mango (the jerky version of dried fruit) as offered in the Notes.

Supermarket papaya with green-yellow skin is ripe and too soft for this salad. Shop at a Chinese or Southeast Asian market for green papaya (pictured, cut open, on page 170). If available, grab a bunch of herbs to jazz things up. Vietnamese balm (kinh giới) is favored in Hanoi, but you have herbal options here. Green papaya keeps in the fridge for 1 week, so there's no need to rush home to make this recipe—unless you're in a hurry to eat a fantastic salad.

Peel and shred the papaya

Using a vegetable peeler, remove the papaya's tough skin. Trim the stem end, then halve the papaya lengthwise. Using a spoon, scoop out the sparkly, space alien–looking seeds. Applying firm pressure on the spoon, scrape out the white nubby layer to reveal the translucent flesh. Do your best in the crevices. Quarter each half.

Ready a food processor with the largest shredder blade attached, add the papaya pieces, and shred, aiming for long thick strands. I usually shred each piece separately, placing it curved- or concave-side down, then hand-cutting the remaining thin pieces to minimize waste and add rustic flair.

Massage the papaya and snip the jerky

In a large bowl, combine the papaya, 1½ tsp salt, and 1 tsp sugar and then use both hands to vigorously massage the strands. Within minutes, the papaya will be wet, a little slimy, and limp. Add water to cover, swish a few times, and then drain in a colander. Rinse briefly with water. Wipe the bowl dry with a dish towel, then use the dish towel to wring out moisture from the papaya. Work in three or four batches, dumping the resulting balls of papaya back into the bowl.

Using scissors, snip the jerky into thin pieces, about ¼ inch wide, so it mingles well with the papaya. Set aside.

Mix the dressing, toss, and serve

In a small bowl or liquid measuring cup, stir together the vinegar, fish sauce, and 2 Tbsp sugar to combine well. Add the chile-garlic sauce. This dressing should taste tart, salty, and sweet with an edge of fire. As needed, tweak the flavor with more vinegar, fish sauce, sugar, or chile-garlic sauce, adding each ½ tsp at a time.

Add the jerky, peanuts, and herbs to the papaya, fluffing to distribute the ingredients well. Pour in the dressing and toss well so it all gets absorbed. Pile the salad onto a plate and serve.

Notes

Ingredients If only shredded green papaya is available, use about 1⅓ lb. This recipe easily scales up or down for different-size papaya; prep a double batch for two salads during the week.

For the dressing, 2 Tbsp of agave syrup or mild honey may be used in lieu of the sugar.

Timing Prep the papaya and cut the jerky (or dried mango) up to 3 days in advance. Store in separate airtight containers, refrigerating the papaya. If opting for mango, season it before using (see Variation).

Variation For Green Papaya Salad with Mango "Jerky," replace the beef jerky with an equal amount of unsweetened dried mango slices. Using scissors, cut the mango into thin pieces, about ¼ inch wide. To add savory, earthy notes, toss the fruit with 2 big pinches of sea salt and ⅛ tsp Chinese five-spice powder. Taste, and work in more salt and spice as needed for a flavorful impact. The rest of the recipe remains the same.

½ cup dried wood ear mushrooms or black fungus mushrooms

1½ lb kohlrabi (see Note), peeled and quartered

6 oz carrot, scrubbed or peeled, cut crosswise into 3-inch-long sections

1 tsp fine sea salt

¾ tsp granulated sugar

8 oz extra-firm or super-firm tofu

1 Tbsp soy sauce

1 Tbsp water

1 Tbsp neutral oil (such as canola or peanut)

¼ cup fresh lime juice

2 Tbsp fish sauce (store-bought or vegan version, page 29), plus more as needed

2 Tbsp agave syrup, mild honey, or granulated sugar, plus more as needed

1 small garlic clove, minced

1 or 2 Thai or small serrano chiles, chopped (use the maximum amount for edgy heat)

3 Tbsp toasted white sesame seeds (hulled or unhulled)

⅓ cup hand-torn Vietnamese coriander or cilantro leaves

⅓ cup mint leaves, torn if large

> For convenience but a less bright flavor, swap out the fresh garlic and chile for 1 to 1½ tsp chile-garlic sauce (see page 37).

Gỏi Su Hào

Kohlrabi and Soy Sauce–Seared Tofu Salad

Looking like the *Sputnik* of vegetables, kohlrabi is enjoyed in Vietnam for its delicately sweet cabbage-ish flavor and crisp texture (imagine super-likable broccoli stems). It may be dried, pickled, simmered in soup, stir-fried, and transformed into salads like this one. The name su hào is derived from French chou-rave (cabbage root), although the vegetable grows as an above-ground bulb, not an underground root. There are many Western ways to use kohlrabi but lively textural salads such as this allow me to tap my Viet heritage. Many cooks favor pork ear for crunch; my vegetable equivalent is wood ear mushroom. The Notes offer many bonuses, including kohlrabi selection tips and protein swaps for the tofu.

Cut and massage the vegetables

Put the dried mushrooms in a small bowl and add hot water to cover by ½ inch. Let soak until softened, about 15 minutes.

Meanwhile, ready a food processor with the largest shredder blade attached, add the kohlrabi and carrot, and shred into the longest strands possible; hand-cut leftover pieces. (I process each kohlrabi piece separately, removing the leftover "cheek" between batches, but I lay the carrot sections as a single layer to process them together.) Transfer the veggies to a large bowl, add the salt and sugar, and then, using both hands, massage the strands for about 45 seconds, until they turn wet and limp and a pool of liquid appears in the bowl. Add water, swish, and then drain in a colander. Wipe the bowl dry. Standing over the sink and using a dish towel, wring out the moisture from the vegetables by the handful, depositing the crisp strands in the bowl. Avoid crushing the strands with too much pressure.

Drain the soaked mushrooms and squeeze them with your hands to expel excess water. Cut the mushrooms into strips about ⅓ inch wide and add to the bowl of vegetables. Set aside.

(CONTINUED)

Sear the tofu

Slice the tofu into eight or nine thin squarish slabs (extra-firm pieces can approach ½ inch thick; super-firm pieces can be about ⅓ inch thick). In a 12-inch nonstick skillet, combine the soy sauce and 1 Tbsp water. Add the tofu and turn twice to coat well. Set the skillet over medium heat, and after gentle bubbling begins, use a thin spatula to turn the tofu.

When liquid is no longer visible in the skillet, drizzle in the neutral oil and shake the skillet to coat the underside of the tofu. Turn the heat to medium-high and cook for 6 to 8 minutes to sear and brown the tofu slabs, turning now and then, until they are a lovely rich brown. Transfer the tofu to a cooling rack (or lean them against the rim of a plate or baking sheet), so air can circulate while they cool and dry, about 10 minutes. Cut the tofu into narrow strips.

Make the dressing and finish the salad

In a small bowl, stir together the lime juice, fish sauce, and agave syrup. Taste, and if needed, add up to 1½ tsp fish sauce or agave syrup for a pleasing tart-sweet-salty finish. Stir in the garlic and chile.

Using a mortar and pestle, pound the sesame seeds to a coarse, aromatic mixture. (Alternatively, pulse in a small food processor.) Scrape into the vegetable bowl, then add the tofu and herbs. Pour in the dressing, toss until it has been absorbed, and then pile the salad onto a plate and serve.

Notes

Ingredients For this salad, select two large kohlrabi bulbs that are heavy for their size; if their tops are attached, trim them for soup or other dishes. Trimmed bulbs keep for weeks in the fridge. To remove kohlrabi's thick skin, use a knife to trim the top and bottom ends, stand the bulb on your work surface, and cut off the skin, working toward the midline; flip it over and repeat. Or, cut in half and use a vegetable peeler, going over the surface well to reveal the luminescent flesh.

Timing Prep the vegetables and tofu up to 2 days in advance and refrigerate them separately; bring them to room temp before tossing.

Lifespan Don't want to store uncooked tofu? Make an extra batch of seared tofu (cook each separately) to keep for sandwiches, fried rice, noodles, or another round of salad. Store in the fridge for up to 5 days.

Variation Instead of the seared tofu, add 6 oz cooked small (bay) shrimp or hand-shredded poached or roasted chicken. Surimi sticks work too: Cut 6 oz crosswise into 3-inch pieces, quarter each, and then pull apart into lithe pieces. Because these proteins may already be well seasoned, you might not need all the dressing; when tossing the salad, add the dressing gradually to taste.

1 (20-oz) can young jackfruit (see Note), drained

4 oz carrot

2 Tbsp neutral oil (such as canola or peanut)

1 Tbsp finely chopped garlic

6 oz oyster mushrooms, torn into bite-size pieces

Fine sea salt

2 Tbsp fresh lime juice, plus more as needed

1½ Tbsp agave syrup, mild honey, or granulated sugar, plus more as needed

1½ Tbsp fish sauce (store-bought or vegan version, page 29), plus more as needed

½ Fresno or jalapeño chile, finely chopped

⅓ cup unsalted roasted peanuts or cashews, pounded or chopped to a coarse texture

½ cup hand-torn Vietnamese coriander or basil (any kind)

Sesame rice cracker rounds (see Note), lightly salted tortilla chips, or tostadas for scooping

Gỏi Mít Non

Young Jackfruit Salad Scoops

In Vietnamese, jackfruit is called mít (pronounced "meet") but it's not solely treated as a meat substitute, as is trendy in the West. The useful jackfruit tree proliferates in tropical Southeast and South Asia, where its huge bumpy-green fruits are commonplace, consumed when mature, sweet, and fragrant, as well as when immature, mild-tasting, and chewy. Its termite-free wood is handy too.

Viet cooks transform young jackfruit into many savory dishes, with plush salads a popular option. Thinly sliced poached pork belly and shrimp are often added to gỏi mít non, but I've found that sautéed oyster mushrooms lend an equally satisfying richness, especially with fried garlic bits added. The salad is scooped up with shards of crunchy, nutty-tasting toasted sesame rice crackers. It's a wild combo of flavors and textures, with the crackers functioning like chips but tasting like pork rinds. Good versions are hard to find, so I often scoop with smaller supermarket sesame rice crackers (such as Trader Joe's Savory Thins), lightly salted tortilla chips, or Mexican tostadas. If you skip the scooping, you'll still have a great salad.

Squeeze the jackfruit and shave the carrot

Cut the jackfruit into small wedges a scant ½ inch wide at the fringy edge. Do your best to cut even pieces. Standing over the sink and working in two or three batches, use a dish towel to gently wring out the moisture from the jackfruit (two or three twists normally do the job). Drop the jackfruit into a medium bowl, then fluff to separate the pieces.

Using a vegetable peeler on the thick stem-end of the carrot, shave off ½ cup of thin, wide pieces and add to the jackfruit. Save the remainder for another use.

Cook the garlic and mushroom

In a 10-inch nonstick or carbon-steel skillet over medium-low heat, combine the neutral oil and garlic. After things begin sizzling, cook for 2 to 3 minutes,

(CONTINUED)

stirring or shaking the pan frequently, until about half of the garlic is golden. Remove from the heat, tilt the pan, and gather the garlic in the pool of hot oil to coax gentler frying for about 45 seconds, until nearly all the garlic turns golden. Using a slotted spoon, scoot and transfer the garlic to a small plate to cool, leaving the oil and any lingering garlic bits in the pan.

Add the oyster mushrooms to the pan, season with 2 or 3 big pinches of salt, and then set over high heat. Cook, stirring, for 2 minutes, or until the mushrooms turn soft and glistening. Remove from the heat and let cool.

Make the dressing, toss, and serve

In a small bowl, stir together the lime juice, agave syrup, and fish sauce. Taste and adjust to your liking. This dressing should be tart-sweet with a salty finish. Stir in the chile.

Right before serving, add the mushrooms, garlic, peanuts, and herbs to the jackfruit and carrot. Using a large spoon, stir to combine everything. Pour in the dressing and mix. Taste to make sure the flavors are balanced; add more lime juice and fish sauce, if needed. Pile the salad onto a serving dish and serve immediately with the scoop of your choice. Invite diners to scoop or use forks or chopsticks to scoot the salad onto their crackers or chips.

Note

Ingredients Buff-colored canned young jackfruit is packed in brine (canned yellow ripe jackfruit is packed in heavy syrup and used for the sorbet on page 275). For a salad with bright flavor, fresh color, and firmish texture, select Asian brands. Brands sold at mainstream markets tend to be softer and darker, which is great for vegan pulled pork or other meaty preparations, but not ideal for salad.

Vietnamese sesame rice crackers, called bánh đa mè, in the northern dialect, and bánh tráng mè, in the southern dialect, are sold at Little Saigon markets, delis, and bakeries; Chinese markets with a large Viet clientele may sell them too. Typically shelved near regular rice paper, these untoasted crackers resemble inedible thin rounds of translucent plastic. I buy the classic version with flecks of white or black sesame seeds. Ones wrapped in flimsy stapled plastic are likely locally made and excellent; otherwise, they're probably imported from Vietnam. Traditionally, the crackers were toasted over charcoal until golden. Nowadays, they contain tapioca starch and are made for the microwave. Use high power for 60 to 90 seconds, turning the cracker midway and carefully monitoring as it expands, puffs, and turns wavy. Let cool completely before breaking into shards for serving. Cook three medium (8-inch) crackers or two large (10-inch) crackers for this salad. If you happen upon the even larger pre-toasted crackers, serve one or two.

Side Dish Gems

ABOUT A YEAR AFTER SWITCHING TO MORE vegetable-centric cooking, I noticed something peculiar about how my husband and I approached dinner. We savored the soup, salad, and sides with rice before diving into the main dish. My husband would make his initial plate of food and jokingly deem it "the vegetarian dinner option." I thought I was the one who loved side dishes, but he does too. In Vietnamese, they are commonly referred to as món ăn phụ (literally "dishes eaten to help"), but rather than cast them in supporting roles, we like to push them to the plate's center. And the more sides, the merrier.

Because building vegetable-centric meals daily means having lots of ideas for fast, tasty side dishes in your back pocket, this chapter's recipes pave a path toward easygoing cooking and eating. They are all vegan but may fit meaty or meatless menus. Recognizing the need to cook with what you've got on hand, the vegetable stir-fry is presented as a blueprint-style method. Recipe tester Diane Carlson voluntarily made it twice, applauding its versatility and tasty outcome. Once you get the hang of it, I hope you'll barely need to refer to the original recipe. Ditto for the zippy cabbage stir-fry, which is seasoned with nước chấm during cooking.

If you've spent any time in Vietnam, you've enjoyed water spinach. As prevalent there as regular spinach is in the West, it's arguably the most-eaten leafy green vegetable in the country. The water spinach stir-fry recipe here is unfussy and fast. You may prepare it with fermented tofu, or season it with my vegan oyster-sauce workaround. Can't get to an Asian market? I suggest worthy stand-ins.

There are many ways that Viet cooks, vegetarians and omnivores alike, enliven everyday meals with nutty sesame salt. In this book, the mixture works its magic on simply cooked greens. The recipe serves as a jumping-off point for your experimentation.

The roasted sweet potatoes with sate sauce are so good they could be a main dish with a salad. You could include them at Thanksgiving for a Vietglish celebration.

Since eggplant has been cultivated in Southeast Asia for eons (plus it is among my favorite vegetables), it's spotlighted twice in this chapter. The stew-y turmeric eggplant with shiso represents old-school northern Vietnamese cooking refashioned for the twenty-first century. The eggplant with fermented-tofu dressing is a chef-y take on a Buddhist dish. Recipe testers Paulina Haduong and Colin Hart served it to friends who had never eaten fermented tofu before. They all adored it.

Speaking of the holidays, in the *New York Times* weekly *The Veggie* newsletter, journalist Tejal Rao once described Thanksgiving vegetable sides as "the actual, low-key superstars of the table." I wholeheartedly agree and would extend that description to dinner throughout the year. In fact, instead of treating side dishes as món ăn phụ helpmates, I'd rather describe them by a less-used, more collaborative term: món ăn kèm (dishes for eating alongside).

Maybe it's time to boost side dishes? You could surely build a meal from this chapter and add ideas plucked from the rice, snacks, banh mi, soup, and salad chapters. It wouldn't be for grazing—it would be for feasting.

1 lb asparagus or other green vegetable (such as celery or green beans)

4 oz carrot, watermelon radish (see Note), or fresh mushrooms (such as cremini, shiitake, or maitake), or a combination

1½ Tbsp neutral oil (such as canola or peanut)

3 slices ginger, unpeeled and smashed with the flat side of a knife

1 large garlic clove, gently smashed

¼ tsp plus ⅛ tsp fine sea salt

2 Tbsp water, plus more as needed

Rau Xào Thập Cẩm

Weeknight Vegetable Stir-Fry

Several times a week, I rely on this versatile vegetable stir-fry to put a fast, tasty side on the table. It features a green veggie that's cut on a steep diagonal to ensure the pieces cook quickly and absorb flavors well. One or two other vegetables play supporting roles by adding contrasting color, flavor, and texture. Simply seasoning with ginger, garlic, and salt during the steam-cooking process allows the vegetable's flavors to brightly shine. Choose what's freshest and in season to produce a winning dish every time. A carbon-steel skillet or wok heats up well to cook this dish up in a flash; whatever you choose, have a lid handy.

Prep the veggies

Trim the ends of the asparagus, then slice the stalks on a steep diagonal into 2-inch-long pieces and put them into a bowl.

Cut the carrot into slices a scant ¼ inch thick and 2 inches long; this ensures they'll cook at the same rate as the asparagus. If using mushrooms, cut the stems and caps into ⅓-inch-thick slices or tear into large bite-size pieces. Add to the bowl of asparagus.

Stir-fry and serve

Set a 14-inch wok or 12-inch nonstick or carbon-steel skillet over high heat on one of your largest burners and swirl in the neutral oil. When the oil ripples, toss in the ginger and garlic. Rapidly press down and stir them to release their aroma. Dump in the vegetables and sprinkle with the salt. Stir and toss for about 1 minute, until the vegetables look glossy with brighter color.

(CONTINUED)

Line up all the ingredients near the stove because the cooking happens fast.

Spread out the vegetables to cover the pan bottom, add the water, cover, and then turn the heat to medium-high. Let the veggies steam-cook for 2 minutes, stirring midway and spreading them out again. When the boiling sounds start turning into a crackling noise (which signals water evaporation), uncover and quickly flip and stir the vegetables, about 1 minute, until no more liquid remains. If needed, turn the heat to high to hasten cooking and thus prevent overcooking. If the vegetables are too firm, add a splash of water and cook 1 to 2 minutes longer. When the veggies are done, they should look lightly glazed. Transfer to a plate or shallow bowl, discard the ginger and garlic if you spot them, and serve immediately.

Notes

Ingredients Peel the watermelon radish if its skin is tough. Kohlrabi may be used instead of carrot or radish; peel and quarter it before slicing.

Variation Don't want to do a mixed-vegetable stir-fry? Use this recipe to cook 1¼ lb asparagus or green beans. The seasonings and cooking time remain the same.

⅓ cup Nước Chấm Dipping Sauce (page 32)

1 Tbsp fish sauce (store-bought or vegan version, page 29), plus more as needed

1½ lb red cabbage, cored and cut into 3-inch-long ribbons about ¼ inch wide

3 large garlic cloves, finely chopped

½ to ¾ tsp recently ground black pepper (use the maximum amount for a mild ring of fire)

2 Tbsp neutral oil (such as canola or peanut)

Squeeze of fresh lime juice (optional)

Bắp Cải Xào

Nước Chấm Cabbage Stir-Fry

Keeping a jar of nước chấm in the fridge means that you can unleash Viet flavors fast. Aside from conventional uses, such as dressing rice-noodle bowls, the condiment is a great seasoning for this quick stir-fry. The sauce's mild acidity brightens the cabbage flavor and color while facilitating the cooking. I tried fresh chile with this dish, but the black pepper more efficiently coats the cabbage with pungent heat. Viet cooks typically stir-fry green cabbage, but red cabbage's sturdy leaves impart body and color to this super-easy side. Try this stir-fry with other vegetables, such as broccoli, or a 2-to-1 combination of broccoli with green or savoy cabbage (hand-tearing the leaves allows the veggies to combine well).

Gather and line up the ingredients

Season the dipping sauce with the fish sauce; add another ½ to 1 tsp fish sauce if needed to achieve a salty, tangy finish. Set this seasoning sauce near the stove with the cabbage, garlic, and pepper so you may work smoothly.

Stir-fry and serve

Set a 14-inch wok or 12-inch nonstick or carbon-steel skillet over medium heat on one of your largest burners and swirl in the neutral oil. When the oil ripples, add the garlic and swiftly stir-fry for 45 to 60 seconds, until fragrant and a few bits are turning pale golden. Dump in half of the cabbage and stir to combine to prevent the garlic from burning on the bottom.

Add the remaining cabbage to the pan and crank the heat to high. Keep stir-frying for 1 minute, or until the cabbage glistens and has slightly softened.

In a circular motion, pour the seasoning sauce over the cabbage to evenly distribute, then stir-fry for 2 minutes, or until the cabbage has further softened and is just cooked through. Sprinkle with the pepper and stir-fry for 30 seconds longer, or until there is little liquid left. Transfer to a shallow bowl or plate, add the lime juice for brightening, and serve.

1 lb water spinach (see Note)

2 Tbsp mashed white fermented tofu (see page 23; preferably without chile)

1½ Tbsp water, or 2 tsp fermented tofu brine and 2½ tsp water (use the mixture for extra oomph)

½ tsp toasted sesame oil

½ tsp cornstarch

Fine sea salt

Granulated sugar for balancing flavor

1 Tbsp finely chopped garlic

1 mild or moderately hot red chile (such as Anaheim or Fresno), halved, seeded, and thinly sliced crosswise (optional, for colorful heat)

1½ Tbsp neutral oil (such as canola or peanut)

Rau Muống Xào Chao

Stir-Fried Water Spinach and Fermented Tofu

If you want to capture elemental Viet home cooking, include the tender spade-shaped leaves and slightly crunchy hollow stems of rau muống (aka water spinach and morning glory, pictured, upper right, on page 192) in your repertoire. The popular everyday leafy greens proliferate in Southeast Asia and southern China, where their mildly nutty flavor is often enjoyed in stir-fries. In Vietnam, rau muống is also blanched for salads, featured in quickie canh soup, and served raw as a noodle-soup add-in. Pairing water spinach with cheese-like, creamy fermented tofu is among my favorite ways to serve the greens. It's easy and luxe-seeming, evoking creamed spinach, a classic steakhouse side dish. I've served this with rice and other Viet dishes as well as a steak. Shop for water spinach at Chinese and Southeast Asian markets; Asian vegetable vendors at farmers' markets may cultivate it too. If it's unavailable, swap in a substitute suggested in the Notes.

Prep the water spinach

With the water spinach still bunched together, use a knife to efficiently trim the often sad-looking cut ends. Undo the ties and rinse the greens, shaking off excess water. Using scissors or the knife, cut the water spinach into 3-inch lengths, dropping the big stem sections in one bowl and the more tender parts (narrower than ¼ inch) in a larger bowl.

Make the seasoning sauce

In a small bowl, combine the tofu, water, sesame oil, cornstarch, and ⅛ tsp salt and, using a fork, mash into a creamy mixture. Taste and add pinches of sugar or salt to yield a salty-sweet, rich, winey finish. Set near the stove with the water spinach, garlic, and chile (if using).

(CONTINUED)

> The water lingering on the freshly washed greens is just enough to coax cooking in the hot pan. When scaling up the quantities, cook in separate batches—there are a lot of greens to manage.

Cook it up

Set a 14-inch wok or 12-inch nonstick or carbon-steel skillet over medium heat on one of your largest burners and swirl in the neutral oil. When the oil ripples, add the garlic and chile. Stir-fry for 15 to 30 seconds, or until the garlic is fragrant but hasn't turned blond. Add the water spinach stems, swiftly stir together, and then turn the heat to high. After about 45 seconds, when the stems glisten and start to soften, dump in half of the tender sections, swiftly stir for 1 minute, until the greens start collapsing, and then add the remainder.

When the water spinach is roughly half its original volume, stir the seasoning sauce and pour into the pan. Cook for 30 seconds, until the water spinach takes on a slightly creamy quality. Turn off the heat, taste, and add more salt and sugar as needed. Transfer to a plate and serve immediately.

Notes

Ingredients Spinach (heirloom Bloomsdale is a personal favorite), kale (Siberian is wonderfully tender), or Swiss chard may stand in for the water spinach. With regular spinach, wash and drain it well; if the leaves are young with nubby root ends attached, keep them that way for texture. Use an additional ½ tsp cornstarch because spinach is super-moist. When cooking kale or Swiss chard, tear or cut the leafy parts from the stems and then into large bite-size pieces. Slice the stems into thin sections on a steep diagonal. Stir-fry the stems 30 seconds to 1 minute longer than you would with those of water spinach, adding splashes of water, until the stems just turn tender, then add the leafy parts.

Variations When fermented tofu isn't on hand, substitute 1½ Tbsp white (shiro) miso to make a Water Spinach and Miso Stir-Fry, which won't be creamy but will still be excellent.

For a Water Spinach and "Oyster Sauce" Stir-Fry, prep the same amount of water spinach, garlic, and chile. For the seasoning sauce, combine 1½ tsp granulated sugar, ½ tsp cornstarch, 1 Tbsp soy sauce, 1 Tbsp water, 1½ tsp fish sauce, and ½ tsp toasted sesame oil. The stir-frying process remains the same.

¼ cup toasted sesame seeds (any kind)

½ tsp granulated sugar

¼ tsp plus ⅛ tsp kosher salt

4 cups lightly packed, cooked leafy greens (such as water spinach, lacinato kale, collard greens, or Swiss chard, include stems for texture; see Note), at room temperature

2 to 3 tsp fish sauce (store-bought or vegan version, page 29) or soy sauce, plus more as needed

1 lime or lemon, halved

Rau Trộn Muối Mè

Greens with Magical Sesame Salt

To enjoy lots of vegetables, you need to have some tricks up your sleeve. One of mine is muối mè (sesame salt), an old-fashioned, magical combination of three ingredients that instantly transforms the mundane into the special. When I was growing up, my mom always had some around for sprinkling onto rice for an aromatic, nutty seasoning. In this recipe, sesame salt functions like a dry sauce to enrich and make cooked leafy greens moreish (you want to eat more of it!).

Muối mè and cooked greens keep well for days, so, to save time during the week, I prep batches of the salt and vegetables ahead, selecting the freshest seasonal greens from Asian and farmers' markets. It's coasting from there: I simply return the greens to room temp, toss them with a bit of fish sauce and lime juice for savory tang, and then finish with the rich nuttiness of sesame salt. It's a delicious side dish that I can put on repeat for perpetuity because I can vary the greens and sesame seeds.

Pound the sesame seeds

Using a mortar and pestle, stir, grind, and pound the sesame seeds, sugar, and salt into an aromatic, finely textured mixture. I usually stop when I can smell the nutty sesame. (If you don't have a mortar and pestle, use a small food processor.)

Toss and serve

Put the greens in a large bowl and season with the fish sauce, 1 tsp at a time. Using your fingers or tongs, work in the condiment so that it's well distributed and there's a slight savory hit when you taste the greens. To brighten the flavors, squeeze half of the lime over the greens, tossing them with your fingers. Taste, and if they're not lively enough, add more lime and fish sauce.

(CONTINUED)

For 4 cups of greens, cook 1 lb trimmed greens that have been cut into bite-size pieces.

Whether black or white, hulled or not, sesame seeds have subtle differences. Try different kinds.

Finally, sprinkle the sesame seed mixture over the greens and gradually work it in, repeatedly tossing to coat well. You may need nearly but not all of it; aim for a rich, nutty flavor. When satisfied, pile the greens onto a platter and serve immediately.

Notes

Ingredients Water spinach (see page 198 for prep tips) should be plunged into a Dutch oven or a 5-qt pot of boiling salted water. Adding 2 pinches of baking soda maintains its vibrant color. As soon as the delicate greens soften, drain in a colander. Dump the greens back into the pot, flood them with water to cool, and then re-drain.

To preserve nutrients, steam-sauté kale, collards, or Swiss chard. Put ⅛ inch water in the bottom of a Dutch oven and add the prepped greens, 2 big pinches of sea salt, and 2 pinches of baking soda. Toss the greens a bit to distribute. Cover and cook over medium heat, checking and stirring, for 6 to 10 minutes, until tender, depending on the greens; if needed, splash in more water. Remove from the heat and let cool.

Variation With Asian greens such as choy sum (aka yu choy, although choy sum technically should be younger and sweeter), steam 1 lb in batches for 2 to 3 minutes each. Cut the cooled greens into short pieces, drizzle lightly with soy sauce, and garnish with some sesame salt. Present the remaining muối mè on the side for diners to sprinkle on as they eat. Choy Sum with Sesame Salt may be made with other stemmy greens, such as broccolini, gai lan, or broccoli rabe.

1 lb globe eggplant

Fine sea salt

2 Tbsp neutral oil (such as canola or peanut oil)

⅔ cup chopped shallots or yellow onion

1½ Tbsp finely chopped garlic

1 Tbsp lightly packed grated, peeled fresh turmeric, or ½ tsp ground turmeric

1½ cups chopped, peeled ripe tomatoes, or 1 (14.5-oz) can diced tomato (include juices)

1½ Tbsp fish sauce (store-bought or vegan version, page 29)

¾ cup water, plus more as needed

3 Tbsp sour cream (dairy-free, if preferred)

1½ tsp Nori Dust (page 27; optional, for briny punch)

½ cup roughly chopped or hand-torn Vietnamese shiso, cilantro, mint, or dill

Cà Tím Om

Creamy Turmeric Eggplant with Shiso

When I come across a big, beautiful, glossy, firm-ish globe eggplant that gives a tad when gently squeezed, I buy it for this slightly funky dish in which large chunks of the purple fruit simmer up to a fascinatingly rich texture and flavor. The preparation is a take on cà tím om, a northern Vietnamese eggplant and tomato dish that is made with turmeric, mẻ (creamy fermented rice), and mắm tôm (fermented shrimp paste). It's finished with garlic and tía tô (Vietnamese shiso). It has a sunny look, yet an earthy flavor. It's a provocative head-turner.

To create a similar experience that's doable with readily available ingredients, I use fresh turmeric or high-quality ground turmeric, which yields bright flavor. Tangy sour cream stands in for the fermented rice, while a combination of fish sauce and ground nori mimics briny mắm tôm notes. Adding garlic builds umami upfront and spikes the finish along with lots of fresh herbs. This eggplant is a side dish, but I've also served it over extra-large (pappardelle-size) rice noodles.

Cut and salt the eggplant

Tear off the flaps from the eggplant stem-end, cut off the stem and a slice of the butt end, and halve the eggplant lengthwise. Cut each half lengthwise into three spears, each about 1½ inches wide. Then cut crosswise into 1½-inch-thick wedges (about five per spear). Put them in a large bowl, toss with ¾ tsp salt, and let sit for 10 minutes, or until the eggplant glistens; a pool of liquid may appear in the bowl. Rinse, drain, and then gently squeeze the spongy pieces to expel extra moisture.

(CONTINUED)

For a nondairy rendition, I use a tofu-based sour cream.

Build a flavorful base

Set a 3-qt saucepan over medium heat and add the neutral oil. When the oil barely ripples, add the shallots and fry gently, stirring frequently, for about 4 minutes, until some pieces are golden. Add 1 Tbsp of the garlic and the turmeric and cook for 30 seconds, until fragrant. Slightly lower the heat and add the tomatoes, fish sauce, and 1 big pinch of salt. Cover and cook 1 to 3 minutes, stirring often, until the tomatoes begin breaking down (they'll be mashable when firmly pressed with the back of a spoon).

Simmer, then serve

Stir the water and sour cream into the tomatoes and then add the eggplant. Turn the heat to medium-high and bring to a simmer. Cover and lower the heat to maintain a simmer and let percolate for 7 to 12 minutes, until the eggplant pieces are tender but not mushy (poke a few with a knife tip to test). Occasionally check their progress and stir gently; if needed, add a splash of water to facilitate cooking.

When the eggplant is done, turn off the heat and let sit, uncovered, for a few minutes to concentrate the flavors. If the sauce is too thick, add water by the tablespoon. Gently stir in the remaining ½ Tbsp garlic, the nori dust (if using), and most of the shiso. Transfer the eggplant to a shallow bowl, garnish with the remaining shiso, and then serve.

Note

Technique To peel the tomatoes, trim a bit of skin from the stem-ends and then use a vegetable peeler in a sawing motion to remove the skin. Fresh tomato yields a livelier result, but canned is available year-round.

3 medium Chinese eggplants (see Note)

2 Tbsp mashed fermented white tofu (see page 23; preferably without chile)

Scant 1 Tbsp granulated sugar, agave syrup, or mild honey

¼ tsp mashed minced garlic

½ to 1 tsp finely chopped Thai or serrano chile (use the maximum amount for edgy heat)

⅛ tsp smoked paprika (optional, for an extra-smoky touch)

1 pinch Chinese five-spice powder (optional, for lively pungency)

2 Tbsp water

1 Tbsp neutral oil (such as canola or peanut)

1 Tbsp unseasoned rice vinegar

1½ tsp soy sauce

2 to 3 Tbsp hand-torn or roughly chopped fresh mint, cilantro, or Vietnamese shiso leaves

Cà Tím Nướng Chao

Eggplant with Creamy Fermented-Tofu Vinaigrette and Mint

Lovely and thơm béo (fragrant and fatty), this plush eggplant dressed in a creamy vegan vinaigrette illustrates the potential of chao (fermented tofu). The elegant dish was created by my friend, Seattle chef and restaurateur Eric Banh, who based the flavors on his childhood memories of visiting Buddhist temples in Saigon, where he was raised. Eric grills or flash-fries the skinny eggplants, but I prefer an easier path, microwaving them first and then briefly grilling over an open flame to add a light smokiness. My approach retains the eggplant's purple skin, which contains nasunin, a potent antioxidant. The Notes offer extra tips for grilling, using miso, and more. No matter how you make this recipe, the result is always splendid.

Cook the eggplant

Tear off the flaps from the eggplant stem-ends. Using a fork, pierce each eggplant eight to ten times to prevent them from exploding during cooking. Rinse briefly under water to moisten, then place on a microwave-safe plate. Microwave on high power for about 6 minutes, until the eggplants are brownish purple and softened (the firmer, skinnier sections are fine). Let cool for a few minutes.

If you have a gas stove and want a light smokiness beyond the smoked paprika that goes into the vinaigrette, hold an eggplant over a medium-high flame, turning frequently, and cook for about 2 minutes, until there is some char and maybe patches of blackened, blistered skin; if you have a small grill rack, place it over the burner to steady the eggplant. (Alternatively, broil the eggplants as close to the heat source as possible for 2 minutes per side, or char them in a ripping-hot cast-iron or carbon-steel skillet for the same amount of time.) Repeat for the remaining eggplants. Set aside until cool enough to handle.

See page 215 for
eggplant selection tips.

Use this dressing on
steamed, roasted,
or grilled asparagus
spears or serve it
with grilled okra.

Prepare the dressing

Meanwhile, in a medium bowl, whisk together 1½ Tbsp of the tofu, the sugar, garlic, chile, and smoked paprika and five-spice powder (if using). Add the water, neutral oil, vinegar, and soy sauce and whisk until well blended and creamy. Let rest for 5 minutes. Taste, and if more creamy, savory depth is needed, whisk in the remaining ½ Tbsp mashed fermented tofu.

Assemble and serve

Cut each eggplant into fork-able or chopstick-able strips, about 3 inches long and ½ inch wide. Transfer to a plate, pour all the vinaigrette over the eggplant, and top with the herb leaves. When serving, include any dressing that has pooled on the plate.

Notes

Ingredients Medium Chinese eggplants weigh 6 to 7 ounces each (if yours are bigger, microwave them for a minute more and make extra sauce). If Chinese eggplants are unavailable, use two small globe eggplants. Regardless, aim for about 1¼ lb total.

Technique If you don't have a microwave or if you want extra smokiness, leave the stems intact on the eggplants and grill them on the grates of a medium-hot grill or stovetop gas burner for about 15 minutes, turning frequently, until the skin turns dark brown (or black) and blisters, and the flesh becomes very soft. Let them cool on a plate or baking sheet for 10 to 15 minutes and then peel off the blistered skin; wetting your hands will aid in rubbing off stubborn bits.

Timing The eggplant and dressing can be prepped up to 5 days ahead. Refrigerate separately in airtight containers and bring to room temperature to assemble.

Variation For Eggplant with Miso Vinaigrette and Mint, trade white (shiro) miso for the fermented tofu. White miso can be sweet, so add sweetener by the teaspoon and taste. The dressing will have greater umami but lack the tofu's fantastic fermented funk and creaminess. But it will be equally delicious.

4 medium-large sweet potatoes (any kind)

1½ Tbsp neutral oil (such as canola or peanut)

¼ tsp fine sea salt

2 to 3 Tbsp Vegan Sate Sauce (page 40)

¼ cup hand-torn soft-leaf herbs (such as mint or dill), or 2 Tbsp thinly sliced green onions, green parts only

Khoai Lang Nướng

Oven-Blasted Sweet Potatoes with Sate Sauce

For most of my life, I baked sweet potatoes like I do russets—whole. But when my mom lit up as she discussed eating slightly charred, ember-roasted sweet potatoes in Vietnam, I had to figure out an easy way to have that sort of experience. High-heat oven roasting intensifies and caramelizes the exposed flesh to evoke open-flame cooking (the nutrient-dense skin is edible too!). Served naked, the potatoes are good; adding spicy, briny sốt sa tế makes them dynamite.

Preheat and prep

Position a rack in the upper third of the oven and preheat to 425°F. Line a large baking sheet with parchment paper or a silicone mat.

Scrub the sweet potatoes with a vegetable brush, rinse, and dry well. If the ends look wizened, trim them. Halve the sweet potatoes lengthwise and put them in a large bowl. Drizzle half of the neutral oil over the potatoes and sprinkle with ⅛ tsp of the salt. Toss to coat, then repeat with the remaining oil and salt to ensure coating all over. Arrange the sweet potatoes cut-side down on the prepared baking sheet, equally spaced to promote air circulation.

Bake, blast, and serve

Bake the sweet potatoes for 15 to 20 minutes, until they are pierceable with a knife tip but there's some resistance in the center. Turn them over and bake for 5 to 10 minutes longer, until they're tender all the way through. (Cooking times depend on the sweet potato type and moisture level.) If there's enough browning on top for you, they're done! Otherwise, turn the oven setting to broil and cook for 2 to 5 minutes, until charred here and there.

Serve the sweet potatoes hot, warm, or at room temperature. Spoon the sauce over them and garnish with the herbs. (Or let diners do it themselves.)

For even cooking, select sweet potatoes of similar shape and size. Aim for 8-oz potatoes. Orange-flesh sweet potatoes are my favorites, but you may roast any kind.

Mains without Meat

MY MOTHER'S CHILDHOOD HOME WAS located next to the neighborhood tofu shop, the East Asian equivalent of the local bakery. How lucky she was to have easy access to freshly made tofu, soy milk, and the tasty concentrated dregs of soy milk, which the shop would press and fry up as crisp yuba (tofu skin) pieces. Her family wasn't vegetarian but, like many Vietnamese, they considered tofu a mainstay. It was a food that celebrated the soybean's potential to nourish, satisfy, and comfort. They cooked it with and without meat, seasoning it with fish sauce or soy sauce, depending on the preparation.

Given its importance in Vietnamese cuisine, tofu is the main protein source in this book. I've cast it in supporting roles in many recipes, but in this chapter, tofu stars in four main dishes—with vegetables in a curry, as a pork belly replacer in a caramel sauce classic, an imitator of ground meat in a spicy crumble, and a twice-fried crispy bed for lemongrass and chile.

Tofu could fill this entire chapter, but vegetables also deserve the spotlight. Mushrooms play a recurring role, for instance. They costar with tofu in the aforementioned curry and caramel sauce mains. The slithery richness of oyster mushrooms gets a spicy lemongrass hit of flavor in a quick stir-fry. Dried shiitake mushrooms inject earthy umami depth to convey meatiness in a super-tasty vegan take on bò kho, a favorite tomato-y beef, carrot, and star anise stew.

Aside from tofu and mushrooms, you'll also use lemongrass many times in this section. If you want to learn more about this aromatic, from buying and prepping to growing it, head to page 44.

Cauliflower typically costars with meat in Vietnamese stir-fries, but here it performs solo, seasoned by a salty-sweet-spicy char siu marinade and roasted. The tender, slightly al dente result is meatlike and best eaten with fork and knife, although it's also at home in banh mi and steamed buns.

And since trompe l'oeil is part of Asian vegetarian cooking craftsmanship, you should also make the veganized "pulled" char siu. It's easy and fast when made with canned young jackfruit. Why so much char siu? The Chinese-style barbecue flavors are beloved by young and old alike. I've prepared char siu pork and chicken, so why not double down on the veggie versions with char siu cauliflower and jackfruit?

These recipes were designed for using standard store-bought fish sauce or the homemade Vegan Fish Sauce on page 29, so cook according to your preference.

Enjoying a plant-forward lifestyle means you need quick, wholesome ideas. Leading this chapter are two of my favorites. The steak-ish eggplant is simple yet lush. Double the prep to keep some around for the week. The herby green egg pancakes are so easy that after making them once, recipe tester Rosemary Metzger said she could already imagine freestyling creative future batches.

This chapter's main dishes are exciting and full-flavored. They are great for all eaters.

2 medium or 1 very large globe eggplant

Fine sea salt

3 to 4 Tbsp neutral oil (such as canola or peanut), plus more for brushing

GARLICKY GREEN ONION OIL

1 cup chopped green onions, white and green parts

2 garlic cloves, finely chopped

2 Tbsp neutral oil (such as canola or peanut)

1 pinch fine sea salt

1½ to 2 Tbsp fish sauce (store-bought or vegan version, page 29)

1 Tbsp water

1 or 2 Thai or small serrano chiles, sliced (use the maximum amount for edgy heat)

You'll need 1½ pounds of eggplant total for this recipe.

Cà Tím Nướng Mỡ Hành

Grilled Eggplant with Garlicky Green Onion Sizzle

Typical versions of Viet grilled eggplant involve charring eggplants, then discarding the skin and presenting the collapsed flesh under a cloak of rich mỡ hành, which entails sizzling green onion in hot oil. It's a personal favorite but, honestly, it's a lot of work for a side dish. To turn this into a main dish, I grill thick meaty slices of eggplant and keep the skin intact to retain as many nutrients as possible. These eggplant "steaks" keep well for days, ready for serving under the luscious green onion–garlic sauce spiked with fish sauce and chile. Who wouldn't want to eat that with rice and a stir-fried veggie or a simple pasta dish and a green salad? This rendition of cà tím nướng mỡ hành is also fabulous stuffed into banh mi.

Grill the eggplant steaks

Tear off the flaps from the eggplant stem-ends, then cut off the stems and a slice of the butt ends. If you're using medium eggplants, cut them crosswise into circles, each about ⅝ inch thick. If your eggplant is bigger, halve it lengthwise and then cut crosswise to yield ⅝-inch-thick half-moons.

Put the eggplant in a very large bowl, season with ¼ tsp salt, and toss with 3 to 4 Tbsp of the neutral oil to coat lightly. Set a cast-iron stovetop grill over high heat and lightly brush with neutral oil (or prepare a medium-hot charcoal fire or preheat a gas grill to medium-high). In batches, grill the eggplant for 4 to 6 minutes per side, or until just cooked through (a knife tip inserted should meet little or no resistance). Transfer the eggplant to a baking sheet or plate, and let cool to warmish or room temperature.

Prepare the green onion oil

To make the Garlicky Green Onion Oil: In a small microwavable bowl, stir together the green onions, garlic, 2 Tbsp neutral oil, and salt. Microwave on high power for 45 to 60 seconds, until bubbly, steamy, and fragrant. Stir, then let cool to lukewarm. Stir in 1½ Tbsp of the fish sauce, the water, and chile. Taste, and if needed, add enough of the remaining 1½ tsp fish sauce to pack extra punch.

(CONTINUED)

Assemble and eat

Arrange the eggplant steaks on a plate. Spoon all the glorious green onion oil over the eggplant and serve.

———

Notes

Equipment Instead of microwaving the green onion oil, put the oil in a 1- to 1½-qt saucepan and set over medium heat. When a green onion piece gently sizzles upon contact, stir in the remaining green onions, the garlic, and salt and cook 30 seconds, until the solids soften. Let cool briefly, then finish as directed.

Lifespan The eggplant can be grilled and refrigerated in an airtight container for up to 3 days. Return to room temperature and microwave on high power for 45 to 60 seconds to warm and refresh before assembling.

EGGPLANT-SELECTION TIPS

When it comes to buying eggplant, I had long followed the notion that firm eggplants are better eggplants. That all changed when I talked to Tra Her and Kou Moua, the Hmong farmers who sell Asian produce at my weekly farmers' market. Kou's family farmed in Laos, and the couple continues that legacy via K T Farms in Fresno, California, where Tra also works full-time as a public school teacher. They consistently cultivate delicious produce, including Chinese, Japanese, Indian, and Thai eggplant varieties as well as globe and Italian.

After recipe tester Tina Ujlaki and I discussed eggplant firmness for the grilled mini steaks on page 212, I wondered: What do farmers look for when picking eggplants? It turns out eggplant isn't picked when ripe, but you don't want them immature and rock-hard either. Years of experience taught Tra and Kou to simply look at the fruits to determine harvest time.

What about eggplant size? That does not necessarily reflect flavor, Tra said, noting that a big eggplant with a pocketlike hollow space inside may taste just as good as a smaller one.

We quickly reviewed K T Farms' eggplant selection that day, which didn't look camera-ready. Some had minor dents or flat patches from sitting. They felt slightly spongy yet dense. These are all good to eat, the couple confidently confirmed, adding that they'd never sell an eggplant that was so soft that you could poke a finger into it (a sign of rotting fruit).

Kou cut open an eggplant that I'd passed over because its skin was a bit matte-looking and it seemed a bit soft when I gently squeezed it. "See?" he said, pointing to the gorgeous creamy interior. "Softer eggplant is sweet. It is like fruit." In a joking tone, he added that there are differences between male and female eggplants. Showing me an eggplant bottom with a deep innie belly button–like dimple, Kou said, "This is male. They have few seeds. The female ones have more seeds, but they taste better."

"Of course. We women are better," Tra responded.

So, don't pass up soft, spongy-ish eggplants as long as they feel dense and are relatively heavy for their size. And when in doubt, ask the farmer.

2 cups lightly packed cooked leafy greens (such as kale, chard, or collards)

1 cup packed chopped raw herbs (such as dill, cilantro, garlic chives, Vietnamese shiso, and wild pepper leaves)

1 Tbsp fish sauce (store-bought or vegan version, page 29) or soy sauce

1 tsp recently ground black pepper

Fine sea salt

3 Tbsp cornstarch

6 large eggs

4 to 5 Tbsp neutral oil (such as canola or peanut)

Viet Chile Sauce (page 39), chile-garlic sauce (see page 37), or sriracha for dipping

For the greens, chop and then microwave or steam-sauté (see Note, page 202) two medium bunches (12 oz total); include any tender stems, chopping them small.

Like green onions? Chop some to add to the herbaceous mix.

Trứng Chiên Rau Thơm

Herby Green Egg Pancakes

Cooking healthful Viet food means I often have a glut of fresh herbs and leafy greens around. Combining those mainstays, I make these egg pancakes. Cornstarch binds the vegetables and facilitates delicately crisp, frilly edges. Use one herb to emphasize a single flavor or mix two or three herbs to vary the flavor notes. Enjoy the pancakes with rice, in a sandwich, or with a salad.

Make the veggie-egg mixture

If there is a lot of cooking water in the greens, pour it off (leave some moisture for tenderness). Coarsely chop the greens into smallish pieces. Put them in a medium bowl with the herbs, then season with the fish sauce and black pepper. Taste for a mild savoriness, working in pinches of salt as needed.

Add the cornstarch and mix with a fork (the starch will disappear as it becomes absorbed). Add the eggs and mix to coat well.

Pan-fry the pancakes and serve

Set a 12-inch nonstick or carbon-steel skillet over medium heat, then add about 2 Tbsp neutral oil to lightly coat the bottom. When the oil ripples, use a ¼-cup measuring cup (or an ice-cream scoop) to deposit the egg mixture for three or four pancakes, using the bottom of your scooper to spread out the mixture to create 3- to 4-inch-wide pancakes. Egg should flow down to create frilly edges. (Drizzle additional egg on top to force them, if you like.)

Pan-fry, flipping the pancakes after 2 minutes, or when the edges look golden brown and crisp. Cook the other side for about 1 minute, then transfer to a rack or platter to cool. Repeat, adding oil and adjusting the heat as needed to make about twelve pancakes total (expect the last ones to be extra-eggy and amoeba-shaped). When the last ones are done, briefly re-fry the first batch to reheat, if you like. Serve with chile sauce for dipping.

Note

Lifespan Refrigerate leftovers in an airtight container for up to 3 days; return them to room temperature and briefly re-fry over medium heat.

1 (14- or 16-oz) package extra-firm tofu, water poured off

Fine sea salt

3 Tbsp neutral oil (such as canola or peanut)

4 large eggs (see Note), boiled or steamed (see box, page 218) until jammy or hard-cooked, and peeled

½ cup chopped shallots or yellow onion

Mounded 1½ Tbsp chopped garlic

12 oz large cremini mushrooms (see Note), halved through the stems

2 cups unsweetened coconut water, strained if pulpy

3 Tbsp Caramel Sauce (page 34; or see Note)

2 Tbsp fish sauce (store-bought or vegan version, page 29), plus more as needed

1½ tsp black peppercorns, coarsely cracked (see Note)

2 to 4 Thai chiles, or 1 or 2 serrano chiles, split lengthwise (optional)

Đậu Hũ Kho Trứng

Black Pepper Caramel Tofu and Eggs

Wanting to make a lighter version of braised caramel pork belly and eggs, a southern Viet classic that's also a Tet must-have, I turned to pan-fried chunks of tofu and meaty cremini mushrooms. They didn't let me down. Once combined with all the seasonings, the mushrooms shared their savoriness while the tofu absorbed the whole shebang; their richness and chew echoed the pork that is traditionally used for the dish. The eggs are typically hard-boiled, but you may employ jammy ones if you like.

Đậu hũ kho trứng is at home with rice and a stir-fried or steamed green vegetable. For a classic pairing, add tangy crunch with Pickled Mustard Greens (page 60) or Pickled Bean Sprout Salad (page 172), as pictured. Leftovers are great with porridge, in banh mi or instant ramen, and even encased in tortillas.

Pan-fry the tofu

If the tofu came as a single block, quarter it before quartering each smaller block to yield rectangular chunks, each about 1 inch thick and 2 inches wide. (If the tofu came as two blocks, halve and then quarter them.) Season all the chunks with a mounded ¼ tsp salt, place on a dish towel, and drain for about 20 minutes.

Set a 12-inch nonstick or carbon-steel skillet over medium-high heat and add 1 Tbsp of the neutral oil. Blot excess moisture from the tofu. When the oil ripples, add the tofu and fry for about 12 minutes, turning the tofu, as needed, to form a golden crust on the four long sides. Set near the stove with the eggs and remaining ingredients to speed through cooking.

Fry the aromatics, then simmer

Replace the skillet over medium heat and add the remaining 2 Tbsp neutral oil. When the oil barely ripples, dump in the shallots and garlic and cook, stirring often, for 3 minutes, until some bits turn golden. Add the mushrooms, tofu, coconut water, caramel sauce, fish sauce, and cracked peppercorns and stir gently to combine. Raise the heat and bring to a gentle boil. Then turn the heat

(CONTINUED)

Coconut water sourced from Thailand tends to have great, bright flavor. Sugar levels range from 9 to 15g per 1-cup serving (check nutrition labels). If you like sweetness, aim for the upper end of the spectrum.

to medium and keep the mixture bubbling for 10 to 14 minutes, turning the tofu three or four times, until the liquid has reduced by nearly half.

Add the eggs to the mixture and continue cooking for 3 to 5 minutes longer, frequently rotating the eggs or spooning sauce over them (the exterior turns a handsome brown). When done, the sauce should be about one-third of the original volume. Stir in the chiles (if using), then let rest, uncovered, for 5 minutes to further concentrate the flavors.

Taste, adjust the seasonings, and serve

Taste the sauce and, if needed, season with additional fish sauce or salt. If it's too strong or you want a little more sauce, splash in water and briefly reheat. Transfer to a shallow bowl and serve.

Notes

Ingredients White mushrooms may be used instead of cremini; the flavor will not be as deep.

No caramel sauce? Substitute 1½ Tbsp agave syrup or mild honey, 2 tsp molasses, and 1 tsp vinegar (rice or distilled white). The color and flavor will be less vivid than with caramel sauce.

Technique To coarsely crack the peppercorns, use a mortar and pestle. Or put them in a small ziplock bag, seal it up, and whack with a meat mallet.

Timing Pan-fry the tofu and cook the eggs up to 5 days ahead. Refrigerate in separate airtight containers; return to room temperature to use.

Lifespan Refrigerate in an airtight container for up to 3 days. Reheat over medium heat, partly covered, with a splash of water, or microwave to warm.

Variation You may omit the eggs.

FOR BOILED EGGS, GET STEAMED!

Boiling eggs to a desired doneness can be tricky, so I prefer steaming, a method spotlighted by Alton Brown years ago. The results are consistent and easy to peel. Simply use a collapsible steamer or a Chinese steamer setup. Once the water vigorously bubbles, add the eggs straight from the fridge. For the large chicken eggs used in this book, my steaming times are the following:

- 8 to 9 minutes for jammy to semi-jammy yolks
- 10 to 11 minutes for creamy to slightly creamy yolks
- 12 to 13 minutes for soft-firm to firm yolks

Cool the eggs in an ice bath for 15 minutes before peeling.

10 oz oyster mushrooms

4 oz snap peas or snow peas

½ small red or yellow onion, cut into ½-inch-thick wedges

3 Tbsp minced lemongrass (see page 44)

1 large Fresno or jalapeño chile, quartered, seeded, and chopped

1 Tbsp finely chopped garlic

1½ tsp Madras-style curry powder, or a combination of ¾ tsp ground coriander, ½ tsp garam masala, and ¼ tsp ground turmeric

Fine sea salt

¼ tsp granulated sugar

⅛ tsp ground turmeric (optional, for extra-bright color)

1 Tbsp fish sauce (store-bought or vegan version, page 29)

2½ Tbsp neutral oil (such as canola or peanut; see Note)

Save leftovers for banh mi or tacos.

Nấm Bào Ngư Xào Sả Ớt

Spicy Oyster Mushroom and Lemongrass Stir-Fry

Delicate oyster mushrooms look as though they lack verve, but in this stir-fry they absorb the spicy seasonings and soften to a chewy-firm texture. When I've applied these same seasonings to chicken, the meat's savoriness muted the flavors of other ingredients. Here, the elements stand in balance with snap peas or snow peas (both called đậu Hà Lan, "Netherlands beans"), contributing vibrant color, mild sweetness, and subtle crispness. Enjoy this bold stir-fry with rice and a simple side, such as the greens with sesame salt on page 201.

Prep the mushrooms and peas

Tear the mushrooms into large bite-size pieces no wider than 2 inches at their fan-like caps; they will lose nearly half of their volume during cooking. It's fine to keep clusters of smaller mushrooms intact.

Using your fingernails, nip each pea at both ends, removing the hard tips and any tough stringy parts that come off. Line them up near the stove with the mushrooms and seasonings—from the onion down to the fish sauce—because cooking goes quickly.

Stir-fry and serve

Set a 14-inch wok or 12-inch nonstick or carbon-steel skillet over medium heat and add the neutral oil. When the oil ripples, add the onion and lemongrass, stir, and fry for about 2 minutes, to soften the onion and start browning the lemongrass. Add the chile, garlic, curry powder, ¼ tsp salt, sugar, and turmeric (if using). Stir for 30 seconds, until aromatic, and then add the mushrooms.

Fold in and stir the mushrooms to coat well. When all the pieces are splotched gold, turn the heat to high and continue stir-frying for about 2 minutes more, until tender-firm. Add the peas, swiftly working to combine them. After 1 minute, when the peas are hot and glistening, splash in the fish sauce. Cook for about 30 seconds to season, hydrate, and soften everything. Remove from the heat and taste. If needed, add 1 pinch of salt. Transfer to a serving plate and bring to the table to eat.

1 (14- or 16-oz) package extra-firm tofu, water poured off

Fine sea salt

3 Tbsp neutral oil (such as canola or peanut)

⅔ cup chopped yellow onion

1 Tbsp finely chopped peeled ginger

1 Tbsp finely chopped garlic

3 Tbsp minced lemongrass (see page 44)

Scant 2 tsp Madras-style curry powder, or a combination of 1 tsp ground coriander, scant ¾ tsp garam masala, and ¼ tsp ground turmeric

¼ tsp MSG, or ½ tsp Asian mushroom seasoning or Marmite (optional)

⅛ tsp cayenne pepper, or ¼ tsp red pepper flakes

6 oz tomato, grated on the largest hole of a box grater (keep juices and seeds)

10 oz medium cremini or white mushrooms, halved through the stems

1⅓ cups full-fat unsweetened coconut milk (whisk before measuring)

¼ cup water, plus more as needed

¼ cup coarsely chopped cilantro sprigs or dill fronds

Medium cremini and white mushrooms have caps about 1½ inches wide; the caps of large ones approach 2 inches wide.

Cà Ri Đậu Hũ và Nấm

Tofu-Mushroom Curry

Here's a confession: I made so-so Viet vegetable curry for years, relying on fish sauce as a cheat but the flavor was off. Finally, I developed this stellar vegan version. It employs the Indian method of browning fried onion to craft a flavorful base. Garlic and ginger lend zip; tomato, fresh mushrooms, and MSG add savory notes. Tofu soaks up all the flavors. Serve this alluring curry with baguette and a salad, or rice and leafy greens. Use leftovers for tacos.

Pan-fry the tofu

Cut the tofu into 1-inch cubes. Season with a mounded ¼ tsp salt, transfer to a dish towel, and let drain for 10 to 15 minutes.

Set a 12-inch nonstick or carbon-steel skillet over medium-high heat and add 1 Tbsp of the neutral oil. Meanwhile, pat the moisture from the tofu (I use a dry area of the dish towel). When the oil ripples, add the tofu and cook for 5 to 6 minutes, turning frequently to brown on two or three sides. Set aside to cool.

Cook the aromatics and simmer the curry

Set a 3-qt saucepan over medium-high heat and add the remaining 2 Tbsp neutral oil. When the oil barely ripples, add the onion and a sprinkling of salt and cook, stirring, for about 5 minutes, until richly browned. Turn the heat to medium, then add the ginger, garlic, lemongrass, curry powder, MSG (if using), and cayenne. Stir for about 30 seconds, until fragrant. Add the tomato, mushrooms, and ½ tsp salt. Cover and cook for 5 minutes, stirring often. The mixture will condense to half its original volume; splash in water if things stick.

Add 1 cup of the coconut milk, re-cover, and lower the heat to a simmer for 5 minutes. Add the pan-fried tofu and water to barely cover the solids. Simmer gently, uncovered, for 5 minutes. Turn off the heat and gently stir in the remaining ⅓ cup coconut milk; let the curry rest for 10 minutes, uncovered.

Tweak, garnish, and serve

Taste the curry and season with additional salt, if needed; splash in water if the flavors are too strong. Stir in 3 Tbsp of the cilantro, transfer to a serving bowl, and crown with the remaining 1 Tbsp cilantro. Serve immediately.

1½ oz dried shiitake mushrooms rehydrated in 3¾ cups water

12 oz large cremini or white mushrooms (choose the biggest ones available)

1 Tbsp Maggi Seasoning sauce, Bragg Liquid Aminos, or soy sauce, plus more as needed

3 Tbsp neutral oil (such as canola or peanut)

¾ cup finely chopped shallots or yellow onion

3 Tbsp minced peeled ginger

1 Tbsp minced garlic

2 large lemongrass stalks, trimmed, cut into 3-inch lengths, and bruised with a meat mallet or a heavy saucepan (see page 44)

1 tsp Chinese five-spice powder

¼ to ½ tsp cayenne pepper (use the maximum amount for a tinge of heat)

2 star anise (16 robust points)

1 bay leaf (optional)

1 cup canned crushed tomatoes

2½ Tbsp fish sauce (store-bought or vegan version, page 29), plus more as needed

1 lb carrots, scrubbed or peeled, then cut into ¾-inch chunks

2 (15-oz) cans cannellini or great Northern white beans (see Note), drained and rinsed

½ cup hand-torn basil (Thai is best), Vietnamese coriander, mint, or cilantro leaves

Nấm với Đậu Trắng Nấu Kiểu Bò Kho

Bò Kho–Style Mushroom and White Bean Stew

I adore bò kho, the southern Vietnamese beef stew with carrots, lemongrass, and star anise, but after years of making and eating it, I realized that the bò (beef) did not hugely define the classic. Yes, meat adds protein and umami, but vegetables—aromatics, spices, tomato, and carrot—are what shape the braise's distinctive taste. Given that, this recipe applies the bò kho flavors to creamy beans and an umami-laden fungus duo (dried shiitakes and fresh cremini) to create a hearty main that holds its own against the beefy original. Recipe tester Terri Tanaka verified my claim through a friend, who ate this beany dish without knowing its intent to imitate and remarked that it tasted like Viet beef stew from a restaurant.

I use canned beans to make this stew fast; see the Note for DIY options. Serve with a baguette, rice, or a grain of your choice (try grits) to soak up the sauce. Add a salad or steamed-sautéed greens with butter, and dinner is done.

Prep the mushrooms

Squeeze each shiitake to expel excess water, letting the liquid drip back into the soaking vessel; decant (or strain) the liquid into a 1-qt liquid measuring cup. As needed, add or remove water to make 3 cups and set aside. Quarter the shiitakes through their stems and put in a bowl. Halve the cremini mushrooms through their stems, transfer to a second bowl, and toss with Maggi.

Set a 5- or 6-qt Dutch oven over medium-high heat and add 1 Tbsp of the neutral oil. When the oil ripples, add the cremini cut-side down and cook, undisturbed, for about 3 minutes, or until browned and slightly softened. Stir, turn off the heat, and scoop the mushrooms into the bowl of shiitakes.

Make the base, simmer, and serve

Add the remaining 2 Tbsp neutral oil to the hot pan, then stir in the shallots, ginger, garlic, and lemongrass. Turn the heat to medium and cook, stirring often, for 2 to 3 minutes, until the mixture is soft and sweetly fragrant (browned bits are fine).

A long rehydration (at least 6 hours) ensures that the shiitakes and their soaking liquid develop superb savors. See page 16 for details on selecting good-quality dried mushrooms, the stew's star.

Stir the five-spice powder, cayenne, star anise, and bay leaf (if using) into the lemongrass mixture and cook for about 15 seconds, until aromatic, then add the mushroom soaking water, tomatoes, fish sauce, shiitakes, cremini, and carrots. Raise the heat to bring to a soft boil, then lower to a simmer. Cover and cook for about 20 minutes, or until the carrots are nearly tender (poke with a knife tip to test).

Retrieve the star anise (it gets difficult to find later) and then stir in the beans. Return to a simmer and continue cooking, uncovered, for 10 minutes longer, or until the carrots are fully tender. Turn off the heat, partially cover, and let the stew rest for 10 minutes to further develop flavor. If it's too thick, add water. Taste the stew, and, if needed, add additional fish sauce or Maggi for more savory depth. Divide among shallow bowls or plates and shower with the basil. Serve immediately.

Note

Ingredients To replace canned beans, use 3½ cups cooked beans (start with 8 oz dried cannellini or great Northern beans). Feel free to use other kinds of beans.

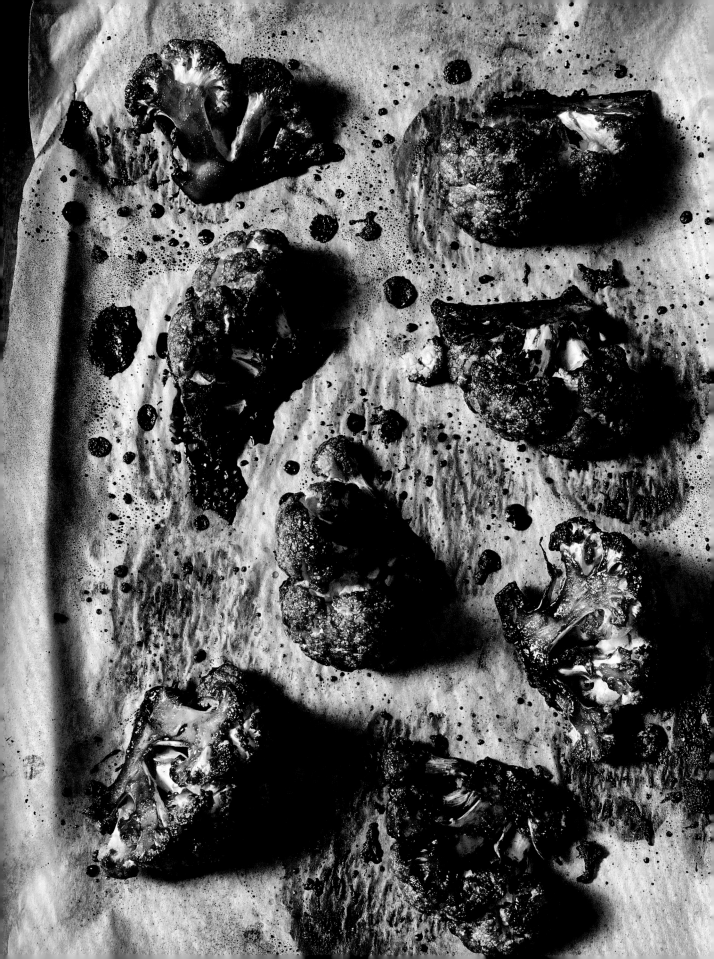

2-lb head cauliflower

3 Tbsp hoisin sauce

2 Tbsp toasted sesame oil

1 Tbsp agave syrup or mild honey

Scant 1 Tbsp ketchup

1½ tsp soy sauce

2 garlic cloves, minced and mashed or put through a garlic press

¼ tsp Chinese five-spice powder

Bông Cải Trắng Nướng Vị Xá Xíu

Char Siu Roasted Cauliflower

In tropical Vietnam, cauliflower is a prized cool-weather crop that's typically stir-fried, added to soup, or pickled. Home ovens are uncommon in Vietnam, so few people roast cauliflower. In my California kitchen, however, I coat cauliflower wedges in salty-sweet-spicy seasonings typically reserved for Cantonese-style char siu barbecue pork, and then high-heat roast them. The contours of the wedges caramelize here and there to develop a deep savoriness that evokes the prized edges and corners of char siu pork. Serve this cauliflower as a satisfying main dish or tuck it into bao (see page 117) and banh mi (see page 128).

Cut the cauliflower

Position a rack in the middle of the oven and preheat to 450°F. Line a rimmed baking sheet with parchment paper.

Pull off or cut away large leaves from the cauliflower, saving them for soup or broth, if you like. Trim a slice from the core end, where it's likely discolored. While holding the cauliflower at a comfortable angle, curved-side down, insert your knife tip into the core. As you push the knife in farther, gently rock the blade side to side and back and forth. In a few seconds, the cauliflower head should crack and naturally break into two halves (mine are always uneven).

Now, cut each half into four wedges, each no thicker than 3 inches on the uneven floret side. (Hold the cauliflower flat-side or curved-side down, whichever is more comfortable. Cut an additional wedge only if you must.) Using a dish towel, dry the wedges so they'll absorb the seasonings well.

(CONTINUED)

Cutting cauliflower into wedges (instead of steaks) is initially tricky, but it minimizes waste.

For a hoisin substitute, see the Note on page 119.

Season and roast

In a big bowl, stir together the hoisin sauce, sesame oil, agave syrup, ketchup, soy sauce, garlic, and five-spice powder. Add the cauliflower wedges and, using a big spoon or spatula, stir to coat well. Most of the seasonings should adhere. Spread the wedges out onto the prepared baking sheet, cut-side down. Drizzle or smear any remaining seasoning from the bowl onto the wedges.

Roast the cauliflower for 15 minutes, use tongs to turn over the wedges, and then roast for 10 minutes longer. Liquid will appear on the pan. Continue roasting for 10 to 15 minutes, during which the liquid will concentrate, bubble, and thicken. As that happens, use the tongs or a spatula to flip the cauliflower pieces about three times so they pick up the seasonings. When done, the cauliflower should look richly browned and be tender yet slightly chewy. A knife tip pierced into the thickest core areas usually meets a little resistance. The total roasting time is about 40 minutes.

To get a slightly deeper color and flavor, keep the baking sheet in its place and switch on the broiler for about 60 seconds, monitoring carefully to avoid burning. Remove the cauliflower from the oven and let it rest a few minutes to develop flavor before serving.

2 (20-oz) cans young jackfruit, drained

¼ cup hoisin sauce

2 Tbsp soy sauce or tamari (tamari is good for rich color)

1 Tbsp toasted sesame oil

2 to 3 tsp Viet Chile Sauce (page 39) or sriracha (use the maximum amount for edgy heat)

1½ to 2 Tbsp brown sugar (light or dark), agave syrup, or mild honey

½ tsp Chinese five-spice powder

¼ tsp garlic powder

⅛ tsp recently ground white or black pepper

2 Tbsp neutral oil (such as canola or peanut)

¼ cup chopped shallots or yellow onion

1 cup water

Fine sea salt

For a hoisin substitute, see the Note on page 119.

For tender-firm texture, choose an Asian brand of young jackfruit in brine, such as Aroy-D. Non-Asian brands, such as Trader Joe's, produce a softer, fall-apart texture.

Mít Non Xé Vị Xá Xíu

Char Siu Pulled Jackfruit

Asian-style barbecue "pulled pork" from young jackfruit? Yes! I imbue immature jackfruit chunks with the savory-sweet seasonings of Cantonese char siu pork and add touches of chile sauce and shallot. The result is salty-sweet-spicy and great for grain bowls, fried rice (see page 67), banh mi (as pictured on page 129), and steamed or baked bao (see pages 113 and 121).

Prep and flavor the jackfruit

Halve each wedge of jackfruit into two skinnier wedges. Then, by the handful, give them a squeeze to expel excess moisture and gently crush the pieces (don't mind the garlic clove–like seeds that appear). Set aside.

In a large bowl, combine the hoisin sauce, soy sauce, sesame oil, chile sauce, 1½ Tbsp of the brown sugar, five spice powder, garlic powder, and pepper. Taste and, if needed, add up to the remaining 1½ tsp sugar for a sweeter flavor.

Cook and pull the jackfruit

Set a 12-inch nonstick skillet over medium heat and add the neutral oil. When the oil barely ripples, add the shallots and fry gently, stirring, for 2 to 3 minutes, until soft and fragrant, with many browned bits. Add the jackfruit and scrape in all the seasonings. Let fry gently for 1 to 2 minutes to develop flavor (it will slightly darken), and then pour in the water.

Turn the heat to high, bring to a strong simmer, and then lower the heat to maintain the steady bubbling action. Cook for 5 to 8 minutes, stirring often and, if needed, pressing on big pieces to break them up. When the jackfruit is done, it will be moist and the liquid mostly gone. Turn off the heat and let cool for 5 minutes. Use two forks to pull and mash the fringelike pieces apart; leave meaty chunks for texture and stir to distribute. Let rest for 10 minutes for the flavors to settle and develop. Taste and add salt, if needed, before serving.

Note

Lifespan Refrigerate for up to 5 days. Warm in a skillet with a splash of water.

16-oz package
super-firm tofu

3 Tbsp white or brown
rice flour

Fine sea salt

¼ cup Vegan Sate Sauce
(page 40)

1½ Tbsp fish sauce (store-
bought or vegan version,
page 29), Maggi Seasoning
sauce, Bragg Liquid Aminos,
or soy sauce

2 Tbsp neutral oil (such as
canola or peanut)

4 garlic cloves, minced

¾ tsp paprika, or a
combination of ½ tsp paprika
and ¼ tsp cayenne pepper

2 green onions, white
and green parts, cut as
thick rings

⅓ cup unsalted roasted
peanuts or cashews

1 large Persian cucumber, or
½ small English cucumber,
thickly sliced

Đồ Chua Pickle (page 56),
Racy Pickled Fennel
(page 58), or Pickled Shallots
(page 57) for serving

Đậu Hũ Bằm Xào Sốt Sa Tế
Spicy Sate Tofu Crumbles

Whether you're a tofu lover or skeptic, you'll likely enjoy these deeply savory, slightly feisty meaty tofu nubs. Their boldness mostly comes from Vegan Sate Sauce, which is loaded with lemongrass, briny umami, and edgy heat.

Serve the crumbles with rice plus refreshing cucumber slices and pickles. Add steamed or stir-fried vegetables for a healthful meal. Or, as recipe tester Alyce Gershenson's husband did—enjoy them all on their own.

Crumble and season the tofu
Blot the tofu dry with a dish towel, then cut or break it into approximately 1-inch chunks. Over the sink, in batches of one or two chunks, give them a squeeze with one hand to slightly mush them. If excess water comes out, flick it into the sink. (Instead of using bare hands, you may re-use the dish towel to squeeze and crush the tofu.) Using your fingers, crumble the tofu into smaller pieces that resemble very coarsely ground meat (think chili grind and expect some tiny bits too); drop the tofu into a large bowl as you work.

Sprinkle the rice flour and ½ tsp salt onto the tofu, then stir and toss to coat well. Mix in the sate sauce and fish sauce, then let sit for 5 minutes.

Fry the crumbles and serve
In a 12-inch nonstick or carbon-steel skillet over medium heat, warm the neutral oil, garlic, and paprika. After sizzling for about 30 seconds and the garlic smells wonderful, add the seasoned tofu and give things a stir. Soon after sizzling resumes, lower the heat slightly and cook for about 10 minutes, stirring frequently with a spatula. As the tofu cooks, the jagged pieces cohere to resemble bumpy clusters of ground meat; scrape the spatula against the pan's rim to return any sticking bits to the mixture. The tofu will darken and brown, depending on the liquid seasoning chosen (fish sauce yields a lighter finish than the others, but any of them will look good). Cook until the crumbles are well seasoned; sneak a taste, but know that the results will be saltier when fully finished.

Stir in the green onions and peanuts. Once the green onions soften, about 1 minute, remove from the heat. Let cool for 5 minutes, taste, and if needed, add salt. Transfer to a plate or shallow bowl and serve with the cucumber and pickle.

> Super-firm tofu yields a fabulous meatlike texture that will wow vegetarians and non-vegetarians alike. Don't be tempted to use extra-firm tofu. The firmness difference matters. See page 22 for sourcing tips.

2 (14- or 16-oz) packages extra-firm tofu, water poured off

Fine sea salt

About 4½ Tbsp neutral oil (such as canola or peanut)

2½ oz chopped lemongrass (see page 44)

¼ cup chopped shallot

1 large Fresno or other medium-hot red chile, coarsely chopped

1 tsp granulated sugar, plus more as needed

¼ tsp MSG, or ½ tsp Asian mushroom seasoning (optional, great for oomph)

¼ tsp ground turmeric

3 Tbsp soy sauce

1½ Tbsp agave syrup, mild honey, or granulated sugar

2 to 3 Tbsp fresh lime juice

Đậu Hũ Chiên Sả Ớt
Twice-Fried Lemongrass Tofu

When I first encountered this tofu dish at a Ho Chi Minh City brewhouse, I didn't know what to make of the mountain of lemongrass bits atop giant scored slabs of deep-fried tofu. I expected old-school cubed tofu in a lemongrass-y stir-fry, but the dish was brash and fun, dipped in soy sauce and nibbled with fresh herbs. Viet food evolves quickly and keeps me guessing.

Back in California, I re-created the dish with pan-fried tofu, stuffing a savory-spicy lemongrass mixture into the score marks and frying the remainder for a fuzzy reddish-hued topping. A touch of MSG brings the mixture together, so I urge you to try it (or its mushroom seasoning kin) in this dish, which can be prepped in advance for easy weeknight meals (see Note). Frying twice yields crispy tofu that's perfect for rice plates, bún rice noodle salads, and even snacking with beer. My skeptical mother ate two slabs at dinner and welcomed the leftovers too.

Cut, season, and pan-fry the tofu
Cut each block of tofu into four rectangular slabs, each about 1 inch thick. (If the tofu was packaged as two blocks per pound, halve each one.) Arrange the eight pieces in a gridlike fashion on a dish towel, season all over with 1 tsp salt, and drain for 15 to 20 minutes. Pat the moisture from the tofu slabs (I use a dry area of the dish towel). Use a knife to score the top of each slab on the diagonal or crosswise, cutting ¼ inch deep and spacing each cut about ⅜ inch apart.

Set a 12-inch nonstick or carbon-steel skillet over medium-high heat and add a brimming 1 Tbsp of the neutral oil. When the oil ripples, add four tofu slabs, scored-side down. Using two thin spatulas, flip the slabs and pan-fry for 3 to 4 minutes per side, until golden and crisp. If you want to avoid an ice-cream-sandwich look, fry the long sides for about 1 minute each. Repeat with the remaining tofu, adding more oil. Let cool on a plate or a small baking sheet for about 10 minutes, or cool completely if cooking in advance.

(CONTINUED)

> To ensure sufficient lemongrass-y results, prep five medium or four hefty stalks and then weigh the result for this recipe. Save any overage for another dish.

Make the lemongrass mixture and dipping sauce

Meanwhile, use a small food processor to mince the lemongrass. Add the shallot and chile, then process to a minced texture. Scrape into a bowl, then season with ½ tsp salt, the sugar, and MSG (if using). Taste to verify a savory, slightly sweet flavor; if you didn't use MSG, you'll need additional salt and sugar. Make any adjustments as needed before adding the turmeric.

In a small bowl, stir together the soy sauce and agave syrup, then add enough of the lime juice for tang. Set this dipping sauce aside.

Stuff the tofu, re-fry, and serve

Tofu tends to stick during frying, so run a dinner or butter knife along the score marks to ensure the cuts remain. Using the knife, stuff 2 tsp of the lemongrass mixture into the cuts of each tofu slab (some lemongrass usually remains on top). Reserve the remaining lemongrass mixture.

Return the 12-inch skillet to medium heat and add 1 Tbsp neutral oil. When the oil ripples, re-fry the tofu in batches, stuffed-side down, for about 2 minutes, until crisp. Turn the tofu slabs and fry for about 2 minutes longer to crisp the other side. Transfer to a serving platter.

Add the remaining 1½ Tbsp neutral oil and reserved lemongrass mixture to the skillet and cook for about 5 minutes, stirring constantly, until it turns fragrant, dark reddish brown, and somewhat dry and crisp. Let cool off the heat for a few minutes to further crisp and dry, then spoon the mixture onto the tofu slabs. Serve with the soy-agave sauce and invite diners to drizzle it on.

Note

Timing Up to 5 days ahead, pan-fry the tofu and prep the raw lemongrass mixture. Refrigerate them in separate airtight containers and return to room temperature before stuffing and pan-frying.

TOFU BUTCHERING TIP

To cut straight and even tofu pieces, steady the tofu block with a flat hand, as pictured opposite. While that hand serves as a low wall and buttress for the tofu block to rest against, your other hand may wield the knife to cut tofu pieces. A tofu block can be wobbly, so fingertips do not provide enough support.

Veggie-Packed Mains

FOCUSING ON VEGETABLES DOES NOT MEAN cutting out meat altogether. When my family lived in Vietnam, my mom would purchase 100g (3½ oz) of animal protein to make a soup, stir-fry, or other dish. Vegetables were usually included in such dishes, so the meat was a costar or supporting actor. If meat played a prominent role in a main dish, her grocery list specified 300g (10½ oz). We were a household of eight people. How well fed were we? In a developing country, I was the rare chubby kid at whom adults marveled.

Among the keys to our low-meat lifestyle was cutting proteins into bite-size pieces. In this chapter, the daikon and pork belly, caramel chicken with mushrooms, and gingery beef and vegetable stir-fry illustrate how moderate amounts of animal protein partner with vegetables to create deliciousness. Spices and aromatics add excitement to those dishes, so you don't miss having a large amount of meat on your plate. Ginger and garlic punch up the seared salmon cubes for a pescatarian take on iconic shaking beef. The resulting main-dish salad is lighter and as equally thrilling as the conventional version.

To echo the Viet knack for making a little meat go a long way, I extend ground beef with tofu and season it boldly for a lower-meat take on lá lốt (wild pepper leaf) rolls. You can make that dish with ground-meat substitutes if you like, because the showstopper is the leaf encasing the rolls. When cooked, lá lốt exudes remarkable aroma and flavor. The oven-baked Vietnamese "meatloaf" also gets an assist from tofu, but in two forms: silken tofu and fermented tofu. Glass noodles, made from mung bean starch, absorb all the seasonings and bulk up the mixture during cooking.

Reaching back to memories of my mother using one whole chicken for many meals, as well as my friends at the Red Boat Fish Sauce company chopping up a whole chicken to serve about a dozen people, I crafted a delectable weeknight roast chicken dinner that's finished with nước chấm and fresh herbs. Cutting the chicken off the bone (practice Thanksgiving carving all year long!) allows the flesh to absorb the sauce.

For a salad-y one-dish meal, make the pan-fried turmeric fish rice-noodle salad, my relaxed version of a complex Hanoi classic. Or, wing it by turning a main dish, such as the beef stir-fry, roast chicken, or grilled lá lốt rolls, into bún noodle salad. The template-style recipe offers parameters for you to build your own from recipes in this book and beyond.

VIET MENU PLANNING

A traditional Viet dinner—of the kind that super-human cooks such as my mother served nightly—consists of a quickie canh soup, a salad or vegetable side, and a main dish, plus rice. It sounds hard to pull off, but the rice is often reheated in the microwave. The soup could be left over from the day before!

In my home, the soup is often loaded with veggies to go along with a vegetarian or vegetable-forward side. If making soup isn't in the cards, I serve the main with a cooked side vegetable (or salad), a pile of pickles from the Pantry chapter, or thickly sliced cucumber.

Noodle soups, noodle salads, or banh mi may be served alone or with a snack or salad for a more substantial meal. Some foods, such as the veganized Hainan chicken rice (see page 72) and Huế rice crepes (see page 81) are wonderful one-dish projects.

When entertaining, I often go for the whole shebang: stand-up snacks with drinks; followed by a sit-down meal of soup or salad, main dish, side vegetable, and rice; and then conclude with fresh fruit, plus a couple sweets.

Vietnamese cuisine isn't about following rules as much as it is about considering parameters. You can bend or break the rules as long as you understand the foundation of Viet foodways—mix and match to blur borders and create cross-cultural menus. Vietnamese food wouldn't be where it is today if cultures didn't mingle.

1⅓-lb center-cut salmon fillet, skin removed and reserved (see Note)

Fine sea salt

Recently ground black pepper

2½ tsp toasted sesame oil

2 tsp minced peeled fresh ginger

1 large garlic clove, minced

1 Tbsp granulated sugar, agave syrup, or mild honey, plus 2 tsp

1 tsp cornstarch

1½ Tbsp soy sauce

1½ tsp fish sauce (store-bought or vegan version, page 29)

¼ cup thinly sliced red onion or shallot

1½ Tbsp unseasoned rice vinegar

2 Tbsp water or neutral oil (such as canola or peanut; choose water for a brighter salad flavor, oil for a richer outcome)

5 to 6 cups lightly packed spring baby lettuce mix or watercress

⅓ cup hand-torn dill, mint, basil, shiso, or a combination

6 to 8 cherry tomatoes or small red radishes, halved

1½ Tbsp white or brown rice flour

1½ Tbsp neutral oil (such as canola or peanut)

Cá Hồi Lúc Lắc
Shaking Salmon

I've shaken cubes of beefsteak and tofu for this iconic Vietnamese main dish salad, so why not fish? Tuna tended to be too lean, and delicate white fish was too flaky, but rich-tasting salmon was just right. I removed the skin so that the salmon cubes would cook up better. I didn't want to waste the skin—a tasty (and pricey) part of the fish—so I baked it into crisp chips to serve with the dish. (If the skin's fishiness isn't for you, discard the skin and skip the prep step.) Coating the salmon cubes in rice flour enables easy searing. Ginger adds a spritely bite to the garlicky, peppery sauce.

In Vietnamese, this warm-cool salad is quirkily named for how the featured protein is cut as large cubes that resemble hột lúc lắc (playing dice). Because *lúc lắc* means "to shake" and that action is involved in cooking the dish, "shaking" became part of the charming English-language translation. No matter what it's called, this salad-y main is great on its own or with a side of rice.

Cut the salmon and make the chips
Preheat the oven or toaster oven to 375°F. Line a small baking sheet with parchment paper or aluminum foil.

Cut the salmon flesh into ¾- to 1-inch cubes and set on a plate. Cut the reserved salmon skin into ¾-inch-wide strips about 3 inches long. Season with a few pinches of salt and pepper and then coat with 1 tsp of the sesame oil. Arrange the skin strips, shinier scale-side up, on the foil.

Bake the salmon skin for 12 to 18 minutes, or until sizzling and crisp (expect oil to pool in the pan). The cooking time depends on the strips' thickness; monitor and remove them as they're done to avoid burning. Transfer to a plate, leaving the oil behind, and let cool completely.

(CONTINUED)

Select a salmon fillet that's about 1 inch thick in the middle; ask the fishmonger to remove the skin if you don't want to do it yourself.

Mix the seasoning sauce and ready the salad

Meanwhile, in a small bowl, stir together the ginger, garlic, 1 Tbsp sugar, cornstarch, ½ tsp pepper, soy sauce, fish sauce, and remaining 1½ tsp sesame oil.

Rinse the onion in a strainer under cold running water for about 10 seconds, then set aside. In a large bowl (suitable for tossing the salad), whisk together the remaining 2 tsp sugar, ⅛ tsp salt, ⅛ tsp pepper, vinegar, and water. Add the onion and top with the lettuce, herbs, and tomatoes. Don't toss yet.

Cook the salmon, toss the salad, and serve

Lightly coat the cubed salmon with the rice flour. Set by the stove with the ginger-garlic seasoning sauce.

Set a 12-inch skillet (I favor carbon steel for its heat conduction) over high heat and add the neutral oil. When the oil ripples, add the salmon and cook, gently turning and tossing it, for about 3 minutes, until the fish is nearly cooked through. To test for doneness, poke the flesh; it should give a bit and the interior should look opaque.

Lower the heat slightly, pour in the seasoning sauce, and cook briefly, tossing and gently stirring, for about 30 seconds to cloak the salmon in the sauce. Remove the pan from the heat and let rest and cool for a few minutes.

Meanwhile, toss the salad, transfer everything (including the dressing lingering at the bottom of the bowl) to a platter or shallow serving bowl, and then top with the cooked salmon and skin chips. Serve immediately, inviting diners to combine the salmon with the salad for a cool-warm finish. Or, ceremoniously combine the ingredients at the table and let diners dive in.

Notes

Ingredients If you skip the salmon skin, substitute crumbled sesame sticks for a rich crunch, if desired.

Technique To remove the skin from the salmon fillet, cut the fillet crosswise into approximately 3-inch-wide sections. Set the fillet skin-side down on the cutting board. Run your finger along the fillet's thicker edge to open a gap between the flesh and skin. Slide a knife (boning, fillet, or chef's) into the gap. Working with the knife nearly parallel to the cutting board, angle the blade downward to cut the skin away from the flesh. When there's enough detached skin, hold on to it to keep the fillet in place and provide slight tension to guide the blade as you saw the knife all the way through to the other edge. When you're done, if you like, flip the skin over and scrape any loose scales off from the shiny side.

TURMERIC FISH

4 (5-oz) mild-tasting fish fillets (branzino, barramundi, trout, tilapia, catfish, or cod)

¾ tsp ground turmeric

¼ tsp ground ginger or galangal

2 tsp fermented shrimp paste or anchovy paste (optional, see Note)

¾ tsp or 1 Tbsp fish sauce (store-bought or vegan version, page 29)

2 Tbsp sour cream (dairy-free, if preferred) or mayonnaise (see pages 48 to 49)

———

6 to 8 oz small, dried round rice noodles (bún or maifun), or 10 to 12 oz rice capellini

6 to 8 cups baby lettuce mix or chopped or hand-torn lettuce

1½ to 2 cups hand-torn or coarsely chopped mixed fresh herbs (such as cilantro, mint, and Vietnamese shiso or balm)

About ½ cup white or brown rice flour

5 to 6 Tbsp neutral oil (such as canola or peanut), plus more as needed

½ cup chopped fresh dill fronds

3 green onions, white and green parts, chopped

1 cup Nước Chấm Dipping Sauce (page 32) or Fermented Shrimp Sauce (see variation, page 33)

⅔ cup unsalted roasted peanuts or cashews

1 cup plain or sesame rice crackers, or 2 toasted Vietnamese rice crackers (optional)

Chả Cá Hà Nội Chiên

Crispy Pan-Fried Turmeric Fish Noodle Salad

One of my favorite northern Vietnamese dishes is chả cá, a Hanoi classic involving grilling and tumbling turmeric-stained fish pieces in sizzling dill and green onions. The fish is enjoyed as a DIY meal, in which diners fashion small, personal bowls of fish, rice noodles, lettuce, herbs, peanuts, and rice crackers, all dressed by a tangy, briny fermented-shrimp sauce. It's a stunning one-dish meal but also a production involving lots of dishware. Wanting to streamline the cooking and presentation but keep some pizazz, I pan-fry crispy fish fillets that have been coated in coarse, stone-ground rice flour. Employing sour cream and ground spices (instead of the old-school fermented rice mash and freshly grated aromatics) minimizes moisture to enable easier pan-frying. Presenting the dish as a big salad encourages eating more lettuce and herbs too. Does my rendition stray too far from the classic? In Hanoi, chefs have served chả cá tacos and risotto. I think I'm good.

Marinate the fish

Using a paper towel, blot excess moisture from the fish and then put the fish on a plate or a small baking sheet. In a small bowl, stir together the turmeric, ginger, fermented shrimp paste (if using), and ¾ tsp fish sauce (use 1 Tbsp if you omit the shrimp paste). Mix in the sour cream to enrich everything. Using a small spatula, spread the sauce onto the fish and turn to coat all over. Cover and let sit for up to 1 hour at room temperature while you prep the remaining ingredients and ready the salad.

Set up the salads

Bring a 3- to 4-qt pot of unsalted water to a boil over high heat. Add the noodles and cook until tender-firm (the cooking time depends on the noodle and brand, so test to verify doneness). Drain the noodles in a colander, dump them back into the pot, and add cold water to cover. Swish for 30 to 60 seconds to quickly cool

(CONTINUED)

Skin-on fish fillets, when available, are extra-tasty. I keep a stash of frozen branzino, barramundi, and trout on hand to make this dish on a whim. Pan-fry a little longer if your fillets weigh more than what's suggested in the recipe.

When a nondairy sour cream is needed, I use a tofu-based one.

Details on Viet rice crackers can be found in the Note on page 190.

and release their starch, then re-drain. Set aside to cool to room temperature (they'll naturally get sticky). Divide the lettuce and herbs among four dinner plates or large soup or pasta bowls. Top with a layer of noodles and set near the stove.

Pan-fry the fish and aromatics, then assemble

Set a wire rack on a rimmed baking sheet. Sprinkle about ¼ cup of the rice flour on one end of a second, large rimmed baking sheet. Coat each fish fillet all over in the flour, adding more of the flour as needed. Place the coated fillets on the clean part of the baking sheet.

Set a 12-inch nonstick skillet over medium heat and add 2 to 3 Tbsp of the neutral oil to film the bottom of the pan. When the oil ripples, add two fish fillets, skin-side down, and let sizzle and fry for about 2 minutes, or until crisp, then use two spatulas to flip the fillets over. Tilt the pan, if needed, to evenly expose the fish to the hot oil and fry for 1 to 2 minutes longer, or until cooked through and crisp. Transfer the fried fillets to the prepared rack. As needed, replenish the oil before frying the remaining fillets.

Add the remaining 2 Tbsp neutral oil to the hot pan, then dump in the dill and green onions and swiftly stir for about 20 seconds, or just until they soften and turn fragrant. Remove from the heat.

Put a piece of warm fish atop each salad, skin- or flesh-side up. Top with the dill, green onions, and all the oil from the pan. Bring to the table and invite diners to dress the salad with the dipping sauce, adding nuts and crackers, breaking the crackers into small pieces for crunch, as they like. Eat with a fork and knife.

Notes

Ingredients Fermented shrimp paste (mắm tôm) is a salty umami bomb with a purplish, toothpaste texture. Just a little is needed to impart a funky, briny edge to food. Sold in jars at Chinese and Vietnamese markets in the condiment aisle (Lee Kum Kee's and Koon Chun's Fine Shrimp Sauce are good), it's traditionally used in chả cá marinade and for the sauce. Anchovy paste sold in tubes at mainstream supermarkets is an okay substitute. Or you may opt for fish sauce, as I also offer in the recipe.

Without ground ginger or galangal, substitute 1 tsp grated fresh ginger or galangal. The fish fries up slightly less crisp but still very tasty.

Variation If you skip the noodles and salad, serve the pan-fried fish with rice (regular or broken) and gingery nước chấm (see variation, page 33) for a zippy Fried Fish with Ginger Dipping Sauce. Mix the sauce into the rice too.

1¾-lb half-chicken (see Note), or 2-lb large chicken thighs or leg quarters

¼ cup chopped shallots or yellow onion

2 garlic cloves, chopped

1 tsp brown sugar (light or dark)

½ tsp recently ground black pepper

Fine sea salt

2 to 3 tsp fish sauce (store-bought or vegan version, page 29), plus more as needed

½ cup lightly packed chopped cilantro sprigs or another tender, fragrant fresh herb

3 Tbsp neutral oil (such as canola or peanut), plus more as needed

1 lb broccoli crowns, cut into florets with ½-inch-thick stem ends

¼ cup Nước Chấm Dipping Sauce base (see page 32)

1 Fresno or jalapeño chile, thinly sliced and seeded

About 1 tsp fresh lime juice, unseasoned rice vinegar, or unfiltered apple cider vinegar

⅓ cup mint leaves, torn if large

Gà Rô Ti

Roast Chicken and Broccoli with Nước Chấm Vinaigrette

When Viet cooks serve whole chicken, they often cut it into bone-in, bite-size pieces to feed a crowd. That's mainly because chicken is still considered a precious food, despite Vietnam's successful economy. Pondering such thriftiness, I began roasting half-chickens, carving them off the bone so diners may enjoy a bit of light and dark meat. The halfsies roasted faster than a whole bird and, moreover, I could easily shove herbaceous seasonings between the skin and flesh. My recipe evolved over time (I use the technique on chicken legs, too), and now I douse the roasted chicken with nước chấm enriched by the roasting pan juices. The sauce penetrates the flesh to imbue extra flavor and is fabulous on rice. Making the most of the oven's heat, I also roast broccoli. Space permitting, you can roast potatoes on a quarter-sheet pan; the timing is akin to that of the chicken.

Pound the seasoning paste and rub it in

Pat the chicken dry with paper towels and put it into an ovenproof skillet or low-sided roasting pan (or set it on a rimmed baking sheet lined with aluminum foil). Using a mortar and pestle, mash, pound, and stir together the shallots, garlic, brown sugar, pepper, and ¼ tsp salt until you achieve a rough wet paste. Add the fish sauce for a strong salty flavor. Stir in the cilantro. (Alternatively, use a small food processor to grind the aromatics and spices, then add the fish sauce and pulse in the herb.)

Using your fingers (or a spoon or a silicone spatula), loosen the chicken skin from the flesh; with the half chicken, you'll be stopped by the drumette and knees. Rub about one-fourth of the seasoning paste onto the underside of the chicken. Use the remaining paste to season the flesh under the skin; do your best to distribute the paste.

(CONTINUED)

What to do with the other half-chicken? Make the Chicken-Vegetable Pho on page 161.

For lovely browned skin, rub 1 to 2 tsp of the neutral oil on the skin (or skip that for a slightly crispier but paler finish). If you're roasting a half-bird, rub a little oil on the exposed breast flesh area where the bone once was. Regardless, finish by sprinkling ¼ tsp salt all over the skin. Let the chicken sit, uncovered, at room temperature.

Roast, sauce, and serve

Set oven racks in the middle and lowest positions and preheat the oven to 425°F. Line a baking sheet with parchment paper or a silicone mat. When the oven is ready, slide the chicken onto the middle rack and set a timer for 25 minutes. Meanwhile, toss the broccoli with 2 or 3 pinches of salt and about 2½ Tbsp neutral oil and transfer to the prepared baking sheet.

After roasting the chicken for 25 minutes, slide the broccoli onto the lower rack. Roast for 10 to 15 minutes more, until the chicken is browned with crisp skin, and the temperature registers 155°F on a meat thermometer inserted into the thickest part of the thigh; its juices should run relatively clear. Remove the chicken from the oven and let it sit at room temperature for 10 minutes. However, keep the oven on and move the broccoli to the middle rack to let it roast for 10 minutes more, or until the stems are just tender and the tops have brown patches.

As you like, cut the chicken into serving portions or carve it off the bone into large bite-size pieces. Arrange on a serving plate. Add the broccoli if there is space or put it on a separate dish.

In a small bowl, combine the nước chấm and chile. Scrape in the pan juices and stir to combine. Taste and spike it with lime juice for a bright note and fish sauce for saltiness. Pour about half of the sauce over the chicken and offer the remainder on the side. Sprinkle the mint all over the chicken and serve.

Note

Ingredients For the half-chicken approach, buy a whole chicken weighing roughly 4½ lb. Cut it in half, removing the backbone. If you want easier prep and carving, remove the breastbone and wishbone. A good butcher will do this for you, if you prefer.

12 oz boneless, skinless chicken thighs, cut into 1-inch chunks

Chubby 2-inch section fresh ginger, peeled, thinly sliced, and smashed with the flat side of a knife

3 Tbsp Caramel Sauce (page 34; or see Note)

2 Tbsp fish sauce (store-bought or vegan version, page 29), plus more as needed

¼ tsp fine sea salt

2 Tbsp neutral oil (such as canola or peanut)

¼ cup chopped shallots or yellow onion

12 oz king trumpet mushrooms, halved lengthwise and then cut crosswise into 1½-inch-thick pieces

½ cup water

2 green onions, green and white parts, cut into short lengths

Gà Kho Nấm Gừng

Caramel Chicken, Mushrooms, and Ginger

Much of Vietnamese cooking is based on simplicity, requiring just a few ingredients. This interpretation of a classic northern Viet kho, a broad range of homey dishes that are often simmered with caramel sauce, originally featured only chicken. For an easy, low-meat makeover, I went with a 50/50 combination of chicken thighs and king trumpet mushrooms, which are coincidentally called nấm đùi gà (chicken leg mushroom). During the quick simmering, the chicken releases its juices to create a sauce, which the mushrooms then absorb. The textural contrast between chicken and mushroom makes gà kho nấm gừng a more interesting dish than the original. Don't worry about all the ginger—it softens and mellows into the background to support the savory-sweet sauce with a hint of heat. Serve with lots of rice and the mixed vegetable stir-fry on page 195 or steamed veggies.

Season the chicken

Put the chicken and ginger in a bowl and add the caramel sauce, fish sauce, and salt. Stir to coat and keep near the stove.

Sauté, then simmer

Set a 2- to 3-qt saucepan over medium heat and add the neutral oil. When the oil begins to ripple, add the shallots and cook, stirring frequently for about 2 minutes, or until about half the pieces are golden. Add the mushroom pieces and cook for 1 to 2 minutes, until glistening. Add the marinated chicken and ginger, stir to combine, pour in the water, and stir again to distribute.

Cover the mixture and bring to a strong simmer. Stir again to circulate the ingredients, then replace the lid. Cook for 8 minutes, stirring occasionally to evenly expose the chicken and mushrooms to the sauce. Fragrant plumes of steam may shoot out from under the lid and the contents will boil vigorously. The sauce will increase in volume as the chicken releases its juices. If the contents threaten to boil over or the lid rattles, lower the heat.

After the 8 minutes, uncover and continue cooking for 3 to 5 minutes, until the sauce reduces and the color deepens to an attractive tan color. Remove from the heat, cover, and let rest for 5 minutes. Stir in the green onions so they slightly wilt in the steamy heat.

Taste, tweak, and serve

Try the sauce and, if needed, adjust the flavor with a dribble of fish sauce. Transfer to a serving bowl and serve immediately.

Notes

Ingredients If caramel sauce is not available, substitute a mixture of 1½ Tbsp agave syrup or mild honey, brimming 2 tsp molasses, and 1½ tsp vinegar (rice or distilled white).

Leftovers For a fast noodle-soup lunch, dilute leftovers with lightly salted chicken broth and water (use a 1-to-1 ratio). Bring to a boil, then add a handful of broccoli florets or sliced cabbage. When nearly cooked, drop in some instant ramen or glass noodles (soak them in hot water to soften and then snip). Or serve over boiled bún round rice noodles.

1⅓ lb daikon radish or turnips

10 oz lean pork belly (with or without skin) or fatty boneless pork shoulder

2½ Tbsp Caramel Sauce (page 34; or see Note for substitute)

1½ Tbsp fish sauce (store-bought or vegan version, page 29), plus more as needed

Fine sea salt

Recently ground black pepper

1 Tbsp neutral oil (such as canola or peanut)

2 Tbsp finely chopped shallots or yellow onion

1 Tbsp minced garlic

½ cup water, plus more as needed

1 or 2 Thai or small serrano chiles, or 1 small jalapeño or Fresno chile, stemmed and split lengthwise

Granulated sugar for balancing flavor

1 green onion, green part only, thinly sliced (optional)

8 oz Persian cucumbers, thickly sliced on the diagonal

Thịt Heo Kho Củ Cải

Peppery Caramel Pork and Daikon

After my siblings left for college, my parents and I shared meals loaded with old-timey (read: low-meat) dishes that they grew up with in Vietnam. Daikon simmered with fatty pork and savory-sweet caramel sauce was among them. I adored thịt heo kho củ cải for its punchy flavors—so much so that I made it after I moved out. It seemed like món ăn người nghèo (poor people's food) when compared to richer classics, such as pork belly simmered with eggs in caramel sauce, so I didn't include it in past cookbooks. Who wants food that signals awful times? But frankly, I crave and prepare this dish often because it's easy, comforting, and doesn't weigh me down. Daikon's earthy funk, pork's savoriness, and the bittersweet caramel sauce create layered flavors. Black pepper accented by fresh chile makes for a never-dull-moment main dish. Serve it with lots of rice to carry its flavors, plus cooling cucumber and a simple green vegetable, such as steamed-sautéed kale or Swiss chard.

Prep the daikon and pork

Peel the daikon, then quarter and cut crosswise into bite-size chunks (imagine fat cherries). Set aside.

Cut the pork into mini-domino-size pieces. If you're using pork belly, cut across the meat grain into 1- to 1¼-inch-wide rectangular chunks. Then slice the chunks across the grain into ¼-inch-thick pieces. (When using pork shoulder, do your best to cut it into similar-size pieces, each about ¼ inch thick. Try to get a little fat with the lean.) Transfer the pork to a bowl, then season with the caramel sauce, fish sauce, ½ tsp plus ⅛ tsp salt, and a mounded ½ tsp pepper.

Fry the aromatics and simmer

Set a 2- to 3-qt saucepan over medium heat and add the neutral oil. When the oil begins to ripple, add the shallots and garlic. Stir and cook for 1 to 2 minutes, until some pieces turn golden.

(CONTINUED)

Scrape the pork into the saucepan, stir in the water, and then raise the heat to bring to a vigorous simmer. Cover, lower the heat to continue simmering, and let cook for 10 minutes, stirring occasionally (scooch the heat down if steam poofs from under the lid).

Uncover the pan, add the daikon and chiles, stir, and re-cover. Return to a vigorous simmer and cook, stirring a few times, for 8 to 15 minutes, until the pork is firm-tender and the daikon are just tender. Test for doneness by poking a knife tip into a piece of pork and a large daikon chunk (turnip takes less time than daikon). If the sauce in the pan isn't rich or potent enough, let simmer, uncovered, for a few minutes to concentrate the liquid. Turn off the heat, cover, and let rest for 5 minutes to finish cooking and meld flavors.

De-fat, taste, and serve

If there's too much fat from the pork, tilt the pan and use a metal spoon to remove as much as you like; save it for other uses. Taste and, if the flavor seems wimpy, add a sprinkling of salt, fish sauce, pepper, and sugar to create a savory-spicy-sweet finish. If things are too salty or you just want more sauce, stir in water by the tablespoon (reheat to combine). Transfer the mixture to a shallow bowl, garnish with the green onion, if desired, and serve with the cucumbers on a separate plate.

Notes

Ingredients Daikon is firmer with a stronger bite than turnip. Choose specimens with fairly smooth skin, a sign that they didn't struggle to grow and aren't bitter.

When caramel sauce isn't available, substitute 1½ Tbsp agave syrup or mild honey, 2 tsp molasses, and 1 tsp vinegar (rice or distilled white); the color and flavor will be good but not as bright.

Instead of pork belly or shoulder, substitute an equal amount of ground pork (80 to 85 percent lean is ideal). As the meat initially cooks with the caramel sauce, mash it into bite-size nubs. Simmer with the seasonings for 5 minutes (instead of 10 minutes), covered, and then add the daikon. Continue as directed.

Timing If you're cooking ahead, after simmering the pork and daikon, partially cover, completely cool, and refrigerate for up to 3 days. De-fat before finishing.

1 (2-oz) bundle dried glass noodles (saifun and bean threads, see page 9)

1 Tbsp neutral oil (such as canola or peanut)

½ cup finely chopped shallots or yellow onion

8 oz ground pork or turkey or chicken dark-meat

1 (5-oz) package baby greens (such as spinach, kale, or power greens mix)

Fine sea salt

¾ tsp recently ground black pepper

¼ cup mashed white fermented tofu (see page 23), or 2 Tbsp fish sauce (store-bought or vegan version, page 29)

1 Tbsp white fermented-tofu brine (optional)

½ tsp granulated sugar (optional)

1 (16-oz) package silken tofu

2 large eggs

¼ tsp ground turmeric

6 to 8 bushy sprigs fresh herbs (such as mint, basil, or shiso; optional)

Chả Trứng Nướng

Vietnamese "Meatloaf"

Compared to jiggly, delicate Chinese and Japanese steamed eggs, Vietnamese chả trứng is sturdy, punchy, and studded with porky nubs and plump glassy noodles. It's traditionally steamed, but many modern cooks bake (nướng) it. No matter how it's prepared, its tender texture recalls a homey crustless quiche to me. Most people, however, describe it as Vietnamese meatloaf, perhaps because it's a beloved comfort food for all ages. Serve it with rice, đồ chua pickle (see page 56), and nước chấm (see page 32), or include it in a Saigon-style broken rice plate (see page 75). I enjoy the meatloaf with a green salad too.

Chả trứng typically gets its umami punch from a fermented condiment. In the main recipe, I season with chao (fermented tofu) or fish sauce, the former lending an alluring depth; see Notes for a third condiment option. I use silken tofu and baby leafy greens to cut down on the eggs and ground meat used. The tasty result bakes up to a marvelous tenderness without needing a water bath to mimic steaming. A mushroom-y vegetarian take is in the Notes.

Prep the noodles

Soak the noodles in hot water, messing them around for 30 to 45 seconds, until they just untangle and soften. Drain well and let them sit for 5 to 10 minutes to further soften and whiten. Using a cleaver, chef's knife, or scissors, cut and chop into pieces no longer than 1 inch. Transfer them to a medium bowl.

Cook the meat and greens

Meanwhile, place a rack in the middle position of the oven and preheat to 375°F. Lightly oil the interior of an 8-inch square baking pan (with at least 2-inch-high sides). For easy removal and cleanup, line the bottom and two sides with parchment paper, allowing about 1 inch of paper to hang over the pan rim.

(CONTINUED)

Set a 12-inch nonstick skillet over medium heat and add the neutral oil. When the oil barely ripples, add the shallots and cook gently, stirring, for 1 minute, or until they turn translucent. Add the pork, pressing it with a spatula to break it into small pieces (meaty bits should be distributed throughout the dish later). Then cook, stirring, for 1 to 2 minutes, until the pork is still a little pink. Add the greens and continue cooking, stirring, for 1 minute, or until the greens soften and the pork is completely cooked.

Remove the skillet from the heat and season the pork with ½ tsp salt, the pepper, and fermented tofu. Taste and, if necessary, add additional salt or the tofu brine to achieve a strong savoriness (nothing else is salted); if you want a slightly sweet roundness, add the sugar. Let the pork and greens cool until warmish, 5 to 10 minutes, before scraping into the noodle bowl.

Blitz the tofu and bake

Pour off any water from the silken tofu tub, then cut the tofu into large chunks. In a countertop or immersion blender, whirl the tofu, eggs, and turmeric into a buttery-yellow, smooth mixture. Scrape into the bowl of noodles and pork, stir to combine, and transfer to the prepared baking pan. Shimmy the pan to even out the meatloaf mixture.

Bake the meatloaf for 30 to 35 minutes, or until it is slightly puffed and dry to the touch, and a toothpick inserted in the middle comes out clean and barely damp. Let cool on a wire rack for 10 minutes before running a knife along the sides of the pan and lifting the paper to remove the meatloaf. Cut into wedges or squares. Enjoy hot, warm, or at room temperature, with the herbs as a refreshing side.

Notes

Ingredients Instead of chao, substitute 2½ Tbsp white (shiro) miso and 1½ Tbsp water for the tofu and brine. Or, opt out of a soy-based seasoning altogether by using 1½ to 2 Tbsp mắm nêm, an extra-funky, purple-gray, opaque fermented anchovy sauce sold in slender bottles at Chinese and Southeast Asian markets. Check near the regular fish sauce for the smallish bottles; their busy labels often confusingly say "SUPER," "Phú Quốc," or "Sài Gòn" so I choose at the upper price range for decent quality.

Technique If you're not using prewashed greens, wash and spin them to minimize moisture; as needed, chop into bite-size pieces.

Variation For Vegetarian Vietnamese "Meatloaf," omit the meat and instead use 8 oz chopped fresh cremini or white button mushrooms (include the stems). After adding them to the skillet, turn the heat to medium-high and cook for about 2 minutes, or until they're nearly half of their original volume. Add the greens and cook for about 1 minute longer, until just softened. Continue as directed.

10 oz well-trimmed top sirloin or another favorite beefsteak

¼ tsp baking soda (optional, for tenderness; see box, facing page)

3½ Tbsp water

2 tsp cornstarch

2 tsp brown sugar (light or dark), agave syrup, or mild honey

1½ tsp regular soy sauce, or 1 tsp dark soy sauce (the latter for dramatic color)

2½ tsp fish sauce (store-bought or vegan version, page 29)

1 tsp toasted sesame oil

3 Tbsp neutral oil (such as canola or peanut)

Generous 8 oz green beans or celery, trimmed and cut on the diagonal into 2- to 3-inch-long pieces

¼ tsp fine sea salt

6 oz large mushrooms (such as cremini, white button, shiitake, or a combo), quartered

Mounded ¼ cup finely slivered peeled fresh ginger

½ small red or yellow onion, cut into medium crescents

3 garlic cloves, finely chopped

2 Fresno or jalapeño chiles, stemmed, seeded, and cut on the diagonal into 2- to 3-inch-long pieces

Rau Xào Thịt Bò và Gừng

Gingery Vegetable and Beef Stir-Fry

Beef and ginger are a classic stir-fry pairing, and many Viet recipes feature them with some green onions added. To tilt the balance toward vegetables, plus add texture and flavor, I include mushrooms and green beans. The mushrooms lend luxurious earthiness and pick up the beefy flavors well. Fried-ginger frizzles crown this stir-fry for a burst of pungent sweet heat. Serve with rice and add a canh-style soup or salad for a great meal. Or top a bún rice noodle salad (see page 256) with this stir-fry to make bún bò xào.

Marinate the beef

Thinly slice the beef across the grain into strips, each about 3 inches long, 1 inch wide, and a scant ¼ inch thick. If you're using the baking soda, in a medium bowl, dissolve it in 1½ Tbsp of the water. Add the beef and massage the liquid into the meat, which will get slippery. Add the cornstarch, sugar, soy sauce, fish sauce, and sesame oil and, using chopsticks or a fork, mix well. Cover and let marinate for at least 15 minutes (I've left it for 1 hour!).

Stir-fry the vegetables

Organize the remaining ingredients by the stove for smooth cooking. Set a 14-inch wok or 12-inch nonstick or carbon-steel skillet over high heat on one of your largest burners and swirl in 1 Tbsp of the neutral oil. When the oil ripples, add the green beans. Using a slotted spoon, swiftly stir and toss them for about 30 seconds to heat through. Sprinkle in ⅛ tsp of the salt and splash in the remaining 2 Tbsp water. Turn the heat to medium-high, cover, and let steam-cook for 1 minute, until the beans brighten in color but are still crisp.

Uncover the pan, dump in the mushrooms, season with the remaining ⅛ tsp salt, and stir-fry for about 1 minute, until both vegetables have slightly softened. Scoop out onto a plate.

Prep a chubby 2-inch section of ginger to yield enough for this recipe.

Instead of a spatula, stir-fry with a slotted spoon to efficiently manage the fried ginger without dirtying another tool.

Fry the aromatics and beef, then assemble

Add the remaining 2 Tbsp neutral oil and ginger slivers to the hot pan and turn the heat to medium. As things sizzle, stir constantly to gently fry the ginger for 2 to 3 minutes, until the slivers resemble nearly crisp wisps and are mostly golden (golden-brown bits are fine). Remove the pan from the heat and gather and scoot the ginger onto a small plate to cool and crisp, leaving the oil in the pan.

Set the pan over high heat and add the onion, garlic, and chiles. Stir-fry for 1 minute, until fragrant, and then move the aromatics to one side of the pan. Add the marinated beef, spreading the strips in a single layer and pushing the aromatics up the wall of the pan, if needed. Let the beef sear for 1 minute, until most of its edges have changed color, then flip and swiftly stir-fry for 1 minute, or until the strips have nearly cooked through (some lingering redness is ideal).

Return the green beans and mushrooms to the pan along with any juices. Stir-fry for about 1 minute, or until hot and cooked through. Remove from the heat and transfer to a large plate. Crown with the fried ginger and serve.

Note

Variation You can swap chicken breast or, as recipe tester Johanna Nevitt suggests, shrimp for the steak.

WHY STIR-FRY WITH BAKING SODA?

Decades ago, a Viet-Chinese chef told my sister, Yenchi, that massaging sliced beef with water was how he achieved a tender, slippery texture in his on-point stir-fries. Naive and curious me tried his technique and got only firm, dryish results. I'd seen Chinese stir-fry recipes call for baking soda in the marinade, but that could add a metallic taste and not have much impact on texture. One day, I put the ideas together, diluting baking soda in water and massaging that solution into sliced beef before adding other seasonings. The beef retained its moisture better during stir-frying and, even with lean cuts such as London broil, it came out luscious and special-tasting. The beef was more tender than usual, with a silkiness as if I'd velveted (flash-fried) the meat.

My idea wasn't original but, rather, floating in the zeitgeist. According to *Cook's Illustrated*, the baking soda solution increases the pH on the meat's surface, which prevents proteins from bonding too much during cooking, thus leaving the meat on the tender side. I use the soda trick mostly on beef and chicken, although I've seen mid-twentieth-century Chinese recipes call for soaking seafood in a weak baking soda solution before cooking. The baking soda massage may seem unnecessary for today's tender meat, but why not experiment to see if you like the transformation?

Bún Noodle Salad BLUEPRINT

Almost any grilled, fried, or stir-fried main dish may star in southern Vietnamese rice noodle salads, which are generically called bún, the name of the capellini-size round rice noodles that define the dish. Bún bowl salads come together easily, so keep the noodles in your pantry (see page 10 for buying tips). Also maintain a supply of nước chấm, lettuce, and herbs in the fridge. This template serves four, but adjust the quantities and get creative with your main feature (leftovers are great, as are seared mushrooms). For a combo salad, use six to eight imperial rolls, plus one of the other main features.

MAIN FEATURE (CHOOSE ONE)

16 Oven-Fried Crispy Shiitake Imperial Rolls (page 103)

16 Oven-Fried Crispy Shrimp Imperial Rolls (page 106)

1 batch Twice-Fried Lemongrass Tofu (page 231)

1 batch Grilled Eggplant with Garlicky Green Onion Sizzle (page 212)

1 batch Beef and Tofu Lá Lốt Rolls (page 259)

1 batch Gingery Vegetable and Beef Stir-Fry (page 254)

1 batch roast chicken (see page 243)

MUST-HAVES

1 cup Nước Chấm Dipping Sauce (page 32)

6 to 8 oz small dried round rice noodles (bún or maifun) or 10 to 12 oz rice capellini

4 to 6 cups baby lettuce mix or thinly sliced lettuce leaves (such as butter, Boston, or green-leaf)

½ to 1 cup coarsely chopped or hand-torn herbs (at least two kinds, like cilantro and mint)

OPTIONAL SALAD EXTRAS (CHOOSE ONE OR MORE)

4 to 5 oz mung bean sprouts

1 large Persian cucumber, or ½ small English cucumber, cut as matchsticks or shaved with a peeler into thin strips

½ to ¾ cup Đồ Chua Pickle (page 56) or Racy Pickled Fennel (page 58)

OPTIONAL GARNISHES (CHOOSE ONE OR BOTH)

⅔ cup unsalted roasted peanuts or cashew pieces, crushed or coarsely chopped if large

3 Tbsp Fast Fried Shallots (page 46) or store-bought fried shallots or onions

3 STEPS TO BÚN SALAD HAPPINESS

Make the main feature or reheat it. To ensure it doesn't wilt the lettuce and herbs, it should be warm or near room temperature. When you use imperial rolls, snip them with scissors for easy eating.

Ready the must-haves to lay the salad foundation. Make the sauce to function as a dressing. Add garlic and chile for pungency and heat, if you like. Set at the table.

In a 4- or 5-qt pot of unsalted water, boil the noodles until tender-firm (the cooking time depends on the noodle and brand, so test to verify doneness). Drain the noodles in a colander, dump them back into the pot, and add cold water to cover. Swish for 30 to 60 seconds to quickly cool and release their starch, then re-drain. Set aside to cool to room temperature (they'll naturally get sticky). Divide the lettuce and herbs among four rimmed dinner plates or large noodle-soup or pasta bowls. For more crunch, color, and tang, add any salad extras.

Divide the noodles among the salads; if they're super-sticky, very briefly rinse them under water to loosen, shake the colander to drain well, and then portion them.

Crown your creation. Add the main feature and optional garnishes; nuts lend texture, and fried shallots offer richness. Present the salad and invite diners to drizzle and dress with the sauce and toss. Use chopsticks (or a fork) and a spoon (or knife)!

3 to 4 oz lá lốt
(wild pepper leaves)

8 oz firm tofu

1 bunch green onions

¼ cup minced lemongrass
(see page 44)

1 Tbsp Madras-style curry
powder, or a combination of
1¼ tsp ground coriander, 1 tsp
garam masala, and ¾ tsp
ground turmeric

1 tsp brown sugar (light
or dark), agave syrup, or
mild honey

¾ tsp recently ground
black pepper

Fine sea salt

1 Tbsp fish sauce (store-
bought or vegan version,
page 29)

1 lb ground beef
(80 or 85 percent lean)

1 (12-oz) package dried fine
rice noodles (see page 10
for bánh hỏi)

¼ cup neutral oil (such as
canola or peanut), plus more
for brushing

1 cup Nước Chấm Dipping
Sauce (page 32)

Leaves from 2 heads soft-
leaf lettuce (such as butter,
Boston, or red- or green-leaf)

1 small handful cilantro sprigs

10 to 12 bushy sprigs of soft-
leaf herbs other than cilantro
(such as mint, Thai basil, or
Vietnamese shiso)

2 cups Đồ Chua Pickle
(page 56; optional)

Bò Nướng Lá Lốt
Beef and Tofu Lá Lốt Rolls

With an aroma of warming spices, these rolls are defined partly by a piquant meat filling but more so by lá lốt, the leaves of *Piper lolot* and *P. sarmentosum* (see page 15). They taste mild when eaten raw, but once heated, they release an intoxicating fragrance. Beef in lá lốt rolls is a Viet favorite, especially during the warmer months when the leaves are most available. I combine meat with tofu for succulent results. Served with bánh hỏi rice noodles for lettuce wraps, these rolls are a great one-dish meal.

Trim the lá lốt
Using scissors, snip the lá lốt leaves from their center stems, making sure to keep about ½ inch of the leaf-stem attached (you'll need it later for securing the rolls). If needed, pat the leaves dry with paper towels. Sort and gather twenty-four to thirty larger leaves (at least 2½ inches wide) for encasing the beef. Finely chop smaller leaves to yield about ¼ cup, then put them in a medium bowl for making the filling. (Save leftover leaves for the herby egg pancakes on page 216 or finishing a stir-fry, soup, or fried rice.)

Craft the filling
Cut the tofu into 1-inch cubes, transfer to a dish towel, and drain for 10 minutes. Meanwhile, finely chop the green onions to yield ⅓ cup and add to the filling bowl. Slice the remaining green onions to yield a brimming 1 cup; set aside.

Add the drained tofu and lemongrass to the filling bowl, then use a fork to mash to a fine texture. Season with the curry powder, brown sugar, pepper, ¼ tsp salt, and fish sauce. Taste and, if needed, add about ⅛ tsp salt for a strong, savory flavor. Add the beef and mix well (your hands are the best tools).

Ready the accompaniments
Rehydrate the fine rice noodles by following the detailed, quirky package instructions, which really do work. If the noodles seem too large and unwieldy, cut them in half. Arrange the noodles on two plates, laying them flat and letting them overlap. Cover well so they don't dry out.

(CONTINUED)

No lá lốt? Use tía tô (Viet shiso). Or, skip the leaves and shape twelve to sixteen small burgers and adjust cooking time as needed; break the burgers into small pieces for wraps.

Instead of beef, substitute ground pork, turkey dark meat, or a plant-based beef alternative.

For bánh hỏi prep pointers, visit Vietworldkitchen.com/ evergreentips.

To grill outdoors, use medium heat and the same cook time. Or, cook the rolls in a skillet, with a thin film of oil, over medium heat, for 3 minutes, turning often.

In a small microwavable bowl, stir together the sliced green onions, ⅛ tsp salt, and neutral oil. Microwave on high power for 45 seconds, or until the onions soften in the bubbly oil. (Or, put the oil in a 1- to 1½-qt saucepan and set over medium heat. When a green onion piece gently sizzles upon contact, stir in the remaining green onions, season with salt, and then cook for 30 seconds, until softened.) Let them cool to room temperature before using.

Prep the sauce, lettuce, and herbs.

Make and grill the rolls

Place a lá lốt leaf on your work surface, dull-side up and the tip pointed away from you (the stem is closest to you). For a 3-inch-wide leaf, use 2 Tbsp filling; shape it into a 1-inch-thick sausage and place it above the leaf's midline—the sausage should span the width of the leaf. Pick up the leaf tip and then pull it over the filling, rolling the leaf downward to encase the filling. Poke the leaf's stem into the leaf, using a paring knife to poke the hole if needed to secure. Place the finished roll on a baking sheet. Repeat with the remaining leaves, adjusting the filling amount for the leaf size. (You'll get the hang of it! If there's leftover filling, shape small burgers.) Lightly brush your creations with neutral oil.

Lightly oil a stovetop cast-iron grill pan and set over medium-high heat. When hot, add the rolls and cook for 5 minutes, or until firm-tender like the flesh by your thumb and forefinger when you make a tight fist, turning often. Lá lốt will wrinkle and hug the meat. Transfer the cooked rolls to a platter.

Assemble and serve

Spoon the green onions and their oil atop the noodles. Serve with the lá lốt rolls, dipping sauce, lettuce, herbs, and pickle. Invite diners to encase a roll in a palm-size piece of lettuce along with the noodles, herb leaves, and pickle, then dip it in the sauce before eating. The pickle may be nibbled as a side.

Notes

Ingredients No bánh hỏi? Boil 6 to 8 oz small dried round rice noodles (bún or maifun) or 10 to 12 oz rice capellini, until tender-firm. Drain, return the noodles to the pot, then add cold water to cover; swish for 30 to 60 seconds to cool, then re-drain. Use your fingertips to pick up small amounts of noodles and twirl them into a tiny nest, setting it on a large platter. Repeat to make twenty-four to thirty snug nests. Cover to avoid drying.

Timing Refrigerate trimmed lá lốt leaves in an airtight container with a paper towel to absorb moisture for up to 2 days. It's fine to chill uncooked rolls for hours before cooking.

Tempting
Sweets and Sips

MANY PEOPLE CONSIDER ASIAN SWEETS mysterious or an afterthought, but if you step inside a Viet bakery or deli, you'll quickly notice a wondrous range of colorful, multitextured goods that merge Eastern and Western concepts as well as borrow from neighboring cuisines. In Vietnam, vendors ply their specialties from morning 'til night to satisfy people's penchant for sweets, most of which are served in smallish portions so one may snack on many of them throughout the day. Ditto for beverage options, which range from coffee and tea to smoothies and chè, dessert-y sweet soups with roots in traditional Chinese medicine. The recipes in this chapter involve low-to-moderate effort but are big-payoff treats.

A trio of easy bakes celebrates crops cultivated in Vietnam. Coffee and cacao unite in a mocha cake that wonderfully tastes like Vietnamese coffee. Cassava and coconut are as important in savories as they are in sweets, and the classic cake herein is on perennial repeat in my home. And Vietnam's warming spices and citrus star in an artful marble cake.

The peanut-y candy recipe includes other ideas for you to play around with. My testers and I enjoyed making them all, and you may too.

Peak-season fruits are top of mind when it comes to kicking off a Viet dessert spread, but since the pleasures of fresh tropical fruits are fleeting, if not rare, I seek gratification in a can. The vibrant no-churn sorbet leads with a jackfruit ditty, but also check out the Notes for equally incredible bonus variations. The sorbet recipe is my way of encouraging you to further explore Chinese and Southeast Asian markets, where there are yards of shelf space dedicated to canned tropical fruit.

And what is corn milk? It's not a typo but a seriously delicious creamy corn-y drink. Corn silk, cobs, and a bit of husk are involved to yield a delightful beverage.

Coffee further revs things up. Make the basic recipe for classic hot or iced Vietnamese coffee. There are two Hanoi-inspired versions to try. Suitable for coolish temps (it can get bone-chillingly cold in northern Vietnam), the eggy coffee is thick and rich, practically like tiramisu. And when the weather is hot and humid, switch to coconut-coffee pops to cool down.

The recipe for jewel-toned chè sương sa hạt lựu summarizes what this book is about—spotlighting the creative use of plants and quirky charms of Vietnamese foodways. This wildly delicious chè dessert soup relies solely upon plants for its playful colors, layered flavors, and varied textures. Its Viet name mentions pomegranate seeds but there are faux ones crafted from water chestnuts. It's loaded with spoonable goodies but is liquidy enough to be served in a glass. The edible, drinkable sweet satisfies just enough so there's room for another nibble afterward (if you're in normal Viet eating mode!). Most important, the plant-based treat appeals to more than just the vegetarian crowd.

These characteristics don't apply to only the one chè preparation but to many foods in the Vietnamese repertoire. They entice, beguile, and sometimes confound to keep you pondering and returning for more. And whether from land or sea, plants play a substantive role in seeding and allowing Vietnamese deliciousness to flourish, attracting everyone to enjoy and consider.

½ cup hulled split (yellow) mung beans or red lentils (see Note)

About 1¼ cups water

1 (1-lb) package frozen grated cassava, thawed, or 1¼ cups cassava flour

1 (13.5-oz) can full-fat unsweetened coconut milk

1 large egg

1½ cups granulated sugar

2½ Tbsp cornstarch

½ tsp fine sea salt

1½ tsp vanilla extract

⅓ cup dried unsweetened shredded coconut

Bánh Khoai Mì

Coconut-Cassava Cake

A dairy- and gluten-free wonder, bánh khoai mì is intriguingly chewy, tropically fragrant, and delicately sweet. You may compare it to Hawaiian butter mochi cake, but there is no rice involved and the flavor is bolder. It's easy to make, requiring just a pot, blender, and pan. When people first try it, they're charmed. "It's like a wonderful dense custard," my neighbor Adrienne said. The cake sings when prepared with shredded khoai mì (cassava), which is sold frozen at Chinese and Southeast Asian grocers. However, more convenient cassava flour, made from grinding the dried root and available at health-food stores, offers a shortcut but the result is less tender. Viet sweets often include legumes. Also sold at Asian markets, buttery mung beans add body to this cake, but red lentils can be substituted for a slightly less-rich result. Recipe tester Jeff Bareilles instinctively served the cake with fresh fruit, which is very Viet.

Cook the mung beans

Rinse the mung beans, drain, and put in a 1- to 1½-qt saucepan with ¾ cup of the water. Set over medium-high heat, bring to a boil, and let bubble vigorously for 2 minutes, stirring, until the beans plump a bit and are barely covered by liquid. Stir once more, turn the heat to low, cover, and cook for 10 minutes. Turn off the heat and let sit for 5 minutes to finish cooking with the residual heat. When done, the beans will be tender but not mushy.

Blend and bake the cake

Position a rack in the middle of the oven and preheat to 350°F. Lightly oil a 9-inch round cake pan (with at least 2-inch-high sides) and line the bottom with parchment paper.

   In a blender container, combine the cooked beans, cassava, coconut milk, and egg. If using grated cassava, pour in ⅓ cup water; if using cassava flour, pour in ½ cup water. Blend for about 10 seconds to get things moving and avoid clumping. Add the sugar, cornstarch, salt, and vanilla and blend until smooth, pausing to scrape the walls of the container as needed. Pour the batter into the prepared pan and scatter the shredded coconut on top.

You have options with this versatile recipe, but for accuracy, weigh the mung beans (100g), cassava flour (176g), and sugar (298g).

Bake the cake for 1 hour 20 minutes, or until the top is dry and richly golden. Insert a skewer in the center of the cake to the bottom of the pan; it should come out clean. Let cool on a wire rack for 1½ hours before unmolding.

Unmold and serve

Run a knife around the sides of the cake. Put a cooling rack over the pan and invert, then remove the pan and paper. Place a serving plate over the cake and invert again so it is right-side up. Cut the cake into wedges and serve slightly warm or at room temperature.

Notes

Ingredients Dried hulled split mung beans (pictured, lower center, on page 262), sold at Asian markets, often have colorant added to make them vibrant yellow. Some of that comes off during rinsing, and I've never had harmful effects from it.

Lifespan The cake can be refrigerated for 3 days, or tightly wrapped and frozen for up to 3 months. Return to room temperature and microwave slices in 15-second blasts to refresh.

2 Tbsp instant espresso, or 2½ Tbsp instant dark-roast coffee granules

1½ Tbsp unsweetened cocoa powder (see Note)

Scant ⅔ cup sweetened condensed milk (coconut, if preferred)

2 Tbsp neutral oil (such as canola or peanut)

6 Tbsp unsalted butter or virgin coconut oil, cut or spooned as 5 or 6 chunks

1¼ to 1½ tsp vanilla extract

1 cup all-purpose flour (bleached or unbleached)

½ tsp baking powder

¼ tsp baking soda

¼ tsp fine sea salt

⅔ cup granulated sugar

2 large eggs, at room temperature

⅓ cup heavy cream, at room temperature

COFFEE-FLAVORED WHIPPED CREAM

2 Tbsp sweetened condensed milk (coconut, if preferred)

¼ tsp plus ⅛ tsp vanilla extract

2 tsp instant espresso, or 2½ tsp instant dark-roast coffee granules

⅔ cup heavy cream, cold

2 Tbsp full-fat sour cream or Greek-style yogurt (dairy-free, if preferred; optional, for extra body and sheen)

Bánh Moka

Vietnamese Mocha Cake

My mom adores this cake and simply calls it "coffee cake," but my husband refers to it as "the cake." I made it about thirty times to craft a sweet imbued by the iconic flavors of Vietnamese coffee with sweetened condensed milk plus a hint of chocolate (coffee and cacao both grow in Vietnam). Cooking the condensed milk with other ingredients was key to avoiding a cake riddled with tunnels. This snacky treat, pictured, in the bottom corners, on page 268, is delicious on its own, but if you buy a half-pint of heavy cream, you'll have just enough for the cake, plus coffee-flavored whipped cream to dress things up. Choose sweetened condensed coconut milk and coconut oil for a coconut-coffee edge. Coconut cream works in the cake batter, but because its flavor impact is minimal and whipping coconut cream can be tricky, I stick with standard heavy cream for the topping.

Cook the mocha base

In a 1- to 1½-qt saucepan, combine the instant espresso, cocoa powder, condensed milk, neutral oil, and butter. Set over medium-low heat for 2 to 3 minutes, stirring constantly, until the mixture resembles soft pudding (the coffee may not fully dissolve). Set aside for about 15 minutes, until lukewarm or room temperature (it will thicken). Stir in the vanilla for a caramel-ish finish.

Meanwhile, position a rack in the lower third of the oven. Set a pizza stone or a baking sheet on the rack to regulate the heat so the center of the cake doesn't sink as it cools. Preheat the oven to 350°F. Lightly oil the bottom and sides of an 8-inch square or 9-inch round baking pan (with at least 2-inch-high sides) and line the bottom with parchment paper.

Make the batter and bake

In a medium bowl, combine the flour, baking powder, baking soda, and salt. Beat with a fork about 20 seconds to combine well.

In a large bowl, combine the sugar and eggs and whisk vigorously for 1 minute, or until smooth, slightly frothy, and creamy yellow. Scrape in the mocha base and whisk to combine. Using the whisk, gently stir in the flour mixture and the cream in this alternating manner: one-third of the flour mixture, half of the cream,

For good measure,
weigh the condensed
milk (184g), butter
(85g), flour (142g),
and sugar (133g).

another third of the flour mixture, the remaining cream, and then the last third of the flour mixture. Between additions, you shouldn't see a trace of the ingredient just added. Scrape the batter into the prepared pan, shimmy it to level the top, and then hold the pan 2 to 3 inches above your work surface and drop it to remove large air bubbles.

Bake the cake for 28 to 40 minutes, or until it is dry on top, springs back lightly when touched, and a toothpick or skewer inserted in the center comes out clean but feels slightly moist. Observe and be patient. When done, the cake ideally should not have pulled away from the pan sides. Let cool completely on a wire rack, about 45 minutes.

Prepare the whipped cream

If it's warm in your kitchen, chill a small or medium metal bowl.

To make the Coffee-Flavored Whipped Cream: In the metal bowl, combine the condensed milk, vanilla, and espresso and stir to dissolve the coffee (it's okay if some doesn't dissolve). Pour in the cream and then use an electric mixer on low to medium speed to whip it until it holds soft peaks (pause to lift the beaters and the clinging creamy tips slump over). Add the sour cream (if using), then continue beating to a voluptuous texture that holds its shape. Cover and keep chilled.

Assemble and serve

Run a knife around the sides of the cake. Put a cooling rack over the pan and invert, then remove the pan and paper. Place a serving plate over the cake and invert again so it is right-side up. Cut pieces of cake and, using two spoons, scoop whipped cream on top of or alongside the pieces to serve.

Notes

Ingredients Select a natural, non-alkalized cocoa powder to add extra bitterness that amplifies Vietnamese coffee's intensity. Use Dutch-processed cocoa for a darker cake with slightly mellower flavor.

Pound instant coffee granules before dissolving if they are huge.

Lifespan Whole or leftover cake can be refrigerated for up to 3 days, or tightly wrapped and frozen for up to 3 months. Return to room temperature, and microwave in 15-second blasts to refresh.

The whipped cream is best used within 8 hours, although you may refrigerate it overnight. As needed, re-whisk to re-volumize and incorporate liquid that has settled on the bottom.

1 Tbsp packed finely grated lime zest (see Note)

2 tsp granulated sugar, plus 1 cup

¾ to 1 tsp ground cinnamon

¾ tsp ground ginger, or ½ tsp ground star anise, plus more as needed

¼ tsp ground cloves, cardamom, or a 50/50 combo, plus more as needed

¼ tsp recently ground black pepper (optional)

Brimming 1 tsp instant espresso or unsweetened cocoa powder

1⅓ cups all-purpose flour (bleached or unbleached)

1½ tsp baking powder

¼ tsp fine sea salt

⅔ cup whole milk or oat milk, at room temperature

½ cup neutral oil (such as canola or peanut)

2 large eggs, at room temperature

1½ Tbsp molasses

Bánh Marble Cake

Spice-Citrus Marble Cake

Reflecting my life experiences and identity, this American marble cake gets the Viet treatment via a bold blending of warm, sweet spices typically found in pho and bò kho beef stew; because of that, I gave the recipe a Vietglish name. This cross-cultural bake is tasty, fragrant, and fun to make. I add lime zest because the citrus is a constant in the Viet kitchen.

When possible, employ Vietnam-grown spices. For example, Royal Cinnamon and Buffalo Ginger, both by Burlap & Barrel, offer vivid, clean flavor. Like moods, spices vary, so this recipe involves crafting your own blend. Be creative with it. I bake this cake in a round pan to maximize the arty marbled appearance on top, but you may opt for a 6-cup Bundt or loaf pan. Enjoy with coffee, tea, milk, or even scoops of no-churn sorbet (see page 275).

Make the lime-zesty sugar and customize spices

Position a rack in the lower third of the oven and preheat to 350°F. Lightly oil the bottom and sides of a 9-inch round or 8-inch square baking pan (with at least 2-inch-high sides) and line the bottom with parchment paper.

In a small bowl, using the back of a spoon, mash together the lime zest with 1 tsp of the sugar to yield a fragrant green mixture. Set aside.

In another bowl, mix 1 tsp sugar, ¾ tsp of the cinnamon, ginger, cloves, and pepper (if using). Taste and adjust with the remaining cinnamon ⅛ tsp at a time, or add pinches of the other spices to create a pleasantly spicy-sweet, slightly zingy blend. Add the instant espresso for a bittersweet, earthy edge. Jot down your formula for future cakes.

Make the batters and marble them

In a medium bowl, combine the flour, baking powder, and salt and mix with a fork for about 15 seconds to incorporate. In a large bowl, combine the remaining 1 cup sugar, milk, neutral oil, and eggs and use a whisk to beat until smooth and creamy yellow. In three additions, gently whisk in the flour mixture, making sure the batter is just smooth after each addition.

(CONTINUED)

> For accuracy, weigh the sugar (198g for the 1 cup) and flour (190g); use bleached all-purpose flour for a more tender cake.

Pour a generous 1¼ cups of the batter into a liquid measuring cup and stir in the lime-zesty sugar. Add the molasses and spice blend to the remaining batter in the bowl and whisk gently to combine well.

Add half of the lime batter in blobs to the prepared pan and then add half of the spice batter to fill in gaps and overlap here and there. Drag a skewer or the back of a knife through the batters about five times to create delicate swirls. Repeat with the remaining batters. To expel large air bubbles, hold the pan 2 to 3 inches above your work surface and drop it.

Bake and cool
Bake the cake for 28 to 40 minutes (the smaller 8-inch pan takes longer), until the top feels dry and a toothpick or skewer inserted in the middle comes out clean. Let cool on a wire rack for 45 minutes.

Unmold and serve
Run a knife around the sides of the cake. Put a cooling rack over the pan and invert, then remove the pan and paper. Place a serving plate over the cake and invert again so it is right-side up. Cut the cake into wedges or squares and serve slightly warm or at room temperature.

Notes

Ingredients Instead of lime zest, try lemon or orange zest. Scrub the citrus to remove the food-grade wax on the peel before zesting. Citrus zest may be refrigerated in a small airtight container for 2 days or frozen in a small jar for 2 months.

Lifespan The cake can be refrigerated for up to 3 days, or tightly wrapped and frozen for 3 months. Return to room temperature and microwave slices in 15-second blasts to refresh.

1 Tbsp coconut oil (virgin or refined) or unsalted butter

1¼ cups roasted peanuts (unsalted or lightly salted; see Note), roughly chopped if huge

¼ cup toasted sesame seeds (white, black, brown, or a combo; see Note for toasting tips)

¼ tsp fine sea salt

¼ tsp plus ⅛ tsp baking soda

¾ cup granulated sugar

2 Tbsp light corn syrup or brown rice syrup

2 Tbsp water

Kẹo Lạc Vừng

Peanut and Sesame Candy

Viet markets often sell this crunchy, not-too-sweet candy by the cash registers as an impulse buy, but you can make this northern Viet nibble from readily available ingredients. Corn syrup sold at mainstream supermarkets or brown rice syrup from health-food stores stands in for the maltose typically used. Tweak the nut-and-seed combinations to prepare other renditions as suggested in the Notes. While you're at it, reuse the parchment paper for multiple batches. This sturdy candy mails beautifully, which is something to remember for the holidays, especially for Tet (Vietnamese Lunar New Year), when it's food-gifting season.

Prep and plan

Because things go very fast, ready your equipment. Gather a rolling pin, knife, metal bench scraper (if handy), and two pieces of 12 by 15-inch parchment paper, one of which is set atop a cutting board for insulation and keeping the candy warm and manipulatable when you roll it out.

Put the coconut oil in a medium or large glass measuring cup and microwave on high power for 30 to 60 seconds, until just melted. (Alternatively, melt it in a 1- or 1½-qt saucepan over medium heat.) Add the peanuts, sesame seeds, salt, and baking soda, stirring well to combine. Set the mixture near the stove.

Make the candy

In a relatively tall 1½- or 2-qt saucepan, use a silicone spatula to stir together the sugar, corn syrup, and water. Using the spatula, scrape along the pan sides to ensure none of the ingredients ride up the walls of the pan and scorch. Clip a candy thermometer to the side of the pan, set over medium heat, and bring the mixture to a frothy boil. Let it bubble away for 2 to 5 minutes, until the thermometer registers around 300°F. (If needed for accurately reading the temperature, tilt the pan to bathe the thermometer tip in the hot mixture.)

(CONTINUED)

Due to weight differences between conventional and organic granulated sugar, weigh 149g of sugar for consistent results.

Turn off the heat but keep the pan on the burner. Immediately add the nut-seed mixture. Stir vigorously for 5 to 10 seconds to combine well. (If the candy is too stiff, turn the heat to low to loosen things as you stir.) Carefully pour and scrape the hot nutty mass onto the parchment paper atop the cutting board.

Press and cut

Immediately use the spatula to press and spread out the mixture to roughly ¾ inch thick to create a slab (mine often looks like Australia). Lay the second piece of parchment paper on top, then use the rolling pin to flatten the slab to about ¼ inch thick (the peanuts dictate the thickness). You can also wield the warm saucepan like an iron to smooth out subtle ridges. As long as the candy is warm-hot, you can manipulate it; neaten the sides with the broad side of a knife or metal bench scraper, if you like.

When you're satisfied, remove the top parchment layer. While the candy remains warm, cut with a knife into rectangular pieces roughly 1 by 1½ inches (or cut diamonds, triangles, or planks). Let cool for 30 minutes before snapping apart. The candy tastes best once it is totally cool.

Notes

Ingredients For good-looking, tasty candy, choose peanuts with a deep color and flavor.

Technique Toast ¼ cup sesame seeds (it's okay to blend different kinds) in an 8-inch skillet over medium heat for 3 to 4 minutes, shaking frequently, until they're slightly plumped and pale golden (try black seeds, if applicable). Slide the pan to a cool burner and let sit for 2 minutes, shaking after 1 minute, to further toast the seeds via the pan's residual heat. When you scale up the recipe, toast in a larger skillet.

Lifespan Store the candy in an airtight container for up to 1 month.

Variations You need 1½ cups of nuts and seeds for each batch. Simply swap and adjust the amounts to make other kinds of candies, such as these:

For Almond and Sesame Candy, swap 1 cup toasted slivered almonds for the peanuts and use ½ cup toasted sesame seeds.

For Cashew and Sesame Candy, replace the peanuts with toasted cashew pieces (or roughly chop whole cashews). Keep the same amount of sesame seeds.

For Sesame Seed Candy, use 1½ cups toasted sesame seeds instead of the nut-seed combo. For bigger sesame flavor, substitute 1 Tbsp toasted sesame oil for the coconut oil or butter.

1½ Tbsp sweetened condensed milk (coconut, if preferred)

2 tsp fresh lime juice

1 to 1½ tsp freshly grated lime zest

1 (20-oz) can jackfruit in syrup, frozen for at least 12 hours

Kem Mít

No-Churn Jackfruit Lime Sorbet

With its intense flavors, canned tropical fruit from Asia is like peak-season fruit on steroids. I've mostly enjoyed it as a fruit cocktail, but my horizons expanded after reading about a 1990s hack by Melanie Barnard, a *Bon Appétit* columnist, who froze canned fruit and then blitzed it in a food processor to make creative no-churn sorbets. (The can will not explode in the freezer.) I tried the brilliant technique with supermarket as well as Asian-market finds. The sublime sorbets were reminders of my time in Vietnam, where many kem (the Viet term for frozen desserts) are plant-forward, light, and refreshing.

Using frozen canned fruit for sorbet offers many pluses: There's consistent flavor and no waste (the sugar syrup contributes to a smooth texture), it's easily concocted without an ice-cream maker, and you can prepare it year-round. I add sweetened condensed milk for a luscious touch and offset it with lime juice or yogurt; the tanginess complements the fruit's brightness. In the main recipe, lime lends sparkle without robbing jackfruit of its unusual flavor that's reminiscent of Juicy Fruit gum. Once you get the hang of this nifty method (keep frozen cans of fruit on hand), play around with the ideas in the Notes and create your own flavors too!

Ready the equipment and seasoning

Gather a medium bowl to hold the can, a can opener, a cutting board, a chef's knife or veggie cleaver, and a full-size food processor. You will need to quickly remove the frozen contents from the can with minimal melting (you want sorbet instead of a slushy).

In a small bowl, combine the condensed milk, lime juice, and 1 tsp of the lime zest and stir to incorporate. The mixture should taste strongly of lime; if not, add the remaining ½ tsp lime zest. Scrape into the food processor.

Chop the frozen contents and blitz

Bring a kettle of water to a boil.

(CONTINUED)

In the medium bowl, lay the can of jackfruit on its side and pour in the just-boiled water to cover it by about two-thirds. Now roll the can back and forth to warm it all over while you count to ten. Using your fingertips or tongs, stand the can upright and take it out of the water. The top should give slightly when pressed, and things may slosh when you shake the can.

Quickly blot the can dry and open it. Pour the bit of melted syrup into the processor. Slide the frozen cylinder onto your cutting board (if needed, remove the other end of the can to push it out). Cut the block into five thick rounds, coarsely chop into chunks no bigger than ¾ inch, and transfer to the food processor. Run the machine for 2 to 3 minutes, or until smooth; as needed, pause to stir the contents. Having a few lingering pieces of fruit is okay; leave them or fish them out.

Firm up, then serve

Although it's scoopable, the sorbet often melts too fast at this stage. Transfer to a container (a metal loaf pan is great to expedite chilling), cover, and freeze for about 2 hours to firm up and meld the flavors. If the sorbet is too hard to scoop, let it sit at room temperature for about 15 minutes, or in the fridge for 30 to 45 minutes, until it's scoopable. Serve in individual dishes.

———

Notes

Equipment Use a high-speed blender if a food processor isn't available.

Lifespan Keep frozen in an airtight container for 1 week.

Variations Instead of jackfruit, freeze, chop, and process other canned fruit. Processing time varies from 1 to 4 minutes, depending on the fruit selected. A few options:

For Lychee-Ginger Sorbet, process a frozen 20-oz can of lychees in syrup with 2 Tbsp condensed milk, 1 Tbsp lime juice, and 2 to 2½ tsp grated peeled ginger.

For Mandarin Orange Sorbet, whirl a frozen 15-oz can of Mandarin orange sections in syrup with 1 Tbsp sweetened condensed milk, 1½ tsp lime juice, and ½ tsp vanilla extract. This sorbet evokes an Orange Julius drink.

For Pineapple-Lime Sorbet, replace the jackfruit with a frozen 20-oz can of pineapple chunks in heavy syrup, keeping the other ingredients as listed. Frozen canned pineapple is stubborn to loosen, so count to twenty when rolling the can in hot water; if it's a pull-tab top, open from the bottom.

For Soursop Sorbet, process a frozen 15-oz can of soursop pulp in syrup with ¼ cup plain Greek-style yogurt and 2 Tbsp sweetened condensed milk; no lime juice is needed. Be patient while processing for 3 to 4 minutes, and you'll be rewarded with a splendid sorbet. (Markets catering to Viet customers often sell canned soursop, which is called mãng cầu xiêm.)

2 large ears corn (yellow or bicolor for vibrancy)

4 cups water, plus more as needed

½ cup full-fat, unsweetened coconut milk (whisk before measuring)

Fine sea salt

½ tsp vanilla extract, plus more as needed

1 to 4 Tbsp sweetened condensed milk (coconut, if preferred), agave syrup, mild honey, or granulated sugar (optional)

Sữa Bắp

Corn Milk

Made from humble ingredients, intriguingly elegant corn milk is an enticing refresher. Many renditions use evaporated milk and sweetened condensed milk, but I combine summertime corn with a touch of coconut milk for a smooth, delicately sweet beverage. Serve sữa bắp as is or offer it as a light soup. Recipe testers Nathan and Kate Schmidt added dark rum to make a cocktail.

Shuck, cut, and boil the corn

If the corn is not shucked, trim the dark wizened portions of the corn silk, then shuck the corn, saving most of the corn silk and six to eight of the inner pale-green husks (it's okay if some silk lingers on the cob). Encase all the reserved silk in the husks, fold the husks over to tidy up the bundle, and tie tightly with kitchen string. Put into a 4-qt saucepan.

Cut the corn kernels off the cobs, then break the cobs in half. Add both to the saucepan, along with the water, coconut milk, and ¼ tsp salt. Set over high heat and bring to a boil, then lower the heat to medium and maintain a gentle boil. Cook, uncovered, for 15 minutes. Remove from the heat and, using tongs, lift out and discard the cobs and husk bundle. Let cool for about 10 minutes.

Blend, strain, and season the milk

Transfer the contents of the saucepan to a blender and whirl at high speed for a good 1 minute, until creamy and milky. Pour the corn through a fine-mesh strainer set over a bowl or a large liquid measuring cup, pressing on the solids with a wooden spoon to extract as much milk as possible. Stir in the vanilla.

If the corn milk is too thick, add up to ½ cup water to thin it out. Corn milk intensifies in flavor and sweetness as it cools; especially once it is chilled. Refrigerate for about 4 hours, then taste and add pinches of salt, drops of vanilla, and, if needed, sweetened condensed milk by the tablespoon. Your tweaks depend on your corn, palate, and serving method (make it strong if serving over ice). Stir before serving.

Note

Lifespan Keeps refrigerated for 1 week.

Including the corn silk, husks, and cobs during cooking pumps up the corn-y flavor.

2 batches Vietnamese Coffee
(page 284), or a generous
1 cup strong coffee, at room
temperature

⅔ cup full-fat, unsweetened
coconut milk (whisk before
measuring)

⅓ cup sweetened condensed
milk (coconut, if preferred)

½ tsp vanilla extract,
plus more as needed

Fine sea salt

Kem Que Cà Phê Dừa

Coconut-Coffee Pops

In tropical Vietnam, frozen desserts are extra-welcome. Beloved ice-cream shops, like Kem Bạch Đằng and Kem Tràng Tiền, enjoy loyal followings. In operation since 1958, the latter is famous for kem que (ice-pops) and was mentioned in *The Mountains Sing*, Nguyễn Phan Quế Mai's historical novel centered on women in war-torn Vietnam. In one passage, the women's intense struggles are momentarily relieved by a rare luxury—a modest frozen snack at Kem Tràng Tiền. The grandmother and granddaughter experience poignant childlike glee, and their joyfulness inspired me to create this coconut-coffee ice-pop. I took cues from the motherland, where kem que is often sweetened by condensed milk and enriched by coconut milk. So aside from enjoying Vietnamese coffee hot, cold, and warm, you may also freeze it.

In a liquid measuring cup, stir together the coffee, coconut milk, condensed milk, vanilla, and ⅛ tsp salt. Taste and, if needed, add a drop of vanilla for fragrance or a pinch of salt for flavor pop. When satisfied, pour the mixture into ice-pop molds. I use ⅓ cup–size ones, so you should get six ice-pops total. Freeze until hard, then unmold and eat up!

To emphasize the
coconut flavor
and make a vegan
version, opt for
sweetened condensed
coconut milk. See
page 22 for buying tips.

Note

Variation To make Corn Milk Pops, season 2 cups Corn Milk (page 277) with 3 Tbsp sweetened condensed milk. If you like, add an additional ¼ tsp vanilla. Pour into six ice-pop molds and freeze as directed.

1 (13.5-oz) can unsweetened full-fat coconut milk

1½ cups water, plus 1 Tbsp

½ cup granulated sugar, plus 2 Tbsp

Fine sea salt

1 Tbsp tapioca starch, plus ¼ cup, plus more as needed

¾ to 1 tsp vanilla extract

½ cup hulled split (yellow) mung beans (see Note, page 265) or red lentils (see Note)

1 (8-oz) can whole water chestnuts

2 tsp red beet juice (see Note), ½ tsp ground turmeric, or ½ tsp matcha powder

1 (20-oz) can grass jelly

1 (20-oz) can longans or jackfruit in syrup (see Note)

2 cups crushed or shaved ice or ice cubes

Chè Sương Sa Hạt Lựu
Jelly and Gemstones Chè

Cheery and summery, this soupy sweet chè is loaded with sunny colors, tropical fruit, silky jelly (sương sa), and buttery mung beans—all punctuated by velvety coconut milk. Once I start eating the dessert soup, I can't stop until I've thoroughly emptied my glass or bowl. I include onyx-colored grass jelly, a cooling (yin) ingredient, to make this southern Viet favorite exceptionally refreshing. Traditionally, red-stained water chestnut nubs are coated in slippery tapioca starch, then boiled to mimic pomegranate seeds (hạt lựu). Modern cooks apply several food-coloring hues for a rainbow effect. I employ beet juice, ground turmeric, and matcha powder, and the results resemble rubies, citrine, and jade—edible gemstones. As with most chè, the components can be prepped ahead so you may indulge on a whim.

Make the coconut sauce

In a 2-qt saucepan, whisk together the coconut milk, ½ cup of the water, ¼ cup of the sugar, and ¼ tsp salt. Set over medium heat and bring to a simmer, stirring occasionally. Mix the 1 Tbsp tapioca starch and 1 Tbsp water and add to the saucepan, stirring for about 30 seconds, until lightly thickened. Remove from the heat and stir in enough of the vanilla for a tropical lilt. Let cool briefly, then scrape this sauce into a heatproof jar or bowl and leave uncovered to cool completely and further thicken. Return the unwashed pan to the stove.

Cook the mung beans

Rinse the mung beans, drain, and dump into the pan. Add the remaining 1 cup water, set over medium-high heat, and bring to a boil, stirring frequently. When the beans are boiling, stir once more, turn the heat to between medium-low and low, and let simmer gently. Partially cover and cook for about 15 minutes, stirring occasionally, until tender (splash in more water if things look dry before the beans are done). Turn off the heat, cover, and let sit for 5 minutes to finish cooking from the residual heat.

(CONTINUED)

Head to a Chinese or Southeast Asian market for mung beans, grass jelly, and canned fruit. Buy water chestnuts and coconut milk while you're there too.

Add 3 Tbsp of the coconut sauce and 2 Tbsp sugar to the mung beans and, using a potato masher, mix and mash to yield a semi-coarse puree (or transfer to a small food processor and blitz). Scrape the mixture into a bowl or container. Let sit, uncovered, to cool completely before using or storing.

Make the edible gemstones

Drain the water chestnuts, pat them dry, and cut into ¼-inch dice. In a medium bowl, mix the beet juice and water chestnuts to stain them ruby red. (If using turmeric or matcha, dilute in 2 tsp water, then add the water chestnuts to stain them golden or jade.) Leave for about 5 minutes to absorb the color.

Fill a 3- or 4-qt saucepan halfway with water, set over high heat, and bring to a boil.

Meanwhile, place the ¼ cup tapioca starch in a small bowl, add the water chestnuts, and use a fork to coat them well, making sure all the nubs are separated. They'll have a matte finish. (If needed, work in a bit more starch.) Dump the coated nubs into a mesh strainer and shake and tap to remove excess starch and prevent clumping.

Set a bowl of ice water near the stove. Add the water chestnuts to the boiling water and cook, stirring constantly to prevent sticking. After they float to the top, let them cook for 30 to 60 seconds, until the tapioca coating looks slightly whitish and puffy (the pot may return to a boil). Scoop up the water chestnuts using a mesh strainer (or drain in a colander) and deposit in the ice water. Let cool completely, pour off the water, and then use these gemstones or store in an airtight container. The gemstones stick when cooled but will separate in the liquidy chè.

Ready the jelly and fruit

Open both ends of the grass jelly can, then push the contents onto a plate to catch any canning liquid. Using a paring knife or a crinkle vegetable cutter, cut the jelly crosswise into five rounds, then cut each round into ¾-inch chunks. Put them in a bowl or other container.

Drain the longans, reserving ⅔ cup of the syrup in a jar or bowl. Combine the reserved syrup with the remaining ¼ cup sugar. Cut the longans into bite-size pieces and set aside.

Assemble and serve

Gather six 1½- to 2-cup-capacity glasses or bowls. Fill each with roughly 2½ Tbsp mung beans, ⅓ cup longans, ½ cup grass jelly, ¼ cup gemstones, 2 Tbsp sweetened syrup, ⅓ cup ice, and ⅓ cup coconut sauce. Adjust the amounts as you like. Garnish with any remaining gemstones. Serve with spoons for diners to stir, eat, and drink up.

Notes

Ingredients In a pinch, use red lentils instead of mung beans; the result is peppery and not as buttery.

Try other canned fruit such as lychee, Mandarin oranges, or pineapple (or even a combo). When refined sugar is a concern, use a favorite substitute. There's no culinary chemistry involved, so the swap is easy.

Technique For the beet juice, finely grate 2 Tbsp packed raw red beet (peeled, if you want). Press the beet through a mesh strainer directly into the bowl that you'll put the water chestnuts into. For two or three colors of gemstones, do simple math to divide the quantities involved; you may boil them together, but the colors will eventually meld and turn muddy.

Lifespan Prep the gemstones up to 2 days in advance; the other components last a good 4 days. Keep all the components chilled and let them sit at room temperature for 10 to 15 minutes before assembly.

CUT POMEGRANATE SEEDS

Pomegranates have been grown in China and Southeast Asia for millennia, and there is a Viet cultivar too. But compared to tropical fruits such as mango and lychee, pomegranate is not commonly eaten in Vietnam. Despite all that, pomegranate seeds play an everyday role in the language of Vietnamese cooking. To dice vegetables, you say "cắt hạt lựu," which literally means "cut pomegranate seeds" and refers to the seeds' shape. It's unclear when the phrase entered the Viet kitchen, but my mom, at the age of eighty-eight, recalls it from her childhood in northern Vietnam. In this chè, pomegranate seeds inspire prep, color, and texture.

2½ Tbsp medium-dark or dark roast coffee (medium or medium-coarse grind preferred)

About ⅔ cup very hot or just-boiled water

Cà Phê

Vietnamese Coffee

You may think that there's only one way to make Vietnamese coffee, but Vietnamese people employ many methods. Cà phê phin (phin filter coffee) has its old-fashioned charms, as does cà phê vợt (stocking coffee), which uses a butterfly net–like fabric filter and charcoal-fueled heat. My mom favored a stovetop espresso maker for years. I like Aeropress's speedy performance and a pour-over too.

Regarding the coffee, pre-ground Trung Nguyên and Café Du Monde were the standard for decades, but some new-wave coffee roasters in Vietnam and abroad are single-sourcing beans for sensational cups. I've used whole beans, pre-ground, and instant coffee. You have options but always aim for a robust, slightly bitter coffee because the sweetened condensed milk will balance the flavors. For the laid-back Viet experience, brew in a standard 6-oz phin, as described in the main recipe. The Notes contain bonus methods and tips for hot coffee (cà phê sữa nóng) and iced coffee (cà phê sữa đá) with condensed milk.

Set up the phin

Remove the screen from the phin's filter chamber. Add the coffee, gently shaking the filter to distribute. (If there's a screw in the chamber, its tip should slightly protrude.) Set the filter on a cup or a glass to monitor progress.

Put the screen atop the coffee, pressing down slightly to ensure it sits flat. (As needed, attach the screen to the screw with a tiny turn; the screen should wobble slightly to allow the coffee to bloom and water to pass through.)

Add water and hang out

Pour about 3 Tbsp of the hot water to fill one-fourth to one-third of the exposed part of the chamber. Let most or all of the water pass through, about 30 seconds, before adding more water to just below the chamber's rim. Put the lid on and wait for all the water to drip through, 3 to 10 minutes, depending on the grind.

If there's little dripping coffee action, loosen the screen to allow more liquid through (use the edge of a spoon if there's a catch in the screen). When no water remains in the chamber, flip the lid and set it down, then place the chamber on top. Enjoy the coffee at the temperature you prefer.

> If using pre-ground canned coffee, the grind is predetermined. The phin works with finely ground coffee but start with a coarser grind and adjust as needed.

Notes

Equipment If you're using an Aeropress, use 3 Tbsp ground coffee, add 3 Tbsp hot water to moisten and bloom the grounds, and then ½ cup hot water before plunging. To make about 2 cups of cold-brewed coffee, in a 1-qt container, combine ¾ cup ground coffee with 3 cups water; cover and let steep for 12 to 24 hours, then strain through a paper coffee filter.

Ingredients If you're using instant coffee granules (select something robust and dark), use 1 Tbsp and a generous ½ cup hot water. Dilute an instant-coffee packet in the same amount too. You can always add water if the coffee is too strong for you.

Want vegan versions of these Viet coffee classics? Use sweetened condensed coconut milk. See page 22 for buying tips.

Variations For Hot Coffee with Condensed Milk, stir together the ½ cup coffee with 1 Tbsp sweetened condensed milk; add hot water if it's too intense.

For Iced Coffee with Condensed Milk, combine the ½ cup coffee with 2 Tbsp sweetened condensed milk. Put four or five ice cubes in a tall glass. Pour the coffee over the ice and stir to combine.

A SHORT HISTORY OF CONDENSED MILK

Sweetened condensed milk (sữa đặc) traveled the globe before it arrived in Vietnam. Its journey started in Europe in the early 1800s when there was a need to preserve fresh milk. French confectioner Nicolas Appert first condensed and canned milk in 1827. To extend shelf life and improve flavor, British civil engineer William Newton added sugar, but he didn't offer his product commercially. In the 1850s, American innovator Gail Borden developed an industrial method for producing sweetened condensed milk, and after it was used as a Civil War field ration, Borden's milk became popular in America.

From the United States, condensed milk returned to Europe and eventually found its way to French Indochina by the early twentieth century. Condensed milk was such a strong staple that during the Vietnam War, American-owned Foremost Dairies operated in South Vietnam to supply milk products to the US military. It also made sữa đặc to sell to locals.

Longevity ("Old Man") has long been a favorite brand of condensed milk for Vietnamese people. Before 1975, it was produced in South Vietnam by Friesland Foods, a Dutch company, which now makes it for the North American, mostly Vietnamese expat community. With such a long history of use by Vietnamese cooks, my pantry always includes condensed milk. For shopping tips and coconut-y dairy-free options, check page 22.

1 egg yolk,
at room temperature

3 Tbsp sweetened condensed milk (coconut, if preferred)

Generous ½ cup Vietnamese Coffee (page 284) or strong coffee, about 90°F

Cà Phê Trứng

Egg Coffee

Among Hanoi coffee specialties is egg coffee—super-warm coffee with a floater of beaten egg yolk and sweetened condensed milk. It dates to the 1950s, supposedly when there was a shortage of milk in Hanoi. Beating egg yolks with condensed milk extends the milk in an elegant, delicious manner. People likely hand-beat the yolks back then. Nowadays an electric mixer does the job in roughly 2 minutes. Egg coffee is rich and sweet, practically fancy-dessert-like. Enjoy it as an afternoon pick-me-up or serve it in small portions after dinner. Add 1 Tbsp whiskey or cognac for extra flourish.

Make the egg cream

In a small bowl, combine the egg yolk and sweetened condensed milk. Using a handheld electric mixer on high speed, beat the mixture for about 2 minutes, until it turns thick and pale yellow. Expect it to resemble slightly aerated, extra-rich condensed milk; you should have roughly ⅓ cup.

Assemble and serve

Keep the coffee in the cup; if you're sharing, divide it between two small cups or glasses, each with a capacity of about ½ cup. Using a spoon, gently add the creamy egg mixture on top. Serve immediately with demitasse spoons for guests to mix and enjoy.

The coffee should be super-warm. In Vietnam, the coffee cup is sometimes put into a shallow bowl filled with hot water to maintain its temperature after it's made. My shortcut is to reheat the coffee in the microwave.

Note

Ingredients If a white ropy strand (chalaza) is attached to the yolk, it's a sign of a super-fresh egg. However, it may not blend into the egg-cream mixture, so I usually remove it by straining through a mesh strainer.

How safe is it to consume raw eggs? Your chances of contracting salmonella are relatively low, given that in the United States, it has been estimated that 1 in 20,000 raw eggs may be bad. To minimize risk, I don't eat raw eggs often and I buy good-quality fresh eggs. I also keep them refrigerated and check for clean, intact shells. You may also try pasteurized or coddled eggs for this recipe.

ACKNOWLEDGMENTS

As a refugee to the United States, I didn't know if I would realize my childhood dream of writing cookbooks, but this is my seventh one. I am grateful to many people. First and foremost, to my parents, Gabriel Nguyễn Quốc Hoàng and Clara Nguyễn Thị Tuyết, and my husband, Rory O'Brien. They supported my desire to become a professional writer and cooking teacher, even though it wasn't a financially "safe" career path. Dad taught me how to garden, and Mom taught me how to cook. Toward the end of my father's life, he often looked out at his garden to savor all that he had cultivated.

I don't make books alone. My online community of smart, curious readers and cooks offer perspectives that shape my recipes and content. I'm also thankful to my intrepid volunteer recipe testers who sourced ingredients during the pandemic, cooked all the recipes, experimented, and provided honest feedback. A big thanks to these individuals (and their family and friends) for diving in and helping me polish this book:

Jeff Bareilles	Hugh McElroy
Linh Bui	Cate McGuire
Diane Carlson	Rosemary Metzger
Alex Ciepley	Johanna Nevitt
John Farmer	Jenny Sager
Alyce Gershenson	Kate Schmidt
Candy Grover	Nathan Schmidt
Doug Grover	Karen Shinto
Paulina Haduong	Terri Tanaka
Colin Hart	Catherine Thome
Kate Leahy	Maki Tsuzuki
Mike Ly	Tina Ujlaki
Laura McCarthy	Dave Weinstein

Many thanks to my mom and my sister, Linh, for proofreading my Vietnamese spelling and testing a few recipes too.

It's a privilege to collaborate with Ten Speed Press to craft enduring books. In particular, I was thrilled to work with the incomparable Lorena Jones, who thoughtfully edited and shepherded this book from concept to market.

The words on these pages benefited from careful work of senior managing editor Doug Ogan, production manager Jane Chinn, copyeditor Mi Ae Lipe, proofreader Rachel Markowitz, and indexer Ken DellaPenta. Art director Betsy Stromberg orchestrated this book's design elements, along with designer Shubhani Sarkar, production design manager Mari Gill, production designer Mara Gendell, and design and production assistant Claudia Sanchez.

At her Good Studios, photographer Aubrie Pick and her assistants, Stephanie Murray and Vanessa Solis, provided an extraordinary environment for crafting these stunning images. Karen Shinto, my dear friend and food stylist, brought her A game to our photo shoot; she could have styled everything on her own but let me, Kate Leahy, and Harumi Shimizu assist her. Prop stylist Glenn Jenkins overdelivered a wealth of dishware and housewares. Publisher Aaron Wehner, marketing director Allison Renzulli, assistant publicity director David Hawk, and marketer Andrea Portanova always have my back.

Cảm ơn nhiều (thank you, very much) for honoring Viet foodways and making this book tuyệt (super)!

INDEX

Published in the United States by Ten Speed Press, an imprint of Random House,
a division of Penguin Random House LLC, New York.
TenSpeed.com
RandomHouseBooks.com

Ten Speed Press and the Ten Speed Press colophon are registered trademarks of
Penguin Random House LLC.

Typefaces: FontFont's DIN Pro, FontFont's More Pro, and Paulo Goode's Yolk

Library of Congress Cataloging-in-Publication Data
  Names: Nguyen, Andrea Quynhgiao, author. | Pick, Audrey, photographer.
  Title: Ever-green Vietnamese : super-fresh recipes, starring plants from
    land and sea / Andrea Quynhgiao Nguyen ; photographs by Audrey Pick.
  Description: First edition. | [Emeryville] : Ten Speed Press, [2023] |
    Includes index.
  Identifiers: LCCN 2022015150 (print) | LCCN 2022015151 (ebook) |
    ISBN 9781984859853 (hardcover) | ISBN 9781984859860 (ebook)
  Subjects: LCSH: Cooking, Vietnamese. | Vegetarian cooking. | Natural foods. |
    LCGFT: Cookbooks.
  Classification: LCC TX724.5.V5 N4695 2023 (print) | LCC TX724.5.V5
    (ebook) | DDC 641.59597--dc23/eng/20220805
  LC record available at https://lccn.loc.gov/2022015150
  LC ebook record available at https://lccn.loc.gov/2022015151

Hardcover ISBN: 978-1-9848-5985-3
eBook ISBN: 978-1-9848-5986-0

Printed in China

Editor: Lorena Jones | Production editor: Doug Ogan
Designer: Shubhani Sarkar | Art director: Betsy Stromberg
Production designers: Mari Gill and Mara Gendell
Production and prepress color manager: Jane Chinn
Prepress color assistant: Claudia Sanchez
Food stylist: Karen Shinto | Food stylist assistants: Kate Leahy and
  Harumi Shimizu
Prop stylist: Glenn Jenkins
Photo assistants: Stephanie Murray and Vanessa Solis
Copyeditor: Mi Ae Lipe | Proofreader: Rachel Markowitz
Indexer: Ken DellaPenta
Publicist: David Hawk | Marketer: Andrea Portanova

10 9 8 7 6 5 4 3 2 1

First Edition

Garlic chive / hẹ lends a mild, garlicky bite to dishes. The flat, blade-like leaf may be tucked into rice-paper rolls, added to noodle soup, or chopped for stir-fries.

Vietnamese coriander / rau răm has a strong cilantro taste with an exciting hot finish at the back of the tongue.

Dill / thì là may be used to finish soup, season fish cakes, and top turmeric-scented fish.

Culantro / ngò gai has a stronger, earthier flavor than cilantro and is not used as often.

Wild pepper leaf / lá lốt releases remarkable incenselike aroma and curry-ish flavors when heated. It may be mislabeled "wild betel." Do not mistakenly buy thicker betel leaves, which are sold stemless.

Mint / húng is the widely sold common mint (spearmint); some markets label it as húng lủi.

sprigs in ziplock bags in the refrigerator, making sure they don't get crushed in the vegetable bin.)

Basil is best washed right before using. To refresh droopy sprigs, trim the stems by ½ inch, then put in a bowl of cool water for about 10 minutes to rehydrate. Spin dry and chill until ready to use.

Lemongrass Technically an herb but used as an aromatic, lemongrass (sà) is an iconic Viet ingredient. For details on buying, growing, and prepping the stalks, see page 44.

Lettuce Soft, bendable leaves of butter, Boston, and red- or green-leaf lettuce are perfect for wrapping and rolling, as are some heirloom lettuces. Crisp romaine is great for noodle soup. To minimize waste, wash and spin dry lettuces as soon as possible after bringing them home or inside from the garden. Refrigerate the cleaned leaves in ziplock bags or recycled mixed-greens plastic containers; add a paper towel to absorb moisture, if you like. Washed lettuce lasts for a week-plus. If you don't have a salad spinner, roll washed lettuce in a clean dish towel, tuck it into a ziplock bag, and refrigerate.

LETTUCE AND HERB SERVING TIPS

When a dish involves lettuce and herbs, present them on one platter when serving four people, and use two platters when serving more people. Consider reachability from everyone's seats. Herbs may be displayed as whole sprigs for diners to snap into shorter lengths or pluck off the leaves. If applicable, serve whole lettuce leaves for tearing into palm-size pieces for wraps, or use scissors to precut them.

Mushrooms (fresh and dried) Members of the fungus family have distinct personalities. They are earthy and meaty in different ways. Recipes in this book employ fresh shiitake, cremini (mini or baby bella), white (button), oyster, king trumpet (king oyster), and maitake (hen of the woods).

Cooked fresh shiitake have a rich, silky texture in addition to their woodsy flavor. Select thick-capped specimens if they're available; they're more intensely flavored than thin-capped, delicate-looking ones. Cremini are an affordable stand-in for fresh shiitakes, but they cook up more chewy than rich. White mushrooms cook up like cremini but with a milder flavor. Ranging from gray to brown, oyster mushrooms taste luxurious after cooking, with a rich, velvety texture that can evoke fatty beef or pork. King trumpet's very firm flesh mimics chicken well. Maitake's slight crunch is reminiscent of beef tendon.

Nowadays, fresh mushrooms are widely sold, but East and Southeast Asian markets consistently offer good selection and prices. Choose domestic over imported ones. Store mushrooms, unwashed, in a porous bag so they can breathe, or let them hang out in their original packaging. Mushrooms that have become dry and wizened in the fridge have awesome bold flavor due to partial dehydration, so don't discard them. However, say goodbye to slimy 'shrooms.

Dried shiitake mushrooms offer incredibly deep umami to help craft excellent veggie-friendly dishes. Resist substituting fresh shiitakes. Purchase dried whole shiitake mushrooms (sliced ones lack taste), and choose a package containing thick curved caps marked by white or dark cracks, often described as "flower" shiitake. If possible, check the package's backside to make sure the mushrooms are of good quality throughout. They may be simply labeled "dried mushroom." East and Southeast Asian markets have great selection and prices.

For deep flavor, the most aroma, and silky texture, rehydrate dried shiitakes in water for at least 6 hours

USE OF COLOUR IN INTERIORS

By 1957 the uninhibited use of bright colours that 'shattered the early 1950s' had given way to a more thoughtful approach. How had 'so many likeable people manage[d] to live with so many shouting walls?' (*House & Garden*, March 1957) The colours themselves had changed little, but the way in which they were used, the proportions in which they were combined and the subtlety with which they were put together began to shift. With experience and confidence, interiors became easier on the eye. Contrasts were less abrupt, although accents remained crisp and even dissonant.

A summary of the trends of a particular decade provides only a small window on the decorating ideas of the time. By no means does it represent general practice. The opportunities presented by different types of houses were varied; some lent themselves more to a traditional treatment rather than a strikingly contemporary one. Whereas a chimney breast wall in a north London flat might be accented in bright red, for example, an interior decorator such as John Fowler might only add a little black to all his colours to produce something mellower for a country house interior.

The magazines were mindful of different tastes, and one published an interview with six London decorators, which described a sitting room with a strong Japanese influence and using colours such as hot chocolate on the walls and mustard on the ceiling, with citron velvet curtains accented with emerald green, lilac and bitter green. Surely this appeared a bit 'shouty' when compared with the more discreet work that Frederick Keeble was producing. He criticized the *House & Garden* paint range for its lack of subdued colours, which he considered essential for pleasant and restful traditional schemes. In an example that Keeble produced for the magazine, willow was used on the walls and in two tones lighter for the ceiling. The panel mouldings and skirtings were painted white, while a dove grey carpet and guardsman red curtains completed the scheme. Perhaps it was among those who put together these less strident interiors that the British Standard range found favour.

SELECTIVE COLOURING

The idea of an accent wall, or 'selective colouring', seems to have originated in the Bauhaus of the 1920s. Architect designers in Germany began to experiment in counter-shading, that is, painting the walls of a room in different tones of white and grey, with the object of minimizing the tonal contrast between light and dark walls. In this way, a wall that received strong sunlight for most of the day was painted a dark tone to reduce glare, whereas the window wall, being the darkest, was painted white or a very light tint to reduce brightness contrast. From this it was but a short step to the introduction of positive colour; walls that received little or no sun were painted a lively 'sunshine yellow', while walls reflecting the direct rays of a hot sun were painted in a deep, light-absorbing shade of blue or cool green. This use of colour recalls the work of Piet Mondrian and it was employed in the interiors of Le Corbusier and his one-time collaborator Amédée Ozenfant.

'Interest' could be provided by the use of a strong colour or by a change in material, such as wallpaper, fabric, wood panelling, brick, marble or stonework. However, caution was advised and the feature had to be selected carefully with regard to its shape and the way it was lit. An awkwardly shaped wall, or one pierced with irregular door or window openings, might not be improved by having a strong colour applied, nor should 'focal' colour be placed where it gave undue emphasis to unimportant features. Several of the more technical works of the time show how selective colouring could be employed, most effectively, to modify the proportions of a room or to emphasize its structural form.

FLUID DECORATION

The reduction in available housing space in the early 1950s was remarked upon by architectural journals of the time. The American Public Health Association went as far as to say 'normal and happy and fruitful family life is possible without modern plumbing and deep-freeze equipment. It is not possible without a reasonable modicum of space.' (*Architectural Record*, 1950). Space-saving innovations appeared and rooms became dual-purpose: the kitchen-diner, living-dining room and even the living-kitchen. Furniture was lighter and easier to move. As a result, decoration became more fluid.

[PP. 309–315] A series of lithographs by Ronald Collins from Noel Carrington's *Colour and Pattern in the Home* (1954).